Mission to Malawi

Mission to Malawi

Memoir of an African American Peace Corps Volunteer, 1967–1969

JOHN E. FLEMING

Foreword by Patricia A. Wand

McFarland & Company, Inc., Publishers
Jefferson, North Carolina

Unless otherwise noted, photographs
are from the author's collection.

LIBRARY OF CONGRESS CATALOGUING-IN-PUBLICATION DATA

Names: Fleming, John, 1944– author.
Title: Mission to Malawi : memoir of an African American Peace Corps volunteer, 1967–1969 / John E. Fleming ; foreword by Patricia A. Wand.
Description: Jefferson, North Carolina : McFarland & Company, Inc., Publishers, 2024 | Includes index.
Identifiers: LCCN 2023058827 | ISBN 9781476693491 (paperback : acid free paper) ∞ ISBN 9781476651293 (ebook)
Subjects: LCSH: Fleming, John, 1944– | Peace Corps (U.S.)—Malawi—Biography. | African Americans—Malawi—Biography. | Malawi—Social conditions—20th century. | BISAC: BIOGRAPHY & AUTOBIOGRAPHY / Personal Memoirs | SOCIAL SCIENCE / Volunteer Work
Classification: LCC HC60.5 .F646 2024 | DDC 361.6—dc23/eng/20231227
LC record available at https://lccn.loc.gov/2023058827

BRITISH LIBRARY CATALOGUING DATA ARE AVAILABLE

ISBN (print) 978-1-4766-9349-1
ISBN (ebook) 978-1-4766-5129-3

© 2024 John E. Fleming. All rights reserved

No part of this book may be reproduced or transmitted in any form or by any means, electronic or mechanical, including photocopying or recording, or by any information storage and retrieval system, without permission in writing from the publisher.

Front cover image: Fleming taking pictures for *The Southern Advisor*; tea farmers below Mt. Mulanje (courtesy of Dana Allen, wildlife photographer, Harare, Zambia).

Printed in the United States of America

McFarland & Company, Inc., Publishers
 Box 611, Jefferson, North Carolina 28640
  www.mcfarlandpub.com

To Barbara, Tuliza, Diara,
Keith, Troy and Jaden

Table of Contents

Foreword by Patricia A. Wand   1
Preface   5

Chapter One
Pre-Departure   9

Chapter Two
My First Year in Malawi   18

Chapter Three
Second Year in Malawi   142

Chapter Four
Departure Home   199

Epilogue   211
Index   217

Foreword

by Patricia A. Wand

The impact of John Fleming on the American public's awareness of African American history is significant. Fleming has provided leadership in the development of six African American museums since 1980 when he was recruited by the Ohio Historical Society to develop a museum of African American history on the old campus of Wilberforce University, a historically Black university.

As a newly minted PhD in history and a civil rights activist, Fleming refocused his career and learned everything possible about building and managing museums. Since then, he has been an administrator or consultant for the development of numerous African American museums in the United States, including the Smithsonian National Museum of African American History and Culture, the National Underground Railroad Freedom Center in Cincinnati, and the National Museum of African American Music in Nashville.

For John Fleming, a widely recognized museum consultant, to take time now from his active career to write his fourth book, focused on two years as a Peace Corps volunteer in Malawi, speaks to the impact of that transformative experience on him personally. It was a story he was compelled to tell.

Since the founding of the Peace Corps in 1961, nearly a quarter million U.S. citizens have cross-cultural experiences as volunteers in 120 countries. The majority of volunteers have been White Americans of European heritage. But from the beginning, the Peace Corps attracted applicants from under-represented and non-majority American groups. John Fleming was one of those.

In those early years of the Peace Corps, founder Sargent Shriver advocated for a color-blind selection process so as not to discriminate against Black and people of color applicants. The Peace Corps' initial policy was not to track the racial composition of training groups.

Shriver, like many northern Whites active in the Civil Rights movement in the mid-twentieth century, was convinced the ground was being laid for America to become color blind. They believed enough time had passed since the Civil War, Emancipation, and Jim Crow that integration could be achieved through a cultural evolution. Besides, they reasoned, ethnicity and race divide people, but the universality of humanity unites us and is the focus of Peace Corps service.

Fleming was the only African American in his training cohort in 1967. Malawi had invited Peace Corps volunteers with specific skills to assist communities in developing segments of the economy. Fleming was assigned to agricultural extension services. In training, he began learning the local language and studying farming techniques. He was sent to a special course in London to learn to create visual aids—including puppets—to use in educating African farmers.

Based primarily on his journal and letters to family and friends, Fleming writes about his two years in Malawi during a critical era in its history and a transformational time in his own life. Malawi had just begun its transition from colonialism under the British to becoming an independent, African-built nation. Fleming brought his heritage as an African American with personal experience of racial discrimination. As was common for American-educated students, Fleming had minimal exposure to African diversity, history, or geography.

Both Malawians and Fleming were familiar with the expected behavior when interactions among Blacks and Whites are based primarily on skin color and racial features. The cultural differences among and within each group, however, were not expected or so readily apparent to either Fleming or his Malawian counterparts. It is that process of recognizing the cultural, along with the racial, differences that gives this story particular depth and significance.

Adding to the race-versus-culture counterplay, Fleming includes candid reflections on what he was experiencing at the time it occurred. In many situations, he narrates his activities or observations as well as his feelings, sharing frank and often personal thoughts with the reader.

For example, Fleming comments on immediately feeling at home when he was in a crowd of Black people, more Blacks than he'd ever seen together in one place. When he unexpectedly encountered a party in a Malawian village, his body immediately moved with the music; the music was in his soul. He relished the deep connection he felt in this Black-majority environment and, over his two years in Malawi, developed close friendships with several Africans and their families.

On the disturbing side, Fleming rankled at the treatment of Malawians when expatriates were disrespectful to locals, demeaned Malawian employees, or refused to promote them just because they were Africans. He resented those Whites who remained in positions of authority in the post-colonial era, denying growth opportunities to Malawians. Fleming worked to get along with his expat host-country counterparts despite their racial prejudices, but within his own scope of responsibility in the agricultural extension service office, he purposefully recruited and mentored Malawians to take over the office including his own position as director.

Born in the mid-twentieth century in a segregated hospital and raised in a mostly segregated town in western North Carolina, John Fleming experienced racial discrimination—based solely on the color of his skin—from childhood onward. His was a lower middle-class family, comfortable within their Black community, whose lives centered on church and school. His family passed down stories of courageous ancestors still in bondage and other relatives who ventured out, losing their lives, or returning with accounts of painful acts that demeaned them and prevented them from reaching otherwise attainable goals.

In this story, Fleming retains the voice of the young man in search of life's purpose. The reader realizes, 50 years after the fact, that without being explicit himself, Fleming has chosen education as his purpose. His primary learning objective—whether delivering content through publications, consultancies, lectures, or museum exhibits and programs—is racial justice.

The late Patricia A. Wand was the president of the Museum of the Peace Corps Experience in Oregon City, Oregon.

Preface

It has been 56 years since I joined the Peace Corps. My two years as a Peace Corps volunteer in the African nation of Malawi were and are the most profound and impactful years of my life. I have wanted to write my memoir of those years and finally found the opportunity when I had completed my work as director of the National Museum of African American Music. Having worked in and developed five national museums relating to African American history, I wanted to take a year off from working on a new project to complete my memoir.

After outlining my plans for the book, I remembered that I had my letters (aerograms) that I had written to my parents while I was in Africa. I was fortunate that my mother had saved all of them. I combined those letters with the ones sent to my sister and my future wife, both of whom had also saved all my letters. I was a voracious writer because I wanted my family and friends to write to me as it was my only form of communication and was the only way that I could keep up with what was happening at home. I had more than 100 letters to draw on in writing this memoir of my Peace Corps experience. I also kept a journal during the first year I was in Malawi. The letters fill in information absent from my journal entries and allow me to be more accurate in my descriptions of events, experiences, and reactions to social-political events in the United States and, in particular, my experiences living in a Black independent country in Southern Africa surrounded by racist White regimes in Southern Rhodesia, South Africa and Mozambique.

The 1960s were particularly tumultuous times both in the United States and Southern Africa. I grew up in a segregated society and had been the victim of discrimination and racism. I was born in a segregated hospital and attended a segregated school. All places of public accommodations were segregated. Since the lowest level jobs were reserved for Blacks, I worked as an assistant janitor for a department store while in secondary school. It seemed natural for me to become active in the Civil Rights movement as a high school student in Morganton, North Carolina, at the beginning of the decade. I continued my activism as a Berea College student helping to organize Berea's participation in the march from Selma to Montgomery in support of voting rights and the March on Frankfort in support of Kentucky's first civil rights act. Later, in my first full-time job after graduation from college, I served as a field representative and an education specialist for the Kentucky Human Rights Commission, where I worked to secure peaceful integration of public accommodations and public school systems. During off-work hours, I was an active member of the more radical Congress of Racial Equality (CORE) that advocated direct and sometimes aggressive action to achieve their goals. Before I left the States for Africa, CORE was advocating Black Power following the example of the Student Nonviolent Coordinating Committee's Stokely Carmichael who called for revolutionary action for all oppressed peoples of the world. This call to action particularly included the countries of Southern Africa.

Mozambique is situated to the east and southwest of Malawi. When I arrived in Malawi in 1967, African freedom fighters had already organized the Mozambique Liberation Front or FRELIMO in southern Tanganyika in 1962 and began incursions into northern Mozambique against the colonial government of Portugal. Toward the end of 1965, the minority White population of Southern Rhodesia adopted the Unilateral Declaration of Independence. The United Kingdom quickly passed the Southern Rhodesia Act of 1965, which reaffirmed Southern Rhodesia as a British colony. In 1948, more than two decades earlier, the minority White population (Dutch and British) of South Africa under the National Party had instituted a system of legalized racial separation called apartheid. This was followed by a Black African defiance campaign, which originally started as passive resistance but eventually morphed into guerrilla warfare. The Sharpeville massacre in March 1960 garnered worldwide attention and condemnation including from the United Nations. Influenced by Malcolm X and Stokely Carmichael's Black Power movement, Africans, with a renewed sense of Black identity and consciousness in the 1960s, started mass resistance and mass strike campaigns. Kenneth Kaunda, president of the newly independent nation of Zambia, and Julius Nyerere, president of Tanzania, were all strong African nationalists promoting a policy of African majority rule throughout Africa but especially in the recalcitrant nations of South Africa and Southern Rhodesia. During the March 1960 Sharpeville massacre, police shot into a group of anti-apartheid protesters in Sharpeville, South Africa, killing 67 and wounding 186. (For additional information, see Tom Lodge, *Sharpeville: An Apartheid Massacre and Its Consequences* [Oxford University Press, 2011].)

Numerous White volunteers have written about their experience in what was then a color-blind Peace Corps organization. But as a Black volunteer, I could not separate my Peace Corps experience from my own history as a Black American. Unlike the majority of Peace Corps volunteers, I came to the Peace Corps as a Black experienced activist in the Civil Rights movement in the United States, so I was definitely aware of the rise of Black African nations from the yoke of colonialism and the continued struggle for liberation in Southern Africa. My experience in the Peace Corps from 1967 to 1969 was also influenced by the international Black Power movement. Against this background, I aspired to re-create my life as a Peace Corps volunteer in Malawi, Africa.

I have used pseudonyms for most people in the book, many of whom have passed. Several friends and of course family members have given me permission to use their actual names and images.

I wish to thank Jack Allison, a returned Peace Corps volunteer from Malawi, my wife, Barbara Fleming, and the late Patricia Wand, who was president of the board of the Museum of the Peace Corps Experience, for carefully reading early drafts of my manuscript. I also want to thank my editor at McFarland. I am especially indebted to Diara Spelmon for giving me valuable feedback and early editing of my manuscript.

Chapter One

Pre-Departure

Why Africa?

It is strange how things turned out. I am not sure if it was predestination or just a fortuitous circumstance. All my life I wanted to be a missionary in Africa. I felt that this was my calling since I was old enough to think about my life's work. As a child, I watched Tarzan movies with all of the stereotypical images of Africa, Black Africans and the White European hero. I did not know much more about African history when I entered Berea College. Berea offered a one-semester course on the entire history of Africa. While I did not know or learn much about African cultures while I studied history at Berea, I was intrigued by the idea of becoming a missionary on the African continent. As a devout Christian, I felt it my duty to introduce Africans to Christianity and to our Lord and Savior, Jesus Christ.

My zeal to be a missionary was grounded in my religious upbringing in Morganton, North Carolina, where I was raised by my parents with my older brother, James (Jimmy), and my younger sister, Patricia. My father, James, and his family were founding members of Slades Chapel African Methodist Episcopal Zion Church, and my mother, Mary, and her family were founding members of St. Stephen's Episcopal Church. It was at Slades Chapel that I learned of the church's missionaries in Southern Africa. Of the three collections during Sunday service, one was devoted to supporting the work of missionaries. Growing up, my brother, sister and I were required to attend Sunday school at my father's church and then attend the regular service at St. Stephen's. Because I was an active participant in the services of St. Stephen's, the ministers knew of my ambitions to be a priest and a missionary. During my high school years, I sang in the church choir, served as an acolyte, taught Sunday school and often read the lessons from the Old and New Testaments during morning prayer services.

The ministers who served our small church supported my calling to be a missionary. The last priest I had was the Rev. Delmar Hare, a young minister in charge of St. Stephen's during my last years of high school. The Reverend Hare took me under his wing and advised me on my future plans. He suggested that I follow in his footsteps that led to his becoming a priest. Hare had gone to Berea College in Kentucky and then to seminary at the University of the South at Sewanee, Tennessee. He encouraged me to apply to Berea because Morganton was within the Appalachian region the college served. I applied and was accepted.

I enrolled in Berea in the fall of 1962 as one of nine Black students in the freshman class, which brought the total population of Black students to 19. Berea was founded as the first integrated college in the South before the Civil War. During the post-war years, Berea had equal numbers of White and Black students. In 1904, the Kentucky legislature passed the Day Law outlawing integrated college campuses. Berea eventually became an all-White school serving underprivileged White students from Appalachia.

By the time I arrived on campus in 1962, Berea had a handful of Black students as it struggled to find its place in this new desegregated society. I would get to know all of these students well, especially Salome David and Michael Ndungi who were both from Kenya. Michael Ndungi and I had originally met when I was a high school student attending a student council conference at Colonial Williamsburg. When we first encountered each other at Berea, we both immediately recognized that we had met before.

While all Black students felt a close affinity to each other, I found myself forming tight bonds with these two Kenyan students. I would often have dinner with Salome, who introduced me to African cuisine. One of her favorite dishes was a curried beef stew served with ugali, a seasonless, thickened porridge of cornmeal and water. It took a while to get used to a different cuisine, but I enjoyed my first introduction to Kenyan culture and would later call on these experiences when I began adapting to Malawian culture as a Peace Corps volunteer.

During my first two years at Berea College, I selected and discarded several majors before settling on American history. I decided that I needed to take some courses on African history to prepare for my missionary work in Africa. Unfortunately, Berea had only one two-hour course on African history. As one can imagine, a two-hour course does not provide nearly enough information for a career as an African missionary. I was an avid reader of African American history, so I began to add books on the history of sub-Saharan Africa and the Atlantic slave trade to my modest library to enhance my knowledge of African history.

As I completed my junior year, I confided in the Reverend Hare that I might not be ready to go to seminary after college; I wanted to know more about living as a missionary in Africa. He suggested that I consider serving

Chapter One. Pre-Departure

in one of the missions to the Anglican Overseas Missions in England in one of their mission schools in Africa. I received a letter from a church official in charge of missions in Central Africa inviting me to serve as a teacher in an Anglican mission school in the British colony called Nyasaland. Nyasaland would become the independent nation of Malawi before I graduated from Berea. Central Africa was where the first missionary, David Livingstone, "discovered" Nyasaland and later established a mission there. Hundreds of missionaries followed in Livingstone's footsteps. I wanted to be a missionary because I took very literally, at that time, the admonition of Jesus to go out and spread the gospel. I could not have envisioned a better place to begin my life as a missionary than Livingstone's Nyasaland.

Between attending classes and working at my job, I managed to complete the application and supplied all the documentation required. I had my health examination at the college hospital, got dark sunglasses to block out rays from the intense African sun and was mentally prepared to meet the challenge of life in the African bush as I imagined it. My assignment was to serve as a teacher at the mission secondary school at Fort Johnston, just south of Lake Malawi.

Before I graduated from Berea in January 1966, I informed my mother and father of my plans to go to Nyasaland as a teacher. My parents did not share my vision for the future. My father thought that I should get a job and make some money as a college graduate. He did not understand why I would want to be a volunteer when I could get a good-paying job as a college graduate. My mother did not like the idea of me being so far away from home, especially for two years.

By the fall of my senior year, all of my preparations were in place for my sojourn in Africa. All I needed to do was to complete my work at Berea and graduate. But then I received a letter informing me that my assignment at Fort Johnston as a teacher would have to be postponed until I completed a master's degree. The letter from the Anglican mission went on to state that the American bachelor's degree was not equivalent to the English bachelor's degree. I would have to earn my master's degree before the church would consider placing me as one of their teachers in their secondary school at Fort Johnston. I was devastated.

I did not know what to do. I had already told all my friends and classmates that I was going to be a missionary in Africa. I fully expected to leave for London and then Malawi after graduating from Berea in January. With my African plans falling through and no job prospects, I could not even think about making alternative plans. That was when I remembered the Peace Corps.

I attended school on campus the previous summer when the Peace Corps had a training program at Berea. I did not know much about the

Peace Corps except that it could be my ticket to Africa to help people. I reasoned I might not be an Anglican missionary, but I would be able to do some good with the U.S. government behind me. I would also use this time in Africa to make up my mind if I wanted to devote my life as a missionary there. I decided to concentrate on graduating and then explore joining the Peace Corps.

I graduated at the end of the fall semester and went home to Morganton. Galen Martin, a Berea graduate who headed the new Kentucky Commission on Human Rights, informed me that they were looking for a field representative for the commission and offered me the job. I said yes immediately and, within a week, I was on a bus to Frankfort.

While working for the commission, I continued to explore opportunities in the Peace Corps. Above all else, I wanted to go to Kenya and work as a teacher. By the time I inquired about volunteering in Kenya, the Peace Corps had filled its quota for that round of teachers. I finally heard from the Peace Corps' Washington office indicating that plans were underway to organize a group of agricultural volunteers destined for Malawi. I immediately filled out the application and was accepted to join Peace Corps Malawi.

Peace Corps Training

Toward the end of summer 1967, we began our training at the YMCA Camp Atkins in rural Macon County, Alabama, about a mile outside of the town of Tuskegee. Our group consisted of 30 all-male volunteers, 29 Whites and 1 Black. The other volunteers seemed nice enough. The weather in Alabama at the end of summer was extremely hot. Our training program was housed in the wooden campus headquarters, which had no air-conditioning. Each volunteer was assigned a shack to live in that previous Y campers had constructed out of wood and tar paper. I could not believe that we were expected to live under such primitive conditions with no electricity, running water or toilet facilities, but I guess they were getting us ready for life in Malawi. Since the only toilet facilities were in the main camp building, if we had to use the bathroom, we just urinated outside of our hut.

We had three full-time White instructors and three Malawi instructors who were brought over to teach us the language and culture of the country. The Peace Corps felt like it was as important to learn about the culture as it was the subject of agriculture. We spent the morning hours learning Chinyanja and the afternoons learning about corn and cotton production.

Chapter One. Pre-Departure

Rural Alabama was chosen as our training site because it was an area that produced two of the major crops of Malawi, cotton and corn. Most of the community in the area lived in poverty. The majority of the residents were sharecroppers who barely made a living farming. Out of the 30 volunteers in the project, seven of us had been selected while in Tuskegee to train in the use of audio-visual aids in a developing country. We were assigned to work with the director of audio-visual services at the Tuskegee Veterans Hospital. Franklin Jones was our instructor. He was Black, as were most of the staff at the veterans hospital. He was also responsible for assigning us resident host families to live with for two weeks so that we gain firsthand experience of subsistence living.

Mr. Jones assigned me to live with Robert Johnson, a widower with two boys, Robert Jr. and Larry, the younger brother. The Johnsons shared their three-bedroom house with Robert Sr.'s sister, Marie, a local schoolteacher. Robert farmed 40 acres of cotton. Marie, who never married, spent her time caring for Robert's boys after his wife died. She would get up in the morning and cook for the entire day. All three of our meals consisted of fried catfish, corn bread, greens and fried okra. I thought it odd that we would have such heavy food for breakfast. Following breakfast, we would head to the fields where we would chop weeds in the cotton field. Mr. Johnson would not allow me to chop weeds because he said that I was a guest even though I insisted that I was there to learn how to plant and care for cotton.

Larry and I would sometimes go fishing to stay busy. We visited neighbors and came across one of my fellow volunteers living with a family nearby. The Johnsons' house was a mansion compared to many of the sharecroppers' houses. Jim Branson was assigned to live with the Perrys, a family of eight. All the children were under the age of 10. The Perrys lived in a four-room unpainted wooden house that stood on large rocks that served as the foundation. They did not have running water or electricity. Jim told me that they had to fish every day to catch their dinner. I thought it was fortunate that Mr. Jones had assigned me to live with the Johnsons.

After two weeks of living with our host families, we returned to base camp where we concentrated on the history and culture of Malawi. Malawi got its first group of education and health volunteers in 1963, shortly after the Peace Corps was formed in 1961. That was before Malawi became an independent country. Westerners were interested in Malawi because of the exploration of David Livingston during the middle of the nineteenth century. Dr. Hastings Banda was elected the first and only president and served as head of the Malawi Congress Party. More than 50 percent of Malawi's gross domestic product came from agriculture, and of that, 60 percent came from the export of tobacco, followed by tea and sugar. Seeing how important agriculture was to the economy, I was surprised that it had taken so long for the Peace Corps office to field a group of agricultural volunteers. Our group was to concentrate on increasing and improving cotton production among other assignments.

Our Malawi instructors provided us with basic information about the country. For such a small country nestled in southeast Africa, it has a diverse climate and geography. It is bordered by Mozambique to the east, south and west, Tanzania to the northeast and Zambia to the northwest. Southern Rhodesia was located south of Zambia and north of South Africa, Malawi is 380 miles in length and has the third largest lake on the African continent. Its largest mountain is Mount Mulanje. Malawi has two basic seasons: the rainy season from November to April and the dry season from May to October. We were scheduled to arrive in the country at the end of the hot, dry season. The temperature can reach into the 90s during the Malawi summer and 60–70 degrees during the winter. We were told that in certain highland areas, the temperature could become much colder. The terrain ranges from grassy slopes to rolling hills to dense forest. The kwacha is the currency and is based on the British pound. Besides Britain, I was disappointed to learn that Malawi's top trading partners at the time were South Africa and Southern Rhodesia.

Members of our group were posted the length of the country, from Chitipi in the north to Nsanje in the south. Malawi is rural, so volunteers were mainly assigned to rural posts throughout the country. We were to be paid the equivalent of $90 per month to cover all of our expenses. Our salary was supposed to be comparable to our Malawi counterparts and thus allowing us to live at the same level as they live.

Our Peace Corps trainers told us that the dress was short pants for men and long skirts for women. The heart of our training programs centered on learning the language of Chinyanja. Much of the other aspects of our training covered cross-cultural experience, health and safety. I would be forever grateful for our medical kits. We had everything in the kits we could possibly need: anti-malaria pills that we took weekly, Benadryl, Sudafed, calamine lotion for rashes, iodine tablets for water purification, Band-Aids, insect repellent and a thermometer.

The best part of our Peace Corps training was the emphasis on understanding the culture. Bringing over Malawians to teach us the language and firsthand knowledge about the culture was extremely helpful. Because of the fight for equality and basic civil rights in the South at that time, I held a lot of resentment toward White people when I arrived in Tuskegee. I found that I quickly identified with my Malawi instructors while keeping the White volunteers at a distance. Although I did not consciously try to separate myself at the time, my numerous negative encounters with

White people growing up always made me keep them at arm's length. I think some of the staff may have held this against me while in training in Tuskegee.

Training in London at the Overseas Visual Aids Office

After leaving Tuskegee, we had two weeks of training in the heart of London. I was the only Black in the group. For a person who had never been out of the States, this was an extraordinary opportunity for me. Our training at the British Overseas Visual Aids (OVA) office involved how to produce visual aids suitable for use in the tropics, including how to make puppets.

During our two weeks in London, the Peace Corps arranged for lodging in a low-to-moderate-priced hotel within walking distance of the training center. The rooms were small with just a bed, dresser, chair and table. There was just one bathroom at the end of each hallway that was shared by all on the floor. Off the lobby on the first floor was a small dining room where we had our breakfast, usually consisting of eggs, cold toast, butter and jam with a baked tomato. The Peace Corps made sure that it was anything but plush. It was a big step above the tar paper shacks that we lived in at the Y camp outside of Tuskegee, Alabama.

The OVA office was located in a four-story building in London. Most of the staff had worked in Africa or Asia in one of the British colonies before the countries gained their independence. They were used to working in the tropics and had developed many projects that could withstand tropical conditions, mainly heat and humidity. We were trained on offset and stencil printing, photography, design and publications. There was a lot to learn in the two weeks we were there. The training was better and more sophisticated than any we had received in Tuskegee where the only specialized training was in photo development taught at the Tuskegee Veterans Hospital.

Margaret Henderson, our primary instructor, had worked in Malawi before. Margaret was single, probably in her late 30s or early 40s. She was nice enough but had a habit of "putting you in your place" if she felt like you thought more of yourself or your abilities than you had a right to feel. Of course, these were her subjective judgments about people.

In spite of being a little eccentric, I must admit that while in London, Margaret made a special effort to show us the sights. We went to the theater every chance we had. We saw two musicals, *Fiddler on the Roof* and *Sweet Charity*. Being on a Peace Corps allowance, we could only afford standing-room-only tickets. This got us about 14 inches of wall space where we could lean for two hours and watch the show. Margaret even joined us for evenings out on the town. One night she suggested to the group of volunteers that we go to a specific pub of her choosing. Not knowing one pub from another, we followed her advice. When we got there, it looked like a typical English bar. There was absolutely nothing unusual about the place. We found a space near the bar and ordered our beers. When I looked around the bar, I noticed that there were only men. There were no women. It never occurred to me that this was Margaret's way of introducing us to an English gay bar.

John Hunter was the Anglophile in our group. He told us that he had English relatives and had been to England to visit them in the past. This made him the expert in the group. A funny thing happened one morning when we came down for breakfast. There were three of us, John Hunter, Roy Adams and me. During our brief English orientation, we were told that if you needed a seat at a table, you were free to sit with others as long as there was a seat available. So, seeing this gentleman alone at a table for four, we decided we would join him. We all sat and waited for the man to lower his newspaper and acknowledge our presence. And when he didn't, John said to the man, "Good morning." Hearing John's greetings, the Englishman then lowered his paper, looked at John, looked at Roy, looked at me and then back to John and asked, "Do I know you?" John replied, "No." The man then raised his paper and continued reading as if we were not there. It was all I could do to keep from laughing out loud at our Anglophile.

Another night we attended a dance concert. It was a little distance from our hotel, so we traveled by subway, or the Tube. A local rock-and-roll band with a singing group were performing. I did not recognize the name of the group, but all English groups sound like the Beatles, so it did not matter that much to me. I was reluctant to ask any of the young ladies to dance since I was the only Black person there and had been sensitized to American racial mores. This was not a problem for the other guys in the group. Roy was certainly the outgoing one and was not reluctant to ask girl after girl to dance. Initially it did not bother him that no one wanted to dance with him. But finally he got the message. I was not sure if it was because we were Americans or because we were strangers.

When the weekend came, I wanted to go sightseeing and visit the British Museum. While in London, we usually traveled by subway or walked. I enjoyed walking around London because I saved money and got a close-up view of the city. We saw an anti-war demonstration in Trafalgar Square where it seemed like everybody in London was either protesting or advocating something. Trafalgar Square is a public square that features many galleries, public buildings, as well as statues and monuments. The Nelson statue is prominently situated in the square. There were so many

Chapter One. Pre-Departure

people in the square that it was difficult to get a clear view. I noticed that the South African High Commission faced the square but did not pay too much attention to it, not realizing what a central role South Africa would play in my future country of Malawi. Some of us went into the National Gallery. We were impressed with the sheer number of paintings.

On Sunday, after breakfast, we went to the British Museum. I was overwhelmed by the size of the building, or should I say, buildings. We entered the museum on Great Russell Street, the entrance that took us into the grand courtyard. Since we were headed to Africa, I wanted to see as much about the continent as I could. My first observation was about the number of things people had taken out of Africa and put into this museum. One probably could learn much more about Egyptian history and culture by going through the museum than you could learn by visiting Egypt.

Our sojourn in London was all too brief. We soon found ourselves on a flight to Blantyre with stops in Zurich and Nairobi.

Chapter Two

My First Year in Malawi

Arrival in Malawi

We joined the rest of our Peace Corps group, which arrived two full weeks before we arrived from our audio-visual (AV) aids training in London. Although our AV group had a wonderful stay in London, my thrill of a lifetime was landing in Nairobi, Kenya, which provided my first glimpse of Africa. I alerted Salome that I would be stopping over in Nairobi where we changed planes from British Overseas Airways to East African Airlines. When we landed and disembarked the plane, Salome was at the gate to greet me. We left the gate and went into the lounge where we caught up on the years since she graduated from Berea. She told me when she returned to Kenya, she was made headmistress of an all-girls school in Nairobi. Our time together passed swiftly. We had only started to catch up on our lives when I had to board my plane for Malawi. I promised that I would return to Kenya during my first vacation.

The plane landed at the Chileka International Airport in Blantyre, the commercial capital of Malawi. The airport in Malawi was much smaller than the bustling airport in Kenya with none of the accoutrements of larger international airports. As my plane approached the airfield, I got a wonderful bird's-eye view of the terrain, the mud and thatched buildings that dotted the gently rolling hillside and the early corn crops that were just beginning to sprout. Howard Carter, the assistant director for the Peace Corps, met us at the gate. Going through customs was uneventful. After gathering our belongings, Howard walked us to the two Land Rovers that transported us into the city. I marveled at the Black faces that lined the nine-mile route into Blantyre. There were women carrying baskets of food and other commodities on their heads. Men and boys dressed in shorts and shirts in various stages of disrepair walked perilously close to the road, or tarmac as the British called it.

The drive into Blantyre did not take long. There were only a few Western-style homes dotted among the many thatched houses. Before I knew it, we were in the heart of Blantyre, a beautiful city and a reflection of its colonial past when Britain controlled Nyasaland. The route we traveled took us to the roundabout where the clock tower signaled the intersection with Kamuzu Highway. We turned left down Kamuzu Highway toward Limbe, a town just outside of Blantyre. Howard took us straight to the Shire Highlands Hotel in Limbe for a rest before beginning a full week of orientation to the Peace Corps and Malawi.

The short ride to Limbe was almost magical for me. The sun was bright, and its warmth provided a pleasant sensation after the long flight to Blantyre. The road between Blantyre and Limbe was lined with tall eucalyptus trees that stretched skyward with leaves and branches curved into umbrella-shaped canopies. There must have been hundreds of Malawians walking to and from Limbe while others rode bicycles with huge loads of cargo attached to the back of their bikes. Along the way, there were various little market stands where people sold all sorts of fruits and vegetables. I don't think I ever saw so many Black faces in one place. I thought at the time that these were my brothers and sisters I had traveled 10,000 miles to serve. I experienced both excitement and a deep sense of satisfaction to be finally in Africa where I would be in the racial majority for the first time in my life.

We soon arrived at the Shire Highland Hotel, which had been built during the colonial era. Before independence from Great Britain in 1964, Africans were not allowed to eat or sleep in the hotel; they could only serve White patrons. Although I grew up in a segregated southern town, I did not imagine that Africans had to undergo the indignity of being second-class citizens in their own country. Our Land Rovers pulled up in front of the hotel where we unloaded our bags.

The hotel lobby was very nice and looked like an old British men's club with overstuffed leather chairs and sofas. The hotel bellman and all of the lower-level staff were Africans. British expatriates served as the desk attendant and the restaurant manager. The whole scene could have taken place in the southern United States during the era of segregation. We were escorted to our rooms, where I quickly unpacked and laid down for a nap before dinner.

Trip to Lilongwe

The day after we arrived in the country, Howard Carter escorted us the 240 miles to the central region. He had planned for our accommodations in Lilongwe, the second largest city in Malawi. Howard informed us that we were invited to have dinner with Mujeeb Patel, mayor of Lilongwe.

I was surprised to see that an East Indian had been elected mayor of what now was going to be the new capital of Malawi. Mayor Patel was either the third- or fourth-generation East Indian born in Africa. So I guess he should be called an African of Indian descent. One could not help noticing that most of the shops in the small towns and even in Lilongwe were owned by Indians.

We arrived at the mayor's house located in the predominantly Indian sector of the town. There were several newly affluent Africans who had been able to purchase or build homes in the area as well as in the part of town that had been reserved for Europeans during colonial days. The Patel family was somewhat of an exceptional Indian family. Mr. Patel made every effort to be part of the larger African community. I suppose that was why he was elected the first mayor of Indian descent. The family had a lovely home with many mementos, furnishings and fabrics from India. Mrs. Patel had her African servants bring us refreshments that were served in their very spacious living room. The food was prepared both in the kitchen and the open-air hearth located outside of the kitchen. Dinner was served in the formal dining room. The food was delicious. After eating somewhat bland English food for several weeks in London, this feast was a gastronomical delight. Just about everything was spicy. I thought I could eat hot food and hot peppers, but I met my match that night. The feast consisted of lamb vindaloo (curry), tandoori chicken, dal makhani (lentils), basmati rice, various types of naan (flatbreads) and samosas. There were various pickles, hot and sweet but all spicy. Jwala (pepper) literally brought tears to my eyes. I was grateful to drink the lassi, yogurt blended with fruit, and eat laddu, a sweet pastry.

We thanked our host and hostess following the feast, gathered our belongings and headed back to the hostel where we were staying for the night. It must have been sometime after midnight that all of us, one by one, became terribly sick. We all had diarrhea and uncontrolled vomiting. The heat of the food attacked us at both ends. I was not sure if the food was prepared in an unsanitary manner or if the cook did not adequately wash his left hand. We were told as part of our training that one never offers to shake hands using the left hand. It was reserved for wiping oneself after a bowel movement. I noticed in public restrooms tins of water next to the toilet, or rather, the hole in the floor that passed for a toilet. Could it have been that the servant preparing the food failed to properly wash his hand with soap? On the other hand, we were not used to hot and spicy food, so the food could just not have agreed with us. Unfortunately, none of us were ready to travel back to the southern region for a tour of the south and getting sworn in by the American ambassador to Malawi.

Chapter Two. My First Year in Malawi

Getting Settled in the Southern Region

After a day's rest, we were finally ready to head south and get ready for our assignments and home locations.

Sometime during our stay in Lilongwe, something bit me on my hip and I noticed that the area had turned red and was swollen. It started to bother me, but I did not say anything until we got back to Blantyre and the Peace Corps office. Howard Carter gave us a tour of the city, stopping off at the Peace Corps warehouse and fix-it shop. We were introduced to Robert (Rob) Johnson who was Black or mixed race (not the Robert Johnson of my host family when I first arrived in Malawi but a different one). He looked as if he could have been part African, Indian and White. He was brown skinned with dark curly hair. We learned through Howard that the notion of race and the accompanying racial separation were a leftover from colonial days as well as an import from South Africa but just not as virulent as apartheid. Apartheid in South Africa was akin to the rigid form of segregation that emerged in the southern United States at the end of the nineteenth century. It seemed that the British in Malawi were practicing a milder form of apartheid or segregation.

Rob's duty was to provide assistance as we gathered our furniture allotment and other needs from the Peace Corps warehouse. Those of us assigned motorcycles were to have them serviced by Rob. He assigned us our vehicle based on our urban or rural locations and duties in the Ministry of Agriculture. Those of us working in the rural areas would get a Honda 175, and those of us living in town would get the smaller and lighter Honda 90. Rob was very helpful and seemed like a nice enough fellow.

By late afternoon, Howard gave us a tour of the Peace Corps building. It was a white two-story building located in downtown Blantyre. Located there were the administrative offices for Matt Rather the director and six American and four lower-level African staff members. Dr. Raymond Flowers was the medical doctor, and Rachel was his nurse. I told Howard that I needed Dr. Flowers to look at a sore I had on my hip from some sort of bug bite.

Dr. Flowers, who liked to be called Ray, looked at my hip and immediately diagnosed the problem. He said that the sore was not caused by an insect bite, but rather it was due to the putzi fly. Evidently in washing my short pants and hanging them out to dry, a putzi fly had laid its eggs inside of my shorts. The egg hatched and the larvae burrowed under the skin of my hip where it was developing into a mature maggot as it fed on my tissue. The maggot was surrounded in pus. I actually felt it moving. Ray injected lidocaine and epinephrine to force the larvae out. Ray quickly popped out the maggot and dressed my wound. He told me to keep it clean and change the bandage daily.

Unfortunately for me, we had to travel to the lower Shire Valley and were gone for two days. The roads were still dusty from the dry season, and it was impossible for me to keep my wound clean. By the end of the second day, my wound had festered and was beginning to smell like rotten meat. I was very concerned. When we got back to Blantyre, I went back to see the doctor. He said that the wound was infected. He cleaned and lanced the wound, drawing out a copious amount of pus. He dressed the wound and told me that in the tropics, it was very important to keep the wound clean by washing the area and applying antiseptic and a clean bandage every day until the wound healed. This time, I followed his advice meticulously.

Our New Home

The Peace Corps office required the Ministry of Agriculture to provide housing for all six volunteers assigned to the Southern Regional Agricultural Office. Initially we were housed in an old tobacco plantation house that had long since been abandoned by European expatriates. The plantation house was located at the Mpemba agriculture station, seven miles from Blantyre. The department decided to use the house to provide temporary housing during our orientation to the work of the ministry. Eventually, four volunteers would be assigned to various stations throughout the region and two of us to the regional office in Blantyre.

Barbara Durr

I had received three letters from my girlfriend Barbara Durr. Barbara would graduate next year from Berea College. I hoped that she might think of joining me in Africa. She brought me updates on race relations in the States and on campus. After reading Barbara's letters, I felt very fortunate to be in Africa and not having to worry about racism and discrimination.

Zomba, Capital of Malawi

As part of our orientation, the AV volunteers traveled to Zomba, the capital city where our Extension Aid headquarters was located. The Peace Corps office found us accommodations at the Zomba Hotel on the outskirts of town. A brick structure with a large wraparound veranda in front extending to both sides of the building, the hotel was obviously built during the early days of British colonial rule. The hotel had about

20 rooms, with a small dining area and a large popular bar. The bar was a favorite hangout for Malawians. The rooms were nice enough, and we all had private ones.

Michael Abrams, the Peace Corps' consulting psychiatrist, joined our group for our final evaluation. During most of our training outside of Tuskegee, Alabama, Doc, as we called him, would stop by our camp and just sort of blend in and observe. I did not know that he was using that time to provide an assessment of each of the volunteers in the program.

Before arriving in Blantyre, Michael traveled to Israel to spend a few weeks at a kibbutz. Doc met us in Malawi and stayed with us in the Zomba Hotel. That night, we all had dinner followed by a beer in the bar when we heard this terrible crashing sound. We rushed down the hall to discover the ceiling in Michael's room had totally collapsed. The ceiling, heavy with thick plaster from wall to wall, fell, covering the entire floor of the room. We all realized that if Michael had been in the room at the time, he would have been seriously injured or even killed due to the weight of the plaster ceiling. He was visibly shaken as we all were. Turns out that termites had attacked the ceiling first and weakened it until the support beams gave way. Michael got another room, and we stayed up all night worrying if the ceilings in our rooms would give way during the night.

By the following night, things had calmed down and the debris from the ceiling had been cleaned up and removed from the room. We had our usual dinner and joined some new African acquaintances in the bar. After a few beers, we retired to our rooms.

Nearly De-Selected from Peace Corps

During our stay at the Zomba Hotel, I got to know Michael better. Over a beer one evening, Michael told me about the selection process and how I was almost de-selected—that was Peace Corps language for not making the cut. I was totally taken by surprise. Nothing could have prepared me for this revelation. I felt as if I was wrongly judged for being the product of my environment and experience.

I had volunteered for the Peace Corps during the height of the Civil Rights movement in the United States where Civil Rights activists were still being beaten, shot and killed. We may never know how many were killed because their bodies were never found. Following James Meredith's march in Mississippi where he was shot, Stokely Carmichael called for "Black Power." I was working for the Kentucky Human Rights Commission where we were supposed to be mediators rather than advocates. Yet I was active in CORE and participated in the regular meetings as part of my job. When Blacks in Lexington, Kentucky, started demanding integration of the schools, CORE took to the streets, demonstrating in front of the superintendent's office, and for the first time, we shouted, "Black Power! What do we want? Black Power!" I still marvel at how quickly the movement went from non-violent action to Black Power advocacy.

By the time I was ready to enter the Peace Corps, I was tired of being a second-class citizen. Even though we had begun to break down the barriers to full citizenship, life for Blacks in the United States had always been a struggle against those who wanted to keep Black people in their place. I came to have some strong feelings against those Whites who tried to block the advancement of Black people. I wanted to go to Africa. I felt like going to Africa as a missionary was one way to escape from the constant racism I faced daily. By the time I had my first job after college, I had very little use for White people and did not mind expressing my feelings. I did not dislike all White people, but a White person had to prove they were not a racist to be my friend.

It never occurred to me that my attitude and behavior toward Whites would reflect on the assessment of my fitness to be a Peace Corps volunteer who represented this country. Now that I am here, I know that I was a better representative of my country in Africa than other Americans here, especially those in the foreign service. I think that as a Black person, I can give an honest assessment of democracy in America. In retrospect, I now know that this was not what the Peace Corps was looking for in their volunteers.

When I reflected on some of the volunteers who made it over here, there was at least one racist in the group, a guy from the Midwest. He did not mind letting people know his opposition to the Civil Rights movement and people on welfare. Obviously, racism did not appear to be a problem for the Peace Corps staff, but he was going to an all–Black country. I wondered just how he was fit to serve. I did not try to hide my dislike and disdain for him even as I was being assessed for my fitness to represent my country. I could only guess that my perceived hostile attitude toward Whites was one more thing our trainers and psychiatrist took into consideration in assessing my fitness to serve in the Peace Corps. I was oblivious to what was going on in their minds. Michael did not tell me any of this until after we were finally sworn in. I was not sure how and why I was allowed to remain as a volunteer. I can only assume that Michael had given me the benefit of the doubt. I still get angry when I think about how an avowed racist got the green light to represent the United States in an African country while I was almost denied a chance to come to my homeland.

Berea College students on the march from Selma to Montgomery, March 25, 1965. I am wearing glasses and am behind the letter H on the banner (courtesy Mike Clark, photographer).

The Extension Aids Office

Our time at the Zomba Hotel was spent completing our in-country orientation before we headed out to the extension aids office at the Ministry of Agriculture. I was surprised to learn that the national office was still headed by a British expatriate by the name of Derrick McKinley. His top assistants were also British, with mid-level and lower-level positions held by Africans. I was the only Black person in my Peace Corps group, and I was not sure how I felt about being the first Black person to serve as a regional officer in the southern region. I would learn that the southern regional office was still controlled by expatriates. The volunteers headed to the central and northern regions would serve among African regional extension officers. By the end of the week, we were ready to depart to our various stations and duty assignments. Six of us were to serve in regional extension aids offices. Two were heading north to the regional capital of Mzuzu, two to Lilongwe and two to the southern region. Rather than serve with us in Blantyre, John Hunter was assigned to the national Extension Aid Office in Zomba, the capital city, where the Ministry of Agriculture was headquartered. So that left Tom Barker, who was assigned to serve in the regional cotton office while my assignment was in extension aids in the same regional office. While the southern regional officer looked for housing for Doug MacDonald, Dick Caldwell, Tom and me, we were all temporarily assigned to Mpemba, an agricultural station.

Our Home at Mpemba

The Mpemba plantation had not functioned as a plantation for who knows how long. To get to our new home, we had to travel about six miles from Blantyre south on Chikwawa Road and make a right turn at the local bar. Once we passed the bar and headed toward our house, we found ourselves on a path that barely passed as a road. The road became one lane that stretched a mile before crossing a bridge over a small stream, then up a slight grade to what looked like a mansion that occupied the most prominent spot in the area. Tobacco had been planted on the surrounding land before the bush encroached on once-fertile soil. Villages were within sight but far in the distance.

The old plantation house was brick with a corrugated metal roof. The most prominent feature was the front veranda that extended the width of the house. There were double doors that allowed entrance into the living

The plantation house at Mpemba.

and dining rooms with a large fireplace in the center of the living room. To the right were a bedroom and a sun porch. To the left of the dining room was a large bedroom with windows both on the front and side. There was a small sunroom that probably served at one time as a reading room. What was to be my bedroom also had a fireplace. Leaving the dining room, there was a bathroom to the left with a real tub, toilet and sink but no running water. Behind the living room was another central bedroom that Tom occupied and a smaller room that led to the kitchen and storage areas. Doug and Dick would temporarily occupy the third bedroom to the right of the living room. Behind the kitchen was a large tank with a hand pump that once drew water from the stream, about a half mile at the bottom of the hill. The kitchen had a built-in sink and a black iron wood-burning stove. The only other building was a carriage house to the right of the house. Tom and I would share this abandoned plantation house for the first year in Malawi.

Dick Caldwell was assigned to work in Nsanje in the lower Shire Valley, Doug MacDonald was assigned to the Balaka/Ntcheu area, John Hunter was assigned to the national extension aids office in Zomba and Tom and I to the southern regional office in Blantyre. Dick and Doug were also assigned to work under the overall supervision of the regional cotton officer. One by one, housing was secured until each volunteer had his own place in his own district. Tom and I were left to live together in the big plantation home.

The Ministry of Agriculture and the Peace Corps office provided our furniture needs: we each got a bed, table, two dining room chairs, a side chair and a paraffin (kerosene) stove. Even with combining Tom's and my furniture allotments, they did not do much to fill up the large space in the plantation house.

Not long after being in the country, I realized that the Honda 90 was too small for all the travel I had to do. I went back to the Peace Corps office and asked Howard if I could have a larger bike. He sent me over to the warehouse where Rob gave me a Honda 125. While there, Rob allowed Tom and me to select some of the old furniture that had been discarded by Peace Corps staff or members of the U.S. embassy in Malawi. I got a well-worn easy chair, some hurricane lamps, one gaslight, a tin for carrying paraffin, a water filter, a sideboard and, above all else, a paraffin refrigerator. We were all set. We had everything we needed to start our new lives in Malawi.

Some Thoughts About Barbara

While in training in London, I told Barbara to send her letters to me addressed to the Peace Corps office in Blantyre. I had been sending her postcards while traveling, but now I was going to write a long letter to her telling her how much I missed her and wished that she were here. I had dated Barbara for a year after graduating from Berea. It was hard for me to leave Barbara, but I promised that I would write every week. I was sure that we would be married if I had been in the States. I thought she understood my commitment to Africa and the need to determine if being a missionary would be my life's work. I hoped that our letters would be enough to cement our love for each other.

The Regional Agriculture Office

The office was located just north of downtown. The offices were in three different buildings that were connected with a covered walkway. Tom was placed in the cotton office under the director of the office, C. JW looked just like the typical British expatriate—mixed gray hair with a handlebar mustache. JW was nice enough and seemed less prejudiced against Africans than his other British colleagues. I was sure it was because his wife was Indian. They had five children, all handsome and brown. Tom liked working for JW, who seemed to like all three volunteers under his supervision.

As the first Black extension aids officer for the southern region, I broke new ground. Malawi had gained independence in 1964, and by the end of 1967, there was not one African regional officer in the southern region. Both the northern and central regions not only had replaced Europeans with Malawians, but each regional office also had an African head. It may have been easier for the British to give up control of the less developed central and northern regions. The last bastions of the British civil service were in Blantyre and Zomba, which was apparent as soon as I walked into the main office building and saw all White faces. Howard introduced me to Nigel Murphy, the regional officer, and his colleague Troy David, the training officer for the region. The two shared the same office and appeared to be close friends.

I reported directly to Nigel, who seemed nice enough, so my first impression was that I was going to enjoy working with him. Nigel, Troy and I talked while enjoying a cup of tea before they showed me to my office. It was a small but adequate room for a one-person operation. The office had a small desk, a draftsman's table, and a filing cabinet. There were windows on both sides of a corner office that faced the street. Nigel and Troy, as they asked to be called, had been working on developing a darkroom located next to my office. The only African of any standing in the office was Frank Bonomi, who was the chief accountant. There were dozens of clerks and messengers spread throughout the office but not high enough in rank for the courtesy of an introduction by Nigel. Nigel showed me the location of the European men's restroom. Even though I was Black, I was an educated American and expected to share the values of other Europeans and thus had the privilege to use the "White toilet." At the time, it never occurred to me that I was viewed as an "honorary" White. During the Jim Crow era in the South, there was no such thing as an honorary White. If you were Black, you had to use the segregated facilities reserved for "coloreds" without exception. The European restroom was kept cleaner than the facilities reserved for the Africans. It did not bother me to use the cleaner facility.

By the end of the day, I had settled into the office and had it somewhat organized. After work, Tom, Dick, Doug, and I drove our motorcycles out of town past the Catholic church and school. We stopped at a little African tavern for a beer before heading home. It had been a long day.

Adjusting to My New Life in Blantyre

As the Christmas holiday approached, the work schedule slowed down. I used the slowdown in work activities as an opportunity to get to know a little about Blantyre, which had a quaint sleepy commercial center even if it was the largest city in the country. I loved going to the African markets. The Blantyre market was full of vendors with their fruit, vegetable, meat and fish stalls. We made regular trips to the market to buy our food and were often surrounded by vendors eager to sell us their produce.

There was also a European grocery store in Blantyre called the Kandodo supermarket. I just learned that President Banda was a big investor in these supermarkets spread throughout the country. The market had everything one could find in an American supermarket, but in Malawi, processed food was imported from South Africa, Southern Rhodesia and, of course, Britain. Shortly after arriving in the country, Britain devalued the pound on November 18, 1967. Malawi followed suit. Most of us had already converted our dollars into Malawi pounds or kwachas and lost about 14 percent of the value of our readjustment allowance. We were told that as long as we purchased Malawi goods, we should be OK.

Malawi government employees worked a half day on Saturdays. We all got Saturday off since Christmas was the following Monday. I used my time off to continue to get to know the area and our new neighbors. Before we even moved into our new lodgings, we met Edward Limbani, who lived with his wife and five children, all under six, at Mpemba. They lived in a government-constructed three-bedroom house that was built for less than 500 pounds. Kitchens and bathrooms were located outside of the house.

Often wives and children ate their meals outside on mats on the ground while the father/husband sat on a chair at a table in the house. Edward had a wonderful family—a beautiful wife and children. Yet he followed the traditional practice of eating separately from his family, at least when company was present.

A Malawi Christmas

On Christmas Eve, Edward Limbani picked us up and took us to his in-laws in a village not far from where we lived. We spent the entire day there. Our host for the day was David Banda, who was a local businessman and headman or chief in the village. Mr. Banda owned the store and bar at the top of the hill and at the intersection of Chikwawa Road and the road leading to Mpemba. He drove a large truck, or as they were called here, a lorry, and always had several workers on the flatbed of the truck. He always waved when he saw any of us. It did not take us long to discover the local bar that he owned. He had invited Edward and his wife to join his family for Christmas Eve dinner. Edward was from Dedza and had no immediate family in the area. He asked Edward to invite the volunteers who lived at Mpemba.

I could not think of a better way to spend our first Christmas Eve than with a Malawian family. There was no commercialism or presents and decorations that we felt were so essential to making a perfect holiday. There was no exchange of gifts as was the tradition in the States. I suppose we could have or should have taken our host family some sort of gift, but we did not think about it beforehand. Therefore, we were the recipients of the generosity of a stranger. When Edward picked us up, we greeted Edward and Mrs. Limbani and their children. We all said, "Muli bwanji?" (How are you?) to which she replied, "Ndili bwino" (I am fine). Mrs. Limbani said, "Mumayankhula Chichewa?" I replied, "Pang'ono, Ndiyenera kuphunzira" (I replied that I speak a little Chichewa and that I need to learn). Edward said that his wife did not speak English and that I could learn how to speak Chichewa just by talking with her.

I thought to myself just how much I hated learning a language, any language. At the end of Peace Corps training, I managed to qualify for level 1, the minimum proficiency for entering the foreign service. I really detested learning French in high school and speaking it with my poor pronunciation. As part of my preparation for the priesthood, I studied Latin at Berea with Miss Ludlum as our Latin teacher. She would always laugh at my translations. It was not just a giggle or a soft laughter. She would laugh out loud and roll from side to side at her desk. I think her ridicule destroyed what little confidence I had left for learning a language.

Chapter Two. My First Year in Malawi

Mr. Banda welcomed us to his home, which was built in a European style with sheet metal roof and cement flooring. There was modern furniture and even electricity, an indication of Mr. Banda's wealth. Mrs. Banda came in from the kitchen to greet all of us and introduced her mother who crawled on her hands and knees from the doorway to where we were sitting. Even though this was a common practice for village women to greet male elders or men with status or education, I was very uncomfortable with how women showed respect.

Mrs. Banda had her house girl bring in some tea for all to drink. The tea was mixed with milk and sweetened with loads of sugar. Christmas carols were being played on the radio in the background alternately in English and Chichewa. Mr. Banda was very curious about where we came from and why we chose to come to Malawi. He was very knowledgeable about current events and what was happening in the States. He asked me if I, being Black, felt like a real American having been treated like a second-class citizen in the States. He wanted to know more about the Civil Rights movement and if children had really been bitten by vicious dogs and bruised by powerful fire hoses. He never seemed to tire of learning more information about America, especially how Black people were treated. While the other volunteers seemed somewhat uncomfortable, I said that our struggle in the United States was similar to the struggle of African people in Southern Africa. I did not mention the slow pace of Africanization in Malawi.

Our conversation was interrupted when Mrs. Banda came into the living room with a basket of swarming termites. While she showed us the basket of termites, her youngest child was snacking on several live termites. I immediately stood up and announced, "Ndikupita ku chimbudzi!" and immediately headed to the outside toilet. When I came back, everyone laughed because they knew that I thought that I was being offered live termites to sample.

When dinner was served, all the men sat at the dining room table while the women and children took their meals on a mat at the back of the house. The meal was delicious. Mrs. Banda prepared curried chicken, lamb stew with onions and tomatoes, okra, nsima and fried termites. The termites had been fried in their own juices or fat. The wings had been removed and the body fried until they were brown and crispy. The nsima was corn meal grounded into a fine powder and then cooked and constantly stirred until a stiff paste formed. Nsima is a staple in Malawi and eaten with a vegetable or meat relish. Everyone laughed again when I kept putting salt on my nsima to give it some taste.

Following dinner, we drove with Mr. Banda to the nearby village to witness traditional dances in celebration of the holidays. Despite the fact

Village farmer's traditional farmhouse with grain storage bins.

that it was getting late, villagers still maintained a large bonfire that burned in the village center. We were greeted as if we were Hollywood celebrities. One by one the villagers came to greet us: first the men and the women, the older ones kneeling out of respect for the Europeans (anyone White was considered a European). Edward told the village headman that we wanted to see traditional dancing. No sooner had he spoken than people began to dance in a circle moving counterclockwise. We were not allowed to be spectators for long. As we gazed at the dancers, we were pulled into a circle. Tom and Doug were awkward in trying to keep time to the rhythm of the drums. Dick must have learned how to dance watching *American Bandstand* back home because he danced with ease and had no problem keeping up with the drumbeats. As for me, I felt like I was home. I soon learned the rhythmic movements of the feet, legs and arms. The whole thing could have been a dance around a bonfire following a football game in my hometown of Morganton, North Carolina. Some people started singing as they danced in a counterclockwise circle, which was punctuated by periodic shouts. We danced until we were exhausted. Edward gathered us up, and we thanked all the villagers for a wonderful entertaining evening.

"Dinners" on Christmas Day

We all slept late the next morning. Nigel Murphy had invited us to his house for dinner. He said that his wife was planning on serving dinner

Chapter Two. My First Year in Malawi

around noon on Christmas Day. Nigel was married to his childhood girlfriend, who had followed him to Malawi some 20 years earlier. All of their children were born in Malawi, went to grade school here but were sent back to England, at the expense of the government, for their high school education. His two boys were back home from boarding school in England while his youngest, the only girl, was still in the mostly White elementary school in Blantyre. Even after independence, only a few of the children of well-off Africans could afford to attend the all–White school. It was reminiscent of the token integration that occurred in the South following the Supreme Court *Brown v. Board of Education* decision.

Mrs. Murphy was very pleasant. She was still a young-looking woman compared to Nigel who had lost most of his hair. The traditional Christmas meal consisted of a goose and all the trimmings. It was the first time that I had had English pudding. The wine served with dinner was from South Africa. Despite my reservations about eating anything or buying anything from South Africa, I must admit that the wine was very good. The dinner gave me an opportunity to see a side of Nigel that I had not seen before. He was nice and was rather jolly outside of the office.

We all enjoyed our dinner but said that we had to leave at 4:00 p.m. to travel to Mulanje to meet up with the other volunteers. We intentionally failed to mention that we were having another Christmas dinner that evening.

Tom, Doug, Dick and I drove to Carl Scott's house in Mulanje. Carl lived in a modern two-bedroom house on the district agriculture department property. I think we were a little jealous of his living conditions because the house has a "real" kitchen with running water, a gas stove, a refrigerator and electricity. He had an indoor bathroom with a sink and toilet. What a luxury for a volunteer. He was not the only volunteer living well. There were some education volunteers teaching in secondary schools who also had similar living arrangements. Secondary schools were residential and all teachers were provided housing. Carl was a good host who cooked an excellent meal. He was quick to hook up with Gloria, the best-looking girl in the office. Gloria and her colleague Penny joined us for Christmas dinner.

By the time we arrived, Carl had most of the food prepared. He had roasted a leg of lamb and several chickens on his grill outside of his kitchen. The meal was a feast by all standards. We had plenty of Portuguese wine, which Dick brought with him from the Lower Shire Valley near the Mozambique border. He routinely crossed the border for Portuguese food and rosé wine. Gloria and Carl made four quarts of eggnog, which was spiked with brandy. I was not sure where they got the brandy. It was imported and probably expensive. When we arrived, people had started on the wine and eggnog, and everyone was in a good mood. We ate late enough in the evening that those of us from Blantyre were ready to eat again. We all enjoyed the dinner. After dinner, we gathered in the living room and sang Christmas carols. Despite the warm weather, we sat on the floor by the fireplace and continued drinking wine. Someone took out some joints, which we passed around. It was not long before we were all high and laughing at anything remotely funny. By midnight, we were all exhausted and decked out in our sleeping bags on the floor by the fire. Although I was the only Black person in the group, I had an unusual sense of camaraderie with my colleagues. It was a nice first Christmas in Malawi.

Getting into a Routine

Several weeks ago, Tom and I wanted to be more involved in our village community and decided that we would teach English classes on our veranda, which covered the entire front of the plantation house. Our local neighbors were anxious to learn to speak English well. While we picked up on some Chichewa words, teaching had not helped us improve our command of their language. The village children and their mothers attended our classes. The children were quick to learn, but we found their mothers were shy or reserved and did not talk very much.

Doug and Dick were now settled in their respective communities. Doug lived in Matope, a little village with a couple of East Indian stores and a small African market. Doug was given a small brick house on the outskirts of town. Dick was assigned to the Lower Shire Valley and was now working out of the local agricultural extension office. Dick was given a small trailer with a bed, kitchen facility, shower and compost toilet. He had a little sitting area with a workstation. So that left Tom and me alone in the large plantation house. I had the front bedroom and Tom had the middle room.

We had fallen into a good routine. We got up in the morning, washed, dressed and ate fruit and maybe an egg for breakfast. We rode our motorcycles together seven miles into town. When we first arrived in the country at the end of the dry season, the roads were dry and dusty. When the rainy season began, the roads initially were compacted and easy for us to maneuver our bikes. Since the rains did not come until early afternoon, we had no trouble driving into town to work. The return trip home was another matter. The roads became muddy, and the bikes became difficult to maneuver.

On the way to work, there were always many people walking along the side of the road heading to their jobs in town. I felt somewhat guilty riding when so many people had to walk. The real lucky ones had bicycles that they use not only for transportation but also to haul their goods to market. It took us only about 15 minutes to travel by bike from our house to the regional agricultural office. Tom parked his bike in front of his office, and I parked my bike next to the Land Rovers on the side closer to my office.

Each regional officer had a Land Rover and driver. Even though they were perfectly capable of driving themselves, the custom, probably from colonial days, provided jobs for hundreds of Malawi men throughout the country. There were four Land Rovers at the office and one Mini Moke. I had never heard of a Mini Moke before, but the car looked more like a golf cart than a traditional car. Nigel told me that the department purchased a Mini Moke shortly after they were introduced by the British Motor Corporation as an off-road military vehicle.

Our work was getting to be routine and enjoyable.

Our Houseboy

Our neighbor and friend Edward Limbani was indispensable in getting us adjusted to our new neighborhood. He showed us where the stream was located and the water well with its hand pump. We had been supplied with five five-gallon buckets to carry our water from the well to the house. The well was a little more than half a mile downhill from the house. Needless to say, the uphill walk from the well to the house with five-gallon water buckets was exhausting.

I found out that it is very common to hire a man to help with chores in Malawi. Edward helped us get a "houseboy" from the local village since our Chichewa was so bad. Stone Chomba, who was really a grown man, had a history of working for Europeans. Stone spoke broken English that was about as bad as my broken Chichewa. I could not help but ask Edward why Mr. Chomba was named "Stone." He said many Malawians like to choose names that have special meanings to their parents. In this case, Stone's father was clearing stones from a field for a garden when his son was born.

Stone moved into the room between the dining room and kitchen. It did not take Stone long to take over. During his first few days, he cleaned the house thoroughly from top to bottom and even polished the red cement floors. Malawians use wax and a cloth to clean and polish the floors on their hands and knees, a practice Stone followed with high efficiency. He was trained to cook traditional British food and had no experience cooking for Americans. So when we purchased a whole chicken at the supermarket and brought it home, we asked Stone if he knew how to fry chicken. He said yes.

I asked him if he could make southern fried chicken. He replied yes. That evening, to our surprise, Stone proudly brought in a perfectly browned "fried" whole chicken to the dinner table. I understood then that I had to be crystal clear and precise in my future communications with Stone.

I had no complaints about the way Stone washed our clothes, which he did in the traditional way, beating them against a stone until they became clean. Whatever he was doing to them, it worked. Our clothes were always clean. He ironed them with a hollow iron that contained hot charcoal bricks. How he managed to keep the ash from the coals from soiling the clothes I had yet to discover.

One afternoon I was out back using the toilet, or *chimbudzi* in Chichewa. That day, I was wearing long pants and had difficulty maneuvering around the toilet hole in the floor and I accidentally dropped my wallet into the hole. Needless to say, I was horrified that my wallet, money and driver's license all fell in the pit. I asked Stone if he might help me retrieve my wallet. He immediately went out and cut two long bamboo sticks and proceeded to pull out the wallet covered in excrement. Stone washed and dried the wallet, my money and my driver's license. Obviously, I never carried that wallet again, but I did bring myself to spend the sanitized paper money.

None of the other volunteers were used to having someone take care of their every need. I think that the biggest problem we had was giving orders. Supervision was complicated by the fact that Stone wanted to do things his way regardless of our instructions. One afternoon, after Stone had been working for us for a while, Tom said that eight pounds were missing from his trunk. Well, by this time, we were the only ones in the house. Tom immediately thought that Stone had taken the money. I was not willing to accuse him of being a thief, but he did have a habit of taking things that did not belong to him with the assumption that we either did not need the item or did not want it. Tom wanted to accuse Stone outright, but I said that I would speak with him. I talked to him about the necessity of being honest and trustworthy. I was not sure I had gotten through to him, but the next morning Tom's eight pounds mysteriously appeared on the table in the dining room. Although Tom was very happy to get his money back, he knew that Stone had taken and returned the money. Tom insisted that he be fired. I told him that he would have to do it. As reticent as Tom was, he got up the nerve to dismiss Stone, which left us once again on our own.

Climbing Mount Mulanje

A group of us decided to climb Mount Mulanje, the tallest mountain in Malawi at 10,000 feet. The mountain itself was very beautiful, and though rugged, from a distance it did not seem challenging. Bob Brown, the volunteer with expertise in veterinary medicine, was the only person from our group who came with practical and useful training. He was stationed at Tuchila Training Center with Carl Scott, and they jointly came up with the idea of climbing the mountain. From Tuchila, you could clearly see the clouds surrounding the mountain, which were constantly shifting and casting shadows on the mountain throughout the day, giving the impression that the mountain itself was ever changing. Carl's house had a terrific view of the mountain. While sitting in his living room, the sunrays crowned the mountain, making it a remarkable sight to behold.

Initially, I was excited about the idea of climbing Mount Mulanje, having never climbed a mountain before. But as the time approached to begin our journey, my enthusiasm slowly waned—in fact, I began to think of reasons not to do it.

The Friday before the trip was filled with confusion. We could not leave until Tom Barker returned from a field trip to Fort Johnston. It seemed like he was always late. While waiting for Tom, our new cook cut his foot and I had to transport him to the local infirmary on my motorbike. I waited until he had been treated and then brought him back to our house at Mpemba. Once Tom returned, we decided to take the government Mini Moke because neither of us wanted to ride our motorcycle to Tuchila.

Tea farmers below Mount Mulanje (courtesy Dana Allen, wildlife photographer, Harare, Zambia).

The Mini Moke was a level above riding a motorcycle but was much more stable because it rode low to the ground. Moke was an old-world word for mule, and that was just how it was treated. Our Mini Moke had open sides and a canvas top and seated four people. The first time I drove the Mini Moke, I must have been daydreaming because I entered the road going to the office driving on the "right" side and nearly ran into Nigel, who stopped, smiled and waited for me to realize that I needed to be on the left side of the road. His only comment was, "You Americans." We met up with Gloria from the Peace Corps office at Carl's house. We still had to travel that evening to get closer to the mountain so that we could start fresh the next morning.

We split into two groups as we headed out to Likabula where we secured our climbing permits and spent the night. The distance to Likabula was 30-plus miles, and even though I did not feel like driving the Mini Moke, I had no choice since Nigel Murphy had assigned the car to me. As we traveled toward the mountain, the tarmac ended and the roads became rougher. I grew steadily more tired as I drove, and as we approached a bend in the road, I knew instantaneously that I was going too fast to make the turn without the car overturning. I couldn't put on the brakes for fear of making matters worse. As I veered around the curve anticipating what I knew would be an accident, I was startled to see a bridge over a deep ravine and a river below. While Gloria dozed in the back, Carl immediately sensed the danger ahead. In a split second, I saw a drainage ditch leading from the road and immediately headed into the ditch with a hope and a prayer that the ditch would stop the car. When Carl saw that we were heading for the ravine, instead of alerting Gloria, his girlfriend in the back, he jumped out of the car alone, landing some 30 feet from the impact of the Mini Moke.

Carl later said that he jumped out of the car because he knew that if we had gone into the river, he would have had to save us. I felt that it was an act of God that saved us. The embankment did prevent the car from traveling on and heading to what I imagined was going to be a serious accident. No one was hurt; not even the Mini Moke was damaged for which I was thankful since it was a government vehicle and I had not been authorized to travel beyond the Tuchila Training Center. If the car had been damaged, the officials in the Ministry of Agriculture would have been furious, not to mention the Peace Corps office. I sat in the car, smoked a cigarette and tried to calm myself while Carl surveyed the situation.

After regaining my courage, I backed up the Mini Moke and we cautiously started up again. Carl had arranged for us to spend the night at his friend's house, which was located at the base of Mount Mulanje. When we arrived, the house was pitch dark with no sign that anyone was home. The

Chapter Two. My First Year in Malawi

house was a relic from the colonial period and looked spooky. It reminded me of our house at Mpemba but not as large. We finally located the night watchman living on the property who could let us in, but he did not speak any English and our Chichewa was not good enough to explain why we were there and what we wanted. It really did not matter because he did not have a key and did not seem interested in helping us, nor did he mind us trying to enter the house. I guess it was because "we" were Europeans. We found an unlocked door on the side of the house. We entered, each found somewhere to place our sleeping bags and quickly settled down for the night.

The next day we were up by 6:00 a.m. We each had a cup of tea and then loaded the car with our sleeping bags and other gear and went off in the Mini Moke to the base of the mountain. We stopped at the Forestry Department outpost where we acquired our Malawian guide and started on what was to become one of the longest and most tiresome journeys of my life.

Our Malawian guide, who obviously had made this journey many times before, helped us with our gear. The guide carried the heaviest knapsack, which had our food and other supplies. Our journey would take us across the plateau to the pinnacle of the mountain where we planned to stay overnight in one of the cabins provided for tourists by the Forestry Department for a modest fee. I followed closely behind the guide as he set a brisk pace up the gentle slope of the mountain. It was not long before I realized that I could not match the guide's pace. The guide was twice my age and carried twice the load of the Peace Corps volunteers. We soon found ourselves on a steeper grade that would lead us up 10,000 feet to the peak of the mountain. I began to breathe heavily. I was sure it was due to being out of shape for this sort of activity and several years of smoking a pack of cigarettes a day. I had been smoking since I was 16 and should have given up the habit now that I was on a limited volunteer income. The concession I made to my restricted budget was instead of smoking expensive American cigarettes while in London, I began smoking a moderately priced cigarette, which I continue to buy in Malawi. I tried a locally made Malawi cigarette that was six for three pence, but they had a horrible taste. So I bit the bullet and paid a little more for cigarettes that had a milder flavor.

Gloria and Carl followed more slowly as they took time to enjoy the scenery and the lushness of the evergreen forest of cedar trees. I told the guide in my version of Chichewa, "Dikinani—pang'ono, pang'ono" (Wait, little by little), in my effort to get him to slow down and wait for the others. Waiting for Carl and Gloria to catch up was my excuse to take a needed break. I could not believe that I was exhausted after just 15 minutes of climbing and we had more than 5 hours of climbing before we joined the other volunteers at the top of the mountain.

We all rested for 10 minutes and then proceeded up and up and up. The incline was never ending. The clouds provided a lot of rain over the mountain contributing to many streams that flowed down the slopes. We passed stream after stream. Initially, they were narrow and we had little difficulty jumping over them. Gloria had some hesitancy in crossing the streams. Her hesitancy and then awkwardness as she jumped over the last stream made me laugh, which I tried not to show. We proceeded. The slope of the mountain seemed to increase the farther we traveled; it felt as if we were walking up a 90-degree incline.

As we moved ever upward, I stepped on a rock and turned my ankle slightly. I suffered from weak ankles as a kid spraining either the left or right ankle occasionally. I fell to the ground on my back barely missing rolling into the stream. I was very fortunate that neither the fall nor the sprain was serious. I soon felt better and was up on my feet. We moved on. Ever upward.

We were told that the water on Mount Mulanje was really pure and safe to drink, unlike in other parts of the country where we had been advised by the Peace Corps not to drink the water without it being boiled. However, our guide would not allow us to drink the spring water until we reached 3,000 feet. We soon came upon a small but swiftly flowing stream where we stopped for a drink and to refill our canteens. We now entered the drainage basin for this magnificent green rainforest. The trees, vines and moss were all various shades of rich green hues that created such beauty that was almost magical. This was a major stop on our journey, which gave us time to appreciate our surroundings. While we stopped for five minutes every half hour, this time we rested for half an hour while drinking the cool water and eating our cheese and biscuits that we had brought with us.

We were soon back on what seemed like a never-ending trail. Carl and I exchanged packs to give me some relief. We climbed one hill after another. I expected to reach our destination as soon as we reached the top of the hill, only to find another hill in front of us. It seemed that there was always a higher hill to climb. I limited my smoking to two cigarettes, which helped my breathing.

When we reached our first plateau on the pinnacle of Mount Mulanje, I believed that we had finally arrived at the top of the mountain. We hadn't, but I was still surprised to see how impressive everything looked from there, which almost made me forget how tired I had become. Looking over the plains, I got a real feeling of communion with nature. We all took in the view as the clouds began to descend on top of the mountain. These were the clouds that we had seen from a distance as we traveled to

Tuchila. The clouds quickly encircled us in a bath of cool, fine mist. There were a variety of flowers along the tall, needlelike grass. The trees were remarkable in that they were stunted and twisted into all sorts of shapes and sizes by the harshness of the changing weather on the mountain.

By noon, we had reached our first major stop and the first rest cabin where we had lunch, which consisted of roast chicken, bread, and cheese. I was surprised to learn that because of our many breaks, we were already two hours behind schedule. The rain began to fall as we finished our lunch under the thatched roof.

By 1:30 p.m., we were on our way across the plateau of the mountain. The clouds now protected us from the sunrays but also became more menacing as they thickened. We continued to walk and walk. When we asked our guide how much longer, he said, "Five hours." By 5:30 p.m., we STILL had five hours to go according to our guide.

We traveled up one trail and down another. My feet, back, legs and whole body pulsed with pain. The only time I smiled through my pain was when Gloria fell into a hole filled with water. For whatever reason, she was clumsy that day. We did not take as many breaks as before, as we were all anxious to get to our destination. There was another peak we had to climb before moving on a more downward slope. I honestly began to feel that I would not make it, as each step was becoming more and more difficult.

As we approached 8,500 feet, I began to fall behind. The higher elevation clouds began to descend on top of us, bringing a chill to the damp air. Nightfall was moving in quickly with all signs pointing to a soaking rain. By this time, I had fallen in the dark several times. The rest of the team wanted to keep moving. I don't remember how I managed to put one foot in front of the other. I told Carl to just leave me. I was ready to give up, to lie down and go to sleep.

When I was almost overcome with the dread of another step and ready to give up, at 7:30 p.m., we saw a light ahead of us that filled us with joy and renewed hope that this journey would end. We rushed toward the light to find Tom and Bob in front of us. We were so happy to see them and to learn that the cabin was only a short distance away. This motivated us to move quickly despite exhaustion. Our rustic cabin was warm and inviting. Bob had built a fire in the fireplace. We laid on the floor in an effort to relax our very tired bones and muscles. We, or I should say Bob, hurriedly cooked our dinner and we all went straight to bed in our sleeping bags.

The next day arrived too soon. Although the journey back down the mountain was much easier and quicker than going up, both Carl and I suffered from a twisted ankle and sore feet. The trip down the mountain was uneventful. It was a steady descent lasting less than four hours. When we reached the bottom, the rains came with a vengeance, but nothing bothered me since we were coming to the end of our journey, or so I thought.

After about a half hour, the rain stopped and the sun came out. The heat from the sun quickly dried our soaked clothes. We found a stream with fresh water and then relaxed under a mango tree. I think I must have eaten a dozen of the sweetest mangoes I had ever had.

We started off again and soon reached the road only to learn that we had crossed the mountain and the return trip around the periphery of the mountain was over 10 miles to where we had left the Mini Moke. We managed to get a lift for the first three miles and then we started walking again. Carl borrowed a bike from a local man and gave it to me. He said since I was in charge of the Mini Moke that I should ride the bike to get the car and return to pick up the team. I agreed, not knowing that as soon as I rode out of sight, the rest of the trip was all uphill. I ended up not riding the bike but pushing it uphill. I was furious with Carl not only for having to walk the remaining miles but also for the added burden of having to push the bike all the way.

I reached our starting point where we had parked the Mini Moke around 4:30 p.m. For a fleeting moment I thought of driving back to Blantyre

I'm driving the Department of Agriculture Mini Moke.

and leaving them stranded, but it was just a passing thought. I drove back to where I left Carl and Bob. After returning the loaned bike and getting gas, we were finally ready to meet the others. I drove back to Carl's house where we had refreshments and then back to Blantyre. Tom and I arrived back at our house at Mpemba after 8:00 p.m. completely exhausted. After grabbing a bite to eat, heating water, and taking a bath, we both retired to our rooms exhausted but thankful for a safe journey to Mount Mulanje and back.

I vowed that I would never climb another mountain or go on such an exhausting trip again. But in spite of the demanding experience, I looked forward to having another adventure soon.

Thoughts on Peace Corps Volunteers

I was happy and had this sense of contentment. My work was going well and the class that I was teaching gave me a sense of having an impact. I did want to meet more people and become part of life here. I had two people over for dinner after returning from Mount Mulanje. It was pleasant enough, but each time I was around some volunteers, they often just reinforced my previous impressions. Except for some members of my group with whom I worked, I didn't seek out the company of other volunteers. I decided early on that I would not go to Peace Corps gatherings. I thought that it was too easy for me living in Blantyre to become involved with other volunteers and isolate myself from the Malawians. It would have been too comfortable for me to fall in with other Peace Corps cliques. I must admit that I was awfully tempted to join the other volunteers for the weekly Peace Corps breakfasts at Todd Mayes's house. Todd was a nice person and a good director, but I did not come to Africa to socialize with Americans. I had to make a concerted effort to reach out to Malawians and not become too involved with other volunteers.

Thoughts on Expatriates

I stopped going to church because I felt it was filled with hypocrisy, which was strange behavior for a person wanting to become a minister. I did go to the Society of Friends' (Quakers') meeting here in Blantyre that met twice a week. I was active with the local Quaker group in Berea. The Berea Friends came the closest thing to being non-racist in the larger, more conservative community. Like me, the Berea Friends were against the war in Vietnam. I was not sure yet about the group here in Malawi. I was willing to give the group a chance before making judgment.

I hoped that I was not becoming racist myself. Sometimes that happens when you live in a racist society. I thought I was escaping racism in coming to Africa, only to be confronted with it from the English expats and White South Africans. I didn't seem to be able to control my dislike of these folks. I felt very angry and bitter at times. I suppose that's what I expressed during Peace Corps training in Alabama. The fact that the British were still in control here in Malawi did not make the situation any better. The expatriates seemed to put roadblocks in front of Malawians as they tried to advance, especially in areas that might threaten the Whites' positions of authority. I knew that the White officers in my regional office would have liked to have viewed me as one of them, but that was not going to happen. As far as I was concerned, neo-colonialism was alive and well in Malawi despite official independence from the British. The fact was that Whites were still in control of this African country; no matter how altruistic they appeared, they were still in control. There was a gulf between the Whites and Blacks and it could not be bridged until the Whites gave up their control and turned over their government positions to Malawians. I was very disheartened at the racism and segregation in this African country.

Nigel Murphy—thought to be a good guy by me initially—turned out to be the epitome of the neo-colonialist. This was brought home to me—hard and fast—while this Malawian woman was using the phone in my office. She asked me earlier if she could use it. Murphy, passing by the office, stopped and demanded with such a harsh tone that she stop talking immediately and put down the phone. I was so taken aback that I had to turn and make sure that this was the Nigel I knew. He surprised the lady who finally just left the office in tears after a minor protest. At the time, I did nothing, and I hated myself for not speaking out. No Malawian man would ever talk to a British woman like that. Since I disagreed with Murphy's behavior, why did I not say anything at the time? That in itself made me an accessory to the act. Malawians had every right to use the phone, especially when they were charged four cents a call, a lot of money for people who made so little. His justification was that the lady was tying up the phone. Well, the British used the phone whenever they got ready, including for personal calls.

Travels in the Lower Shire Valley

I missed Barbara most when I was lonely and rather depressed. She was a good sounding board for my thoughts and feelings even if it was a long-distance correspondence. I began my last letter to Barbara by telling her of a trip to the southern tip of Malawi that I took the previous week. I'd spent a day in Ngabu and then went on to Nsanje and on to Mozambique. I'd met up with Dick Caldwell, the volunteer in our group, who was part of the cotton team and assigned to the area. We'd gone to his house for a late lunch. It was odd that Dick and I became friends—a White southerner from Alabama and I, a Black man from North Carolina. Dick and I did not have much in common during training. I saw him as a White man who had been the star of his football team who was able to attract all of the girls in high school and then in college. He was best friends with Doug and Carl Scott. I was standoffish with all the volunteers.

Only after we arrived at our post, prior to Dick's final assignment, did Dick and I get to know each other better at our plantation house at Mpemba. We talked during the evenings and had some serious conversations about life, the South, integration and racism. It was not until he was assigned his post at Nsanje in the Lower Shire Valley that Dick and I became friends.

As the extension aids officer for the region, it was my responsibility to supply all of the audio-visual needs of the field staff and especially the staff of the district and divisional training centers. I liked my job because it took me to all corners of the region. It allowed me to get to know a lot of Malawians and to keep in touch with members of our agriculture group. I was glad that I was able to swap my Honda 90 for the heavier Honda 125 because I never would have made the trip to Nsanje on the lighter motorcycle. As a regional officer, I could use the office's Mini Moke for long trips. Otherwise, I had to secure an office Land Rover and driver from one of the other officers for travel outside of town. There was something about having a driver that did not sit well with me. I knew that I should not have felt that way because having drivers for the office provided a lot of work for Malawians.

The next day, we all went to Ngabu where I did an assessment of the needs of the rural training center and what support was needed to help the staff carry out their educational programs among the farmers. I talked with individual instructors and field staff to determine the visual-aid needs of the staff. It was remarkable how effective these simple tools were in helping farmers understand ways to improve their crop. For example, the use of before and after posters showing the effect of fertilizer helped farmers visualize the impact of fertilization on increased crop yields. Malawi farmers were poor and anything that increased their crop yield had a direct impact on their standard of living. After completing my work with the staff, we decided to go over the border into Mozambique to buy beer and wine.

The Lower Shire Valley had been carved out over time by the Shire River. Lake Malawi empties into the Shire and travels southeast until it enters Mozambique. By the time it is in the Lower Shire Valley, the river is wide and somewhat swift. The land it traverses is low and flat, good alluvial farming land. The drawback of living in the Lower Shire Valley is that at night the mosquitoes swarm in droves. I did not believe how bad it was until I wiped my arm one evening to find it full of bloody mosquitoes.

During the rainy season, a simple trip of 20 miles often took over one and a half hours. We arrived across the border around noon and proceeded to the local bar and restaurant to have a cold Portuguese beer. It seemed as if we were always drinking beer, but when you could not trust the local drinking water, a beer was the next best thing. We started drinking and eventually lost count of how many beers we had consumed. We were high by the time we were ready to leave. We purchased a large jug of Portuguese wine and left.

The area supervisor suggested that we go to his house for food and, of course, more beer. We ate, drank beer and danced to American-style rock and roll.

The day after I returned to Blantyre, I went to Nchalo to the rural training center there. On the way, I picked up Doug and another White Peace Corps volunteer and took them with me. Nothing really happened out of the ordinary, with the exception of going into a bush store at Nchalo where a Malawian came up to greet us. He said to me, "Moni Abambo" and to Doug, "Moni Bwana." We both immediately understood that I was being addressed with the term for "father" while Doug was addressed as "master" or "boss." I did not think too much about it at the time but later found it to be both gratifying and amusing. Doug, like so many other Whites here, had such big guilt complexes. I told Doug that when Malawians begin to see you as a friend rather than just another European, they would stop calling you bwana or master. Nevertheless, Doug said that he hated the term. My only concern was that language continues to pose a barrier between me and other people. I wanted to be treated as much like a Malawian as possible and develop friendships. Yet I was not learning the language anywhere near as well as Dick, so language was a barrier I had to overcome. If a person called me bwana, it was unlikely that I would ever develop a friendship on equal terms because of their worldview and how I fit into it as a perceived European.

The next day when I returned to Blantyre, I decided that I would go to Troy David's party at his house Saturday night. Troy was Nigel's colleague and friend in the regional office. I continued to have mixed emotions about socializing with the British whom I generally disliked for the way they treated Malawians. At the same time, I hated to turn down free food and good booze. In the final analysis, it was in my best interest to attend. I needed both Troy and Nigel's help in setting up the type of office

I wanted to establish and outfit. They had already told me that we may be doing the audio-visual work for the Department of Health and Community Development. If this happens, there would be sufficient funds to add an associate director that I would train to take over my job when I leave. I could also get an assistant messenger and maybe even a secretary. In the area of equipment and office space, I would be moving into a larger space with four office rooms, a darkroom, a drawing/design room with duplicating equipment and other extras that I need to carry out the work of the office. This was not only what I wanted, but it was also far beyond what I thought was possible. I decided that I would humor Troy without accepting or being overcome by his implicit racism.

It was not only the British who got on my nerves when it came to race relations. Tom Barker, my housemate, was beginning to get on my last nerve pretty much the whole evening. He bugged the hell out of me by the way he generalized about Malawians. He would say things like, "You can't trust them," or "The whole country is adulterous." Admittedly, there were bars where prostitutes hung out, but these were places most Malawi women would not visit. I tried to tell him or show him how the whole country had conservative morals and values. I thought that Tom came from a midwestern, middle-class, conservative Republican background, which in my mind explained a lot about his conservative ways. I was not sure why Tom joined the Peace Corps. We never talked much about his upbringing. I did know that I didn't want to continue to share a house with him. We didn't have enough in common to really become friends and to get along well. On the other hand, I had made friends with lots of Malawians. Friendships were something you had to work at and I didn't think that Tom was trying very hard. He seemed pretty satisfied working hard at his job and staying pretty much to himself.

Invasion of Soldier Ants

I thought all through the night that daylight would never arrive. I was so relieved when Sunday arrived and the war with the army was over—that is, the army of ants, soldier ants. I could not believe what we went through the previous night. We were invaded by an army of soldier ants. I mean, millions of ants. Tom and I did not know what to do. We woke up in the middle of the night being attacked—I mean, actually bitten by tiny ants. I jumped out of bed onto the floor to find my feet covered with ants, all attacking and biting. I went into the dining room and lit a kerosene lamp. I could not believe my eyes. Tom came out of his room with his flashlight in hand while trying to brush off these ants. They were everywhere. We heard lizards hit the floor as they fell from the wall because they too were being attacked by hundreds of ants. It was too difficult to see exactly what was happening. We both grabbed our Coleman mantle wick lanterns that had been issued by the Peace Corps and quickly lit them. The brightness of the lamps lit up the room.

Our eyes confirmed what our bodies already felt—we were being invaded by an army of ants. Millions of them had invaded our house. They had trails coming in from the windows, under the doors and down from the ceiling. They formed bridges as if to protect the long phalanx of soldiers. At first, we had no idea what we would do. It occurred to me that kerosene might stop them. I then told Tom to get the kerosene and we would pour it around the window and doors. We poured enough kerosene to burn down the house several times, but even that did not stop them.

Now I was really getting worried. I thought of the movie I saw some years ago, *The Naked Jungle*, where people on a South American cocoa plantation were being attacked by army ants. The plantation owners had gotten word that legions of ants were on the move and would arrive at their plantation homes in a few days. Refusing to leave, they decided to fight. In addition to barricading the house, one man rigged explosives to the nearby wooden dam and, as a last resort, blew up the dam and flooded the area just as the ants arrived.

Lacking access to a dam to blow up, I just knew that we were doomed. We did not leave the house for fear that the ants were all over the yard and

John Hunter in front of his African township house in Zomba.

beyond. As we battled our own army of ants, I could not put out of my mind what happened in the movie. Not even the blown-up dam could stop the army on the move. Eventually, the humans were all eaten alive, and this was the image that came into my mind as we faced terror in the night. I felt surely we would not make it to dawn alive.

Physically and mentally exhausted, we came up with a plan. We placed each leg of our beds into our metal dinner plates and poured kerosene onto them. We finally crawled back into our beds and tucked our mosquito nets under our mattresses. While hoping for the best, we fell asleep from pure exhaustion.

When we woke up the next morning, the ants were gone but left a path of destruction in their wake. The kitchen was decimated. They had consumed any and all goods they encountered including the poor wall lizards. Outside, we found several of our baby chickens had been killed. All in all, we were thankful that we were still alive. I never forgot that ordeal and nothing in our training had prepared us for this encounter.

Work in Zomba

By March, it was difficult to believe that we had been in Malawi for almost half a year. We survived the rainy season and the attack of the army ants and were in the time period between the wet and dry season in Malawi. I had already made several trips to Zomba where the national visual aids or extension aids office was located. John Hunter was a Peace Corps volunteer stationed at the national office. He had been assigned a house in the African part of town where most of the mid-level African civil servants lived in this government-sponsored housing project. The complex consisted of a series of modest dwellings with two bedrooms and a living/dining area with an indoor and outdoor kitchen. The outdoor kitchen was used for cooking while food preparation took place inside. John's place was comfortable enough. I usually stayed with him when I was in town. John was tall and lanky and loved being in Africa. He loved being around Black folks and seemed to lack any hint of racism. He enjoyed his beer and loved to dance, even if his rhythm was a little off sometimes. He caught on quickly to how Malawians danced.

John worked at the extension aids office located at the top of a hill, one of the highest points in town. The office complex had several offices connected by covered walkways. The office was run by a large British expatriate by the name of Derrick McKinley. Derrick was a career civil servant in the old colonial office prior to independence. He was stationed in Nigeria until independence when Nigerians, unlike Malawians, quickly

Africanized their civil service. Derrick then came to Malawi. He seemed pleasant enough but constantly complained about Nigerians whom he considered too assertive and aggressive. Of course, I thought that was just the opinion of an Englishman used to being in charge without anyone, especially an African, questioning his authority. This view of Nigeria only made me more interested in visiting the country where Black people acted "whiter" than the Europeans. To the European mind, Nigerians did not know their "place."

I liked traveling to Zomba, the capital of the country. It reminded me of what I imagined a colonial town looked like in the old days. In addition to going to the Zomba Inn for beer with our African colleagues, sometimes an expatriate invited us to the Zomba Club. It, too, was a relic from the colonial days with few African members. It was not that Africans were barred from being members; most just could not afford membership. Maintaining high membership fees was one way of keeping Africans out of social clubs. The club was nice with facilities for eating and a separate bar for the consumption of alcohol, where most expatriates headed after work. There was a tennis court and a golf course. I did not play either, so I didn't take advantage of these amenities. And even if I could play, I would never have joined a club filled with expatriates.

British volunteers did not have a problem belonging to the club, nor did Bill Wyatt, a Peace Corps volunteer stationed in the area. Bill was tall, dark, charming and handsome and could be, at first glance, taken for an African. He played tennis, so he had a club membership. Bill, a native of Virginia, arrived in Malawi about a year before I did and had quickly lost his southern accent in exchange for a British accent. I first thought he was just putting on airs, but he seemed very comfortable speaking the King's English. Bill dated a British volunteer named Margaret who, with her blond hair and blue eyes, was quite attractive. They seem very fond of each other. We all went to the club a couple of times for gin and tonics, the only place in town where you could get an ice cube in your drink. Bill's whole orientation was to the British, which kept us from becoming close friends, even though he was one of the few Black volunteers in the country. It was too bad because overall I thought Bill was a nice guy.

Mail and Communications in Malawi

My first hire was a messenger. I would always address Joseph Kapanela as Mr. Kapanela. We spent most of the afternoon talking as we collated the staff newsletter. I was always interested in learning about a person's background and family. Mr. Kapanela finished elementary school but did not score high enough for a coveted slot in one of the few secondary schools. Earlier we had gone to the town and had lunch at one of the African restaurants where we had a traditional meal of fish relish and nsima. I did not think it was particularly good, but I ate it anyway. I was sure that this was the first time Mr. Kapanela had a meal with a Westerner. After lunch, we returned to the office and finished our work.

Peace Corps volunteers living in Blantyre received their mail at the Peace Corps office. At least once a week, I would send Mr. Kapanela to the office to pick up any mail I had received. I wrote a lot of letters or aerograms to people because I wanted to receive lots of letters from home. I finally notified my family and friends to send my mail to the regional agricultural office in Blantyre. Only occasionally did I get a notice to collect a letter from the Peace Corps headquarters in Blantyre.

I felt it was my lucky day when I received both a letter and package from Barbara. We had been separated for nearly six months. I thought that my love for her grew more with each passing day. I carried her picture in my wallet everywhere I went. I guess we both wondered if our relationship was strong enough to survive two years of being apart.

Barbara was a beautiful young lady with perfect brown skin and long straight hair. She impressed me immediately. I thought she was so sophisticated when we first met in Berea. I certainly thought that she was more sophisticated than I. She had such good taste in clothes, always looked like a model. I knew for sure that I could wait for her, but I was afraid that she might be wooed by someone else. I saved Barbara's letter to open once I got home. I wanted to savor it. I described all sorts of scenes and adventures in my last letters to her. She said that she thought that I might love Africa more than I loved her. Obviously, I loved Africa and loved every minute of being here in this beautiful country with warm, welcoming people. It felt like I was home. I loved the experience of being in a majority Black country, where I didn't have to worry about being discriminated against because of my color. I wanted to return to Africa once my tour of duty was up. The big unanswered question for me was whether Barbara would share my love for Africa and its people. Her early responses indicated that she was keeping an open mind. She also told me that a friend read one of my letters and thought it was rather impersonal. As I read Barbara's letters, I often detected a note of sadness in the tone of her letters as if she was lonely.

After I finished reading my letter, it was time for my English class with the local village kids and their mothers. The women seemed shy and were reluctant to speak up. I think it was because I was both a male and an American. On the other hand, the children were all very anxious to learn English because they knew that English was the official language of

Malawi. When Hastings Banda, the president of the country, returned to Malawi after being away for nearly 50 years, people said that he could not speak Chinyanja. Banda was Chewa and officially changed the name of the language to Chichewa. He spoke only in English and had his speeches translated in Chichewa. He made a point of correcting his Malawi translator to make sure that the people knew he understood the language. I think that the whole thing was rehearsed to make him look good. At any rate, English was the official language and children knew that they must learn it to get ahead. So here I was, teaching English as a foreign language. This was one of the few things that Tom and I did together. I should have spent the time having them teach me Chichewa since I got only an FS-1 on my foreign service exams. I just did not have an ear for language. Often, I found myself too tired to teach, but the day was a good day and it was such a pleasure teaching the kids. They were such a joy.

New Living Arrangements

I didn't know how Tom and I managed to end up living in the same house, but I had made up my mind to move out. I planned to talk with Howard about building my own little house with the Peace Corps putting up part of the money if I was able to secure the remainder of the funding. I had tried to live with Tom, but we just did not get along. Tom was right out of college with little worldly experience when he joined the Peace Corps. He had little patience with Malawians and often got frustrated in having to deal with them. He would have made a good expatriate during colonial times. I was not sure why Tom joined the Peace Corps. He did not seem like the typical Peace Corps liberal volunteer wanting to do good in the world. Since it was obvious that he had not been around many Black folks, especially from another culture, he did not seem to be able to put himself in their shoes. Maybe that was something the Peace Corps should have emphasized in cross-cultural training.

Tom evidently had never been on his own and did not know how to do a lot. Since I'd worked for several years and had lived alone, I knew the rudiments of cooking. Cooking only became a problem for us when our cook took off for the weekend at the end of the month; then I usually would cook for both of us. The previous week, Tom decided that he wanted to cook. Reluctantly, I agreed. He was going to make fish and chips. After waiting for a long while in our living room to be called to dinner, I walked into the kitchen to find Tom hunched over on the floor peeling potatoes and washing them in a teacup. He had not started cleaning the fresh fish he had purchased at the market. That was the sort of thing that made me frustrated with Tom and want to do the cooking myself. Plus, I didn't think Tom was very sanitary in handling food. We had a small table in the kitchen, so why he decided to stoop on the floor to prepare food was beyond me.

Ghosts

To tell the truth, I was always a little wary of living in this old colonial house. It seemed rather creepy from the very beginning. It was not so bad when the other volunteers were here. It was full of life, and I gave little thought to the house being haunted. Once the other volunteers left, it was just Tom and me in this big house. One night, I swore I heard the front door open with the hinges making a squeaking sound. It was enough of an unusual sound to wake me up. I then heard footsteps slowly move toward the dining room. I was startled by something bumping into the table causing the flashlight to fall to the floor. I jumped out of bed and hurried into the dining room. Once I lit the lantern and could clearly see, whatever caused the noise was gone. I looked around the house and found nothing or no one. Tom was still asleep, so I did not wake him. I then thought that I must have been dreaming, but the front door was still ajar and the flashlight had fallen to the floor. I thought that I should keep this to myself. I did not want anyone to think that I believed in ghosts.

But no sooner had I dismissed the thought of ghosts than Tom and I drove home late one night to find our cook sitting under a large tree next to the old carriage house. He had a lantern next to him. We found out that he was scared to stay in the house alone. We later learned that he was not the only one in the area who thought the house was haunted. Many villagers felt the same way. I continued to wonder why the house was abandoned. Although it was old, it still had its charm and was quite livable. Could the former residents have been chased out by ghosts, I wondered.

One of the area supervisors, James Katembe, lived near our house. We had become friends and his wife often had me over for dinner. I told Mr. Katembe that I wanted to build my own house. He thought that this was a good idea and offered me use of a portion of land he owned at the top of the hill above where we currently lived. He said that he planned to build his house there once he left government service. The plot overlooked rolling bush-lined hills with no other houses in sight except for this hut where his farm assistant lived. Earlier during the day, we walked up the hill to survey the area. I told him that all I needed was a living room, a small bedroom, a kitchen and a bath. I had designed the house at work and showed him my plans. I wanted the house to have a cement floor and metal roof with plastered mud walls. I suggested that we plaster the outer walls with cement to ensure that the walls would not deteriorate during the rainy season. These plans seemed to be agreeable to Mr. Katembe.

Howard Carter thought my plans were sound and the house a good idea but wanted to know what would happen to the house when I left. I told him that I would leave the house to my friend and neighbor Mr. Katembe. He agreed that the Peace Corps office would provide me with 150 pounds to purchase materials for the house. This would allow me to secure the metal for the roof and the cement for the floor and walls. Mr. Katembe suggested that we go to the forest department and secure small four-inch poles that would be spaced a foot apart to construct the wall and frame the roof. Mr. Katembe paid for the poles. He would have his laborer find old bricks from the plantation grounds that would be placed between the poles, secured with lateral bamboo stripes, and then plastered with mud with the outer layer plastered with cement. Mr. Katembe liked the design and said that it would be easy for him to add to the house to accommodate his large family once my tour of duty ended. By the time I was ready to depart, I was sure the Katembes would have another addition to their family. Mr. Katembe had a trip out of town and when he returned, we started planning for construction.

Life was good. I had made many friends and I enjoyed visiting the families of my friends.

A New Hire

Troy David hired Sandy Mphiri as my new assistant. He was 21 and tall, about the tallest Malawian I had ever seen. He was fresh out of secondary school. There were only 30,000 students in elementary school in the entire country and only 3,000 went on to secondary school, schools that were mostly run by missionaries. A lot more students passed their qualifying exams than got admitted to secondary school, which was very disheartening for them. But out of all the secondary school graduates, only 300 would gain admission to college. So, successfully completing secondary education was a pretty good achievement and very important for getting a good job. Mr. Mphiri seemed pretty intelligent but inexperienced. He also seemed eager to learn. I thought that he would catch on quickly to his new duties. I also thought that we would get along, even with my temperamental ways.

The weather was getting cooler. When the clouds and mist descended over the area, I was told that this type of weather was called chaperone. Because Blantyre was located on a plateau, it was colder here than in the surrounding lowland areas. I expected that the coming winter would really bring some cold weather on the plateau. We had already experienced

Chapter Two. My First Year in Malawi

My new house and motorcycle out front.

the cold where everything was surrounded in a damp, cold mist. It was bone chilling when riding my bike. I had written to my sister, Patricia, to send me some warmer clothes, long pants, a jacket and the like.

I made final arrangements for the construction of my house. Building would actually start in April, and I hoped to move in by June. Volunteers got around $90 every month on the first. It sounded like a lot, but we spent every penny of it. That's the main reason why I needed the support of a Malawian to get my house built. I did not have extra money for construction outside of what the Peace Corps provided.

The Peace Corps was now planning to have our group conference on the lakeshore. I didn't plan to go, using the excuse that I had too much work to do. Tom and I decided to invite folks to our house for a party on Sunday.

New Help

After Tom fired our cook, allegedly for stealing, we hired this young boy who could not finish school because he did not have school fees. Everson Kachale was his name and he had not worked for anyone before, so we would have to train him. I had to train him to cook since Tom did not know how, even though he thought that he could. We planned to pay Everson the same five pounds we had paid the others, but our neighbors and friends objected when I raised the subject. They did not want us to pay Everson any more than what they were paying their household help. Anyway, I promised Everson that to save a pound a month from his pay for him so that when we left, he would have funds to pay his school fees. Everson agreed. He still lived with his parents and would move in with us. We provided food and shelter, and his cousin, a driver for the department, provided transportation for him when and if it was needed so he could save most of his earnings. It seemed as if we had found a system that would work for all involved.

The Assassination of Martin Luther King, Jr.

We found out that Dr. Martin Luther King had passed on the day after he was shot. I was totally devastated by the news. I found out on BBC radio and was alone when I heard the news. I could not believe my ears. Our beloved leader, winner of the Nobel Peace Prize was assassinated! Lord have mercy. "Bless that good man who only wanted to bring peace and justice." I had cried for Dr. King. Maybe I also cried for myself, my people and the general state of the world—how could this have happened? It was not as if I did not expect it, but when I expected that he might be killed organizing in the Deep South, it did not happen. Somehow I thought that if one of our leaders was to be killed, it would be H. Rap Brown or Stokely Carmichael, NOT Dr. King, not at this time.

In contemplating the death of Dr. King, I felt that the whole structure of American society was rooted in racism since slavery. What would it take for White people to change? Must Black people have to resort to violence to bring about meaningful structural change in American society? White people were so selfish that they would not even save themselves from the impending destruction. I prayed that God have mercy on us, on those who were so unmerciful.

I could not help but feel that racism was widespread and seemed to be so deeply embedded in Whites and their relationship to non-Whites. I found that many of the British in Malawi were racists. I saw very little difference between them and those racists who continued to govern South Africa and Southern Rhodesia. Dr. King's death was a turning point in my life here. I did not see how much more I could tolerate—it was far too much to bear. I felt like my people were Black people whether here in Africa or in the States—they/we were all being oppressed/suppressed. I didn't think that I could be silent anymore and remain faithful to what I believed in and who I was as a Black man, as a human being. Although I didn't want to be expelled from the country or to be asked to leave or be fired from my job, I did not see how I could remain here for any length of time and remain true to myself. I didn't think that I had spoken out against racism as much as I should. I had been too silent and had acquiesced too often when I saw a racist act or heard a racist comment. If I said that I loved Malawians, then I had to prove it by words and deeds. I had no doubt that Banda was wrong in the policies that he implemented. He allowed the Whites to maintain control as if his own government and rule were still dependent on Whites. You can't have a multi-racial society and have a harmonious racial atmosphere when Blacks were in the majority and Whites were in control. It was wrong, and for me to condone it tacitly through my silence was just as wrong. I vowed henceforth to speak up. I would say the truth as I saw it, even if it meant I had to leave Malawi. King's death and the racism I witnessed here were making me rethink my philosophy of non-violence. I wondered how I could remain non-violent in the face of such oppression. I wanted to believe that non-violence was a way of life. Yet, that very philosophy was taught to me by White people. How could such men teach Black and brown people to practice non-violence when they had not convinced their own people to do the same. The very sane White people who practiced genocide on Black people around the world told us to accept whatever comes and be non-violent in our response. The murder of Dr. King changed me a great deal. I felt even more separate from Peace Corps volunteers and staff. Even though they all regretted what happened, it seemed to have impacted me more than I can describe. I knew that the changes I experienced with the death of Dr. King would be reflected in my relationships with White folks in Malawi.

In spite of all that had happened, I still loved it here. The country and people were lovely despite all of the poverty. This was a beautiful place and I enjoyed being here in spite of the British. I could not have been assigned to a better location than the Blantyre plateau. The elevation moderated the temperature so that it did not get too hot in the dry season or too cold in the winter. I may have complained about the cold, damp weather because I didn't have the proper clothes. I could have used a raincoat, a heavier jacket, and gloves. I could also have used a car, but I knew I would not get any of those things. And why should I? We were here to experience life as Malawians experience it. Despite the Peace Corps' intentions that we live at the level of our colleagues, we were much better off than most people. My home was surrounded by lush green grass and woods. There were flowering trees and many mango trees. My neighbors had welcomed us to this village and would do anything to help us out, and I would do the same for them.

The Vietnam War and the President

President Johnson decided not to seek re-election. I was glad. His Vietnam policy was too much. Now that he had made his decision not to run, he decided to stop the terrible bombing of Vietnam. I hoped that the war would end with his decision to step down. I was not going to be hypocritical, like some Peace Corps volunteers and say that I regret seeing him leave office. I do not. I was glad. I had consistently opposed the war. I never bought into the logic of why we were there in the first place. The fact that France could not win its war in Indochina should have told us something. The conventional wisdom was that we were there now to try to stop the spread of Communism. I did not, and still don't, believe that destroying a country, a people or their culture was the way to stop Communism. I began to see the struggle of Black Americans with the struggle of people of color around the world before Dr. King voiced his opposition to the war.

Although I thought that the war in Vietnam had overshadowed Johnson's administration, I still had to admit that he had done a good job in civil rights at home. It was interesting that it took a southerner, maybe even a former racist, to get the Civil Rights Act of 1964 and the Voting Rights Act of 1965 passed. It was as if all our work during the Civil Rights movement came to a head during the Johnson administration. Johnson did a good job getting the Medicare and Medicaid bills passed. I was sorry that he could not see the folly of his ways in pursuing the war so relentlessly. It was as if he was blindsided. From what I had read in the newspapers here in Malawi, the United States was pretty much divided over the war and the continued Civil Rights struggle had turned into the Black Power movement. Somehow, I felt that I should have been at home in the midst of the struggle. I had always been active in the movement and felt guilty sitting on the sidelines here in Southern Africa. I began to think that I could in my own way help bring Black Power to the people in Malawi.

I had been giving a lot of thought about race in America. I still had not gotten over the death of Dr. King, but I had also been thinking about the death of Malcolm X and the conversation that I had had with my Berea roommate Charles Ward. I never thought that Charles and I would become best friends after our freshman year. Although we were all poor, Charles came from a really impoverished family in Jenkins, Kentucky. When he came to school, he had $35 in his pocket; his church had collected and given that to him. Charles had to work 20 hours a week, 10 more than most of us, to help cover the cost of his education since his mother did not have any money to send him. His mother was blind but did not let that disability keep her from doing everything she needed to do to raise her family.

The one thing I can say about Berea was that it served the poor residents of Appalachia well. Under any other circumstance, Charles, being Black and poor, would not have gotten an education even though he was about the smartest person I knew. Upon entering Berea, we both were avid readers trying to catch up on what we were not exposed to in high school.

Charles was a math major. I took great pleasure in seeing all the boys in our dorm coming to Charles for help with their math assignments.

Charles was very perceptive and could analyze anything. It was good to see Charles again when we returned to Berea from school summer break in 1964. I had been on an American Friends Service project in Philadelphia while Charles went to New York to work and live with his uncle in Harlem. There, he was exposed to the teachings of Malcolm X. We both had read *The Autobiography of Malcolm X* and talked about the difference between King's philosophy and Malcolm X's philosophy. I was adamant that King's approach to non-violent direct action was the course we should be taking. Charles, on the other hand, thought that Malcolm X was espousing a philosophy of race pride, manhood and self-determination. By the time Malcolm broke with Elijah Muhammad, traveled to Mecca and joined the Sunni branch of Islam, he became more of a civil rights advocate promoting racial justice. I think Charles knew that Black people, especially the downtrodden, needed a philosophy of racial pride and self-assurance. He also understood well before I did that we needed to be strong men ready to fight for our rights as human beings. Since living in Malawi and having to deal with racism here, I had come more and more to respect the teachings of Malcolm X. I think if he were alive today, he would have definitely been our national leader and a pan–African leader as well. Of course, people still suspect that the FBI was involved in his murder, even if three Black men were indicted for the actual killing. One also had to wonder about the circumstances surrounding the murder of Dr. King.

Thoughts on the Peace Corps

I still couldn't talk to anyone in the Peace Corps office about King's death. His assassination made me hate the expatriates even more. I guess they had become a stand-in for racist Americans. I believed the other Black volunteers were experiencing the same thing that I was going through, but we had never gotten together to talk about these and other matters of importance to us as non–Whites.

I found out that there were nine of us here. Most of us didn't like the expatriate situation or the fact that Malawi had such close ties to South Africa. After King was killed, a Black volunteer wrote a letter to the president. Somehow it got back to the ambassador, who then called in the Peace Corps director. The volunteer basically wanted to know when and if President Banda would comment on the death of Dr. King. After all, Banda could not wait to compliment the president of South Africa on his recent elections, probably the only Black African leader to do so. I told Howard that we as Black volunteers do not look to the Peace Corps to take up for us matters regarding race relations. The Peace Corps was barely willing to support the White volunteers. So I didn't expect anything more than a transfer or being sent home for any ruckus we made here.

I was tired of people who were not willing to stand up for what they believed in and for what was right. We all should be promoting the advancement of Malawians, which means the Africanization of the civil service and the dominant White corporations in the country. I told Howard not to be surprised if all the Black volunteers decided to leave in protest over race relations in this country and the failure of the Peace Corps to act on our behalf. I understood that the director of Africa Peace Corps would be in Malawi soon. I hoped to get a chance to meet him and talk about our grievances. I was not sure that the Peace Corps understood how all these things had impacted us. It was even worse because the Peace Corps did not take a stand against racism here in Malawi. They said that we were not to get involved in local politics. But how could we not get involved when it was really a matter of human rights when it came to race relations? I wished that there was an opportunity for the few Black volunteers to get together to talk about our experiences. At least it would make us feel that we were not alone here.

On Malawi Friends

I sent Barbara some African carvings for her graduation from Berea College. She told me that she accepted a job at IBM in New York and would leave for the city after graduation. Barbara said that the conference on racism at Berea went well even though the college initially opposed the idea. Fannie Lou Hamer spoke; I wished I had been there to hear her.

Time only increased my love for Barbara. Not only did I ask her to marry me; I also asked her to come to Malawi to live. I knew that I was lonely. But it was not just that; I loved her very much and wanted to spend my life with her. I was not sure when I left the States, but since being here, I now realized how much I missed her and loved her. I was not ready to marry when I joined the Peace Corps but felt that I was ready now. I was ready to give up my "freedom" and live the rest of my life with Barbara. I asked her in my last letter to come to Malawi as soon as possible so that we could be married. I told her the house that I had built with Mr. Katembe would be our home. It was finished and looked very good. It had a veranda with two large windows in the sitting room and one large window in the bedroom. I had a paraffin stove and table in the kitchen, and I found an old bathtub at the Peace Corps warehouse for the bathroom, still with no running water, unless Everson or I ran with the five-gallon buckets filled with water. I also had a discarded old, upholstered chair for the living room. I took the old paraffin refrigerator from the plantation house and put it in my living room. Tom could store his perishable food in it anytime he liked. So, that was the picture I painted for Barbara as our first house. I was anxious to hear her answer to my proposal.

Mark Chiphwanya and his wife were my very best friends. Mr. Chiphwanya was educated in the States and was the highest ranking Malawian in the region, at least in the Department of Agriculture. He must have been about 10 years older than me. He and his wife, Beatrice, were a very handsome couple and had beautiful children. They had become my family here. I was often invited to their house to eat. They made me feel totally at home, apart from the language issue. I did not think that I have improved my ability to speak Chichewa. I know that Mark would have liked for me to be able to speak his language. He couldn't help but make remarks about the level of my language skills or rather my lack of language skills. With that exception, I felt like I had become one of the people here. I knew that I should have devoted more time to learning the language and stop making excuses.

The first time I was invited to the home of the Chiphwanyas, I was still trying to get used to eating nsima. Most Malawians eat their food with their hands. They are very careful to wash their hands and eat with only their right hand. Mrs. Chiphwanya's mother was visiting the day I arrived for dinner. When she entered the room, she got on her hands and knees and crawled over to greet me with the right hand extended and the left hand held to her side. I felt bad, but I knew that this was the custom among older female adults. Mrs. Chiphwanya was educated and westernized. She joined us at the dining room table where we used forks and knives like the British with the fork in the left hand and the knife in the right. We still had nsima as the staple. When I put salt on my nsima, Mrs. Chiphwanya explained that I was to put the salt on the relish or side dishes. I learned to like nsima with a good relish, but I preferred the coarser ngaiwa made from coarse corn meal. Of course, well-to-do Malawians considered ngaiwa food for poor people who couldn't afford the refined grained corn.

I felt very comfortable around Mark and Beatrice. I called Beatrice Mrs. Chiphwanya, but Mark preferred that I use his first name. When we were alone, we talked politics, but we both knew better than to share our views of the president and his policies outside of his house. Mark had been able to move up in the department because he was very intelligent and was well liked by all. That was the one characteristic that most Malawians had, likeability. There was also the issue of Malawians telling you what they think you want to hear. That in itself was a form of politeness, but it could be an issue in the workplace when you need an accurate assessment of a problem or issue. It was not as much of a problem once Malawians got to know you personally. Mark would have no problem telling me something if he thought that it was for my own good. We got along well and had much in common.

Another Accident

When we first arrived in the country and were assigned motorcycles, the volunteers in our group were told that the accident rate among volunteers was 100 percent. Of course, I did not believe them at the time, but I came to realize how right they were. This was the third accident I had had in a year. I was out in the bush on my bike following a Malawi agricultural worker on our way to a local village. I did not know the terrain, so I wanted to stay close to my colleague in front of me, who without signaling, made a 90-degree turn. We were traveling about 30 miles an hour, and I was too close to make the turn without overturning my bike. I could not put on the brakes fast enough to stop. So I ended up flying across a stream with my bike landing in the middle of the stream and with me landing on the other side of the water on the muddy bank. All I could think of at the time was that I did not want to catch Bilharzia. Bilharzia, or schistosomiasis, was one of the dreaded parasitic diseases the Peace Corps warned us about during our in-country training. We were told not to wade in stagnant water or water that was not flowing. The disease is caused by a snail releasing a parasitic flatworm that penetrates the skin. Once in the body, it attacks the spleen and liver and can lead to death if not properly treated. The Peace Corps told us that one or two volunteers who contracted the disease had to be flown to a military hospital in Germany. So I did not want to get the disease and had to watch my stool for blood for the next several weeks. I was thankful that I was not seriously hurt and villagers helped me retrieve my bike from the stream.

The Assassination of Robert Kennedy

Senator Robert Kennedy was assassinated. Once again, I was shocked and overwhelmed with sensations similar to those I had experienced on learning of the death of Dr. King. Senator Kennedy worked so hard for the disadvantaged, which cannot be said about too many politicians.

The Peace Corps office reacted immediately by closing the office for the day. I also heard that they received a death threat, which turned out to be false. Did they even know how it looked and how we Black volunteers felt to see them immediately close the office when Kennedy was killed but not when Dr. King was killed? I could not help seeing racism where it existed. I thought that there was racism in the Peace Corps office. Otherwise, why would all the White people have the higher level jobs and the Black people the menial jobs? We Americans were raised in a racist society, so it would be unusual for any American to escape the scars of racism. It was not an overt form of racism in the Peace Corps office, but it existed. So many White Americans were not even aware of their racism. I was sure that it never occurred to the office staff to close the office when King died. When Kennedy died, it seemed to be a natural response. If we cannot recognize the racism in ourselves, how would we ever hope to rid ourselves of this evil? I did not mean to single out the Peace Corps for racism. After all, we were citizens of the United States where we all were raised in a racist society. I didn't think that I would ever get over the fact that our trainers considered at one time that I might have been unfit to represent the United States as a Peace Corps volunteer. Of course, I was angry and bitter about the treatment of Black people in this country, but why couldn't they see that I had been scarred by this racist society I was raised in? Was my pain invisible? What they saw in me was my bitterness, but how many times can you be told "Go to the back of the bus" or "We don't serve coloreds here" and not be bitter? The Peace Corps blamed me rather than the society that had permanently injured me. They thought in terms of keeping me from serving my country, while overlooking the racism in another White Peace Corps volunteer.

The Answer Was No

I finally heard back from Barbara telling me that she could not join me in Malawi. What a blow! I thought that I had fantasized to the point where I had it in my head that she would join me in Malawi, get a job as a teacher and we would stay for an extra year and have a wonderful romantic time as newlyweds. Barbara's letter brought reality home to me. Initially, I felt depressed, even more so than my usual state. I guess that I felt awfully lonely and wanted companionship. I also wanted both worlds: to live in Africa and to have Barbara enjoy the life I was enjoying. Barbara was frank about how she felt. First and foremost, she said that now that she had a good paying job working for IBM, she felt a need to help her mother out. Her mother struggled to raise four girls after she separated from Barbara's father. Rosa Durr was a very proud woman, and Barbara said that she insisted on paying her way through life without help from anyone. Barbara

Lake Malawi with Mozambique mountains.

emphasized the sacrifices her mother made to ensure that all her daughters had the opportunity to go to college. Now she felt it was payback time. She also told me that her younger sister had entered college and Barbara felt the need to help her sibling out.

Holiday on Lake Malawi

I spent a few days on holiday at the Agriculture Department's "resort," which consisted of two Quonset huts made from corrugated steel situated right on Lake Malawi. They were furnished with two beds, chairs and table with a small kitchen outfitted with running water and a paraffin stove. There was a small toilet and shower. It was plain, nothing fancy, but was nice enough to spend some time relaxing; above all, it was free. The lake water was warm with gentle breaking waves over the sandy beach. There were several large rocks that emerged from the water and an island in the distance. I had heard that Lake Malawi is large enough to sink an ocean-going ship during a severe storm. There were a couple of chairs situated to the side of my Quonset hut with several palm, mango and pawpaw trees, which provided shade and fruit.

The market was in Fort Johnston. I drove down to secure some chambo, a fresh fish caught from the lake. I thought that chambo was the best tasting fish I had ever eaten. It looked like a tilapia but was much better with a sweeter taste. Malawians liked to cook chambo with onions, tomatoes and peppers. We had dried chambo that way several times in the office. Even dried, the taste was quite good. I had learned to appreciate dried fish despite its smell.

Fort Johnston was already familiar to me. I was supposed to have served as a teacher in the Anglican school there, so I was anxious to see the school where I was rejected as a teacher for lack of "proper" British credentials. I had since learned that Fort Johnston was named after the British officer Sir Harry Johnston, who established a British post there. The area was also well known for its slave market. Today, it is just a quaint little village at the southern tip of Lake Malawi where its waters empty into the Shire River before meandering down through southern Malawi into Mozambique, where it eventually flows into the Indian Ocean. In Fort Johnston, there was an open air market that sold vegetables, fruits, meat and fish in addition to household items. There were a number of Indian stores, a Catholic cathedral and a large mosque. A clock tower was erected in the early twentieth century in honor of Queen Victoria. Then there was the Anglican school. It was located in an old store or warehouse-like building. In talking to a Malawi teacher there, I found out that none of the teachers had a bachelor's degree, not even the principal. How ironic that I was rejected because I did not have a master's degree. So much for English standards of education. If I had been assigned to the school, the living conditions would have been about the same as they were for Peace Corps volunteers. The big difference was that I would not have had the support of the Peace Corps office or the U.S. government. Being in the Peace Corps turned out to be a better choice for me.

I was glad that I decided to spend my holiday at Lake Malawi. I felt like I was on the verge of becoming exhausted and needed time alone to do some thinking. Being at the lake for three days gave me time to think about my reactions to expatriates. I thought that I was becoming so sensitive to everything. I realized that my responses to simple actions from expatriates were much too sensitive. I finally had to apologize to Nigel Murphy for reacting to restrictions on the use of the office camera. It was a very expensive camera, and he did not allow it to be used for personal reasons. Nigel had been nice to me and I guess we could have been friends if I had been White instead of Black. After having a chance to reflect on my behavior, I decided that I would try to get along with him, but I thought that we could never be friends in the true sense of the word.

It was after our little altercation over the camera that I decided to come up to the lake. Tom Barker and another volunteer joined me on the lake. Since we had nothing else to do when evening came, we decided to drive down to the Palm Beach Hotel and have a few beers. The hotel was run-down and a sad reminder of what colonial life was like before independence. However, we could not be picky since that was the only place that served bottled beer. Over the course of the evening, we had about three beers each. We were mostly silent as we enjoyed our beers. We finally left around 9:30 p.m. and immediately went to bed.

The next morning, we were up and out early. We drove back to the hotel and walked along the lakeshore. I wondered about the former residents of the old colonial houses and mansions that dotted the shore. Some of the houses were falling apart from abandonment. We had lunch in the old Yacht Club where older members, the remainders of a bygone society, now got drunk as early as mid-afternoon. We enjoyed our fish and chips before heading back to the Quonset huts. We spent the rest of the day reading, relaxing and preparing the evening meal.

After dinner, I decided to go for a swim in the lake and take a bath. I still had not overcome my inhibitions regarding bathing nude or swimming nude in the lake. In Malawi, it was common for men to bathe where they pleased, but women were more modest. An elderly woman passed by carrying firewood on her head and said, "Odi, odi" to let me know that she was excusing herself as she walked by. After she was gone, I finished my bath, dried off and went to bed.

The next morning, Tom had to make a quick trip to the area cotton office. I decided that I would relax before we began our trip back to Blantyre. I got up late and took a dip in the lake for my daily bath. I dried off and relaxed under a palm tree. There were a number of fruit trees in the area, so I picked a grapefruit and a papaya for breakfast. I fried some chips and hoped that that would hold me until we reached home. I decided to lie in the hammock and enjoy the view of the lake with the mountains on the distant shore. I assumed that Mozambique was on the other side of the lake. The water was very placid with the occasional ripple caused by two young girls washing metal dishes along the shore. One of the girls had a baby on her back wrapped tightly with a cloth. The other wore only a skirt and was just beginning to develop breasts. Women in the villages often did not cover their breasts. Even in the city market they would only cover their breasts if they found Europeans looking at them; the gaze of foreign men made them uncomfortable. Uncovered breasts were so common that I was no longer distracted by bare-breasted women.

When I looked across the lake, I could see that the haze on the Mozambique mountains had lifted. I could clearly see that the mountain range was smooth, interrupted only by the occasional jagged peak. A few clouds remained overhead. I saw several birds flying toward the island in the middle of the lake. An African man in a dug-out canoe slowly passed. I was captivated by the beauty of the moment.

My thoughts were interrupted by the sounds of an approaching motorcycle. I saw that Tom had returned. We quickly packed our few belongings, locked the Quonset huts and headed back to the city. It did not take long before we arrived in Zomba. We were fortunate that the road between Zomba and Blantyre was paved. Most of the time, the government had only enough money to pave one lane. As a result, when two cars approached each other from the opposite direction, the proper road etiquette was for each car to move from the center of the road leaving only one front and one rear tire on the tarmac. It was a system that seemed to work; however, a volunteer told me that once the driver of an approaching car stayed in the middle of the tarmac forcing him on the dirt road and nearly causing him to crash while he was driving his bike.

It was late in the afternoon when we arrived back at Mpemba. We were both tired. Tom parked his motorcycle in front of his house, and I continued up the hill to my little house. Mr. Katembe's farmworker had a mud hut just to the right of my house. He did not speak English, so our conversation was limited to what I could communicate in Chichewa. I was glad that he lived next door because he could keep an eye on my house when I was away. The trip to the lake had been both enjoyable and relaxing. I was glad that I went.

Letters Home

I had just finished writing a letter to my parents. One of my great pleasures was receiving mail from home. Letters took a while to arrive in the country's central post office, then on to the regional office where I was now receiving all my mail. Each government office had a messenger to deliver and pick up mail locally. To get mail, I spent a lot of time writing to all my family and friends. I wrote consistently to Barbara, Mom and Dad and my sister, Patricia. I also wrote to Aunt Lillian and Aunt Lucille. I loved the letters from Lucille because they were long and so full of information about the family. In my last letter to Mom and Dad, I let them know that I was finishing up my course at the Polytechnic Institute where both Tom and I attended. The weather was cold at night, so I hated having to ride back home when the temperature dropped. Nevertheless, I had enjoyed the course and I had become friends with Dick and Anne Oliver.

The previous night, we had a presentation from the American consul, who gave a glowing report of race relations in the United States in spite of the death of Martin Luther King and the riots that followed. I was surprised at the spin he was able to put on the denial of rights to Black people and how long the United States had struggled to live up to the ideals of liberty and justice embodied in the Constitution. He also spoke of American foreign policy as if altruism was at the core of our foreign policy, especially as it related to Africa. I doubted that we would even be in Africa had it not been for the Cold War. I asked the consul what he thought about the United States promoting democracy in Africa while denying equal opportunity for Blacks at home. He said that the United States was making great progress in extending civil rights to Blacks. When I asked about the assassination of Dr. King and ensuing riots, he became visibly irritated and said that I needed to give others the opportunity to ask questions. He ignored me for the rest of the evening. I wondered if I was reported to the U.S. embassy as a person to be watched.

I often complained about how cold it was here. Although I had adequate clothes for the cold weather, I really felt sorry for those who had to endure the cold, damp weather we were having. I saw many Malawians who had nothing more than a pair of shorts and a shirt to keep them warm. But there was very little I could do to help them. When I arrived in Malawi, I had $200 in my savings account in the bank at home. The Peace Corps provided about $90 a month for living expenses. The British devaluation of the pound followed by Malawi also devalued our monthly allowance. Of course, as long as we spent our money on local goods and services, the Malawi pound, or kwacha, went a long way. But even so, that left us with about $3 a day for all expenses. Overall, that made our status roughly the equivalent of lower middle-class Africans. Although I could not contribute much monetarily, I felt good about my work and its contribution to the development of the country.

I thought the Peace Corps was wise in emphasizing teaching and agricultural development. Education was valued among Malawians more than anything else because they knew that it would lead to success in life and allowed them to provide for their families. Their attitude was similar to the attitude of Black people in the South toward education and work following emancipation after the Civil War. Having been denied an education during slavery, the first thing the freedmen did was to establish schools throughout the South, first elementary schools, then high schools, and finally colleges and universities. The British, through their mission schools, provided elementary education to ensure a supply of low-level clerks for their colonial government. Today, Malawi parents go to great lengths to secure school fees to allow their children to take advantage of still-limited educational opportunities.

Our group was the first Peace Corps agricultural group in Malawi. I thought we would have an impact—maybe not change the world but in our small way improve conditions for several people that could have a ripple effect. I loved my job, and I thought that I was being helpful in a minor

Malawi farmer having his crop weighed.

way. We were all trying to get farmers to understand how such simple things as adding fertilizer to their crops could substantially increase their yield and how the production of cash crops such as cotton and tobacco could provide additional income for their families.

On Independence

Whereas July 6 was Independence Day in Malawi, the U.S. embassy, USAID, and U.S. Peace Corps all celebrated July 4 on the embassy grounds. Most volunteers in town went by the embassy, if for nothing else but good food and beer. Doug was in town and so was Dick. We decided to skip the festivities and stop at the local bar just outside of town on the way back to Mpemba. That turned out to be one of our favorite places to hang out after work. When we first arrived in the country, people were still talking about the uprising of Malawi young Turks against President Banda. Malawi gained independence from Great Britain in 1964, and two years later on July 6, 1966, the country became a republic. Malawians celebrated their independence two days following our July 4 celebration.

Throughout our Peace Corps training, we were told not to get involved in politics. I think this was general Peace Corps policy but was really emphasized to us new volunteers in Malawi. I wondered if it was because of the political upheavals that had taken place here. Shortly after we arrived in the country, we heard of the attempted coup by Henry M. Chipenbere, one of President Banda's former cabinet members. Chipenbere was a "Young Turk," who eventually became impatient with the slow process of Africanization. After all, what was the meaning of independence if the British continued their economic control of the country? I was in total agreement with Chipenbere. I heard privately from my Malawi friends that Chipenbere and other freedom fighters sought independence from Great Britain in the 1950s. When protest led to violence in 1959, Chipenbere was arrested and imprisoned. He was prosecuted for sedition and imprisoned until 1963.

When it was evident that Britain would grant independence to Nyasaland, Hastings Banda, a medical doctor trained at Black colleges in the United States, was invited back in anticipation of independence and potentially to serve as the leader of the new country. Banda was probably the most educated Malawian at the time, but he had been abroad for decades. Some of Banda's young ministers felt he was out of touch with the culture and the younger activists of his country. They eventually rebelled against Banda's autocratic rule, his continued close relationship with South Africa and the slowness in Africanizing the country, which created the cabinet crisis of 1964. Although reluctant initially to join the rebellion, Chipenbere eventually joined in an attempted bloodless coup. The coup attempt failed. Many of the insurgents were captured and allowed to leave the country. Chipenbere resigned and settled in his home district in Fort Johnston. In February 1965, his rebellion against the government failed.

Our favorite beer joint became a place where we fantasized what we would have done if we had been in the country when the Malawi Young Turks rebelled. On one occasion, when we were drinking beer with some Malawians who were regulars at the beer hall, the conversation turned to Chipenbere and the rebels. It was obvious that our friends were rebel sympathizers and posed a danger to themselves and to us just by talking about the incursions into the Lower Shire Valley from posts in Mozambique. We fantasized about joining the group and helping to overthrow the government. After all, we had been in the country long enough to experience firsthand how the president not only encouraged expatriates to remain in the country but also turned a blind eye to their racist behavior. Now I was sure if the attempted coup by members of his cabinet was a major contributing factor to the way he ruled the country with an iron hand today.

Of course, the rebellion was stamped out quickly. Despite rumors, there was no hope that the rebellion could be revived no matter how willing we were to serve in the insurgency.

When Malawi Independence Day came, we celebrated with the rest of

Chapter Two. My First Year in Malawi

President Hastings Banda waving to a group of farmers.

the country. Instead of going to the U.S. embassy for our own celebration, I went to the Malawi celebration near the stadium. We watched the parade of Malawians march toward the stadium. Women all wore wraps that had images of Banda on the red, green and black colors of the flag. Most prominent were the Malawi Young Pioneers in their khaki uniforms. Originally conceived as a progressive development organization, the Young Pioneers slowly became a paramilitary wing of the Malawi Congress Party. I heard rumors where they would harass and sometimes beat dissidents who spoke out against Banda's policies. It never occurred to me and my friends that we might become the subject of harassment by the Young Pioneers.

Tom, Dick, Doug and I viewed the festivities but did not join the crowd in the stadium. Instead, we headed back to the plantation house at Mpemba. We invited Carl Scott and other volunteers to join us for a celebration. Carl turned out to be a pretty good cook and made some excellent pizza.

Even though I had moved out of the house, Tom and I still entertained visitors together in the old plantation house. When we got back to the house, Carl was already there with his supplies for the pizzas. Dick had brought up a huge jug of Portuguese rosé wine. The wine was exceptionally good. Whenever Tom and I purchased one of these jugs, the wine would last us a month drinking wine every day. With the beer and Malawi gin, we thought we had enough beverages. Carl proceeded to make lots of dough and sauce for the pizzas. He had to go to the European market to secure the cheese and seasoning. We had become efficient at cooking on a wood stove. There was only one firebox that produced heat for baking in the wood stove, so we had to keep turning whatever was in the oven to prevent it from burning on one side.

Carl did not need help from me or anyone else in the kitchen. By the time volunteers and our Malawi neighbors began to arrive, Carl had made five pizzas, some with cheese and some with a combination of meat and cheese. Mr. Katembe and his family lived close to us on the old plantation. He was kind enough to bring his hand-crank record player. He had some nice Congolese and West African highlife music. For some reason, the music was so familiar to me. I loved to dance to the songs even if I could not understand the words. It did not take much for the Peace Corps volunteers and guests to start dancing. They had already started drinking the wine and beer, so they were beginning to lose any inhibitions they may have had. Whereas there were female Peace Corps volunteers at the party, none of the Malawi women came. Perhaps their husbands did not allow them to come because of their tradition of not socializing in mixed company.

It was well past midnight when the guests began to leave. Some of the volunteers like Dick and Doug spent the night. While cleaning up the mess, we noticed our dog, Thako, lying on the floor with a stomach that looked like he had swallowed a watermelon. Thako could barely wag his tail or raise his head. He had eaten all of the pizza sauce Carl had left on the table. He had climbed up on the table and evidently kept eating until almost a quart of sauce was consumed.

Thako was a stray pup who wandered up on our porch one day out of the blue. He was less than a year old. He was golden brown. His name in Chichewa means "buttocks." Everson gave him that name. I was not sure why. He was no trouble at all. Everson basically cared for the dog, especially when we had to travel. Malawians don't have a lot of money to spend on their pets. They were fed whatever was left over from the meals, usually nsima that might have a touch of some ndiwo for flavor, and that was about it. So, when Thako saw his opportunity to eat until his heart's content, he did just that. What could we say? The party was over and we had no use for the sauce. We left him in the kitchen on the floor and went to bed.

New Office on Kabula Hill

I believed that Nigel Murphy had come to the realization that I knew what I was doing and that this Peace Corps thing would probably work out. Nigel told me earlier in the month that he had a conversation with Derrick McKinley, and they decided to expand the extension aids office

Chapter Two. My First Year in Malawi

My new office on Kabula Hill, Blantyre.

under my supervision. It was obvious that the small office in the regional headquarters was not suitable for an expanded operation. Nigel said that they had rented a vacant house on Kabula Hill across town in Blantyre that would serve as my expanded office. Despite my feelings toward Nigel and other expatriates, I was pleased that they had enough confidence in me to expand my office's operation.

Nigel and Troy drove me to my new office. We passed the new Soche Hotel, which was the most beautiful and modern hotel in Malawi. I understood that some South African businessmen put up the money to build it. I thought that much of the new development money that came into Malawi originated in South Africa, Southern Rhodesia or Britain. We continued to drive until we reached the entrance into a "White" neighborhood with bungalow-type houses that were obviously built during the colonial era.

I was impressed with the location and size of my new office. The house, though in a residential area, was somewhat isolated in the neighborhood, so I would not have to worry about neighbors complaining. The house itself had four rooms with an indoor toilet. There were eucalyptus trees on both sides of the house, which gave the feeling of being in the tropics. There was a veranda that stretched across the entire front of the house. The house was a brick structure with a metal roof. There were large windows on each side of the door. On entering the front door, there was a large room that would become my office. The other three rooms would serve as offices for the soon-to-be-hired and greatly anticipated staff.

I immediately began to secure office furniture and to interview candidates for the new positions. Joseph Kapanela was now assigned to my office as a messenger and would deliver and pick up any mail from my new office to and from the regional office. He had his own bicycle which helped him secure the job. Joseph had completed standard eight, the equivalent of the eighth grade in the United States. That was a high achievement for the average Malawian, which allowed him to apply and get the job as messenger. It paid eight pounds a month, a good salary for a young Malawian.

Several months before, I created a very primitive-looking newsletter, which I named the *Southern Advisor*. It was designed to serve the needs of regional agricultural extension staff as well as the teachers in the area and district agricultural training centers. The first issue was mimeographed. As editor, I researched and wrote the stories, typed them, ran the mimeograph machine, collated the pages, and stapled them together. Obviously, I needed help. The good thing about having had to do the work myself was that it made it easier for me to teach others.

I hired a bright young man who had finished form four (high school graduate) when he applied to be my assistant. He was much taller than I was, dark brown and had a big, wide smile. He wore a tie to work every day, whereas I dressed in shorts and a short-sleeve shirt. Troy had told me soon after I started work in the regional office that I should have some everyday work shorts made. He suggested that I go to an Indian store to purchase khaki cotton cloth and take it to any of the men with sewing machines in front of the store to make my shorts. He said that the British style of shorts required you to always sit with your legs together or crossed, otherwise with the large opening for the leg, anything could be exposed. Based on Troy's advice, I commissioned several pairs of shorts that would be my uniform for most of my work except during the cold season, when I wore my long pants.

I did not call any of my African colleagues by their first names. All, no matter the status, wanted to be called "mister." I thought that it was a leftover from colonial days when African men were called either "boy" or by their first names. Even today, the British supervisors almost never use mister to address an African employee. So my messenger was named Mr. Kapanela and my assistant was Mr. Mphiri. I want everyone to call me John, but that was easier said than done since Malawians had great respect for a person's education and status.

My job as regional extension aid officer was becoming more defined. I would have to produce a monthly newsletter in English for the extension area supervisors and the training centers' staff and provide educational materials for both groups. Doug and Tom were working on a handbook about the best methods for growing cotton and they wanted my office to print it. Only that week, we got word from the Zomba office that we would be producing puppets and mini theaters as a teaching tool for the field staff. I guess the training I received in London was coming in handy.

The regional office and the extension aid office in Zomba were combining their resources to purchase an offset press. I had already decided to put my new hire, J.B. Ntungama, in charge of the press. It was a logical choice because he was already helping me with the newsletter. The process of producing a newsletter was more than I had bargained for. Word was now out among the regional agricultural staff that we were accepting articles from the field. Initially, only a few came, which meant that I had to write several myself. I asked my Malawi friends if they would also write some of the first articles to encourage their co-workers to contribute to the newsletter. I typed each article and then did my editing on the typed copy. I retyped the manuscript and laid the copy out in the format for printing. I then typed the copy on stencils for mimeographing. I had to draw my own illustrations. I published at a very fundamental level with the two weeks of training I received at the Overseas Visual Aids office in London. It took a couple of weeks before I got the printer from South Africa. Meanwhile, I continued basic production.

The week before, I also traveled to Zomba to meet with Derrick McKinley. He informed me that he was retiring from his job and going to

I'm sitting in the Kabula Hill office.

Nigeria to work and live. Derrick was nice enough. He was a big heavy-set guy who exuded confidence, although he did not look or act like the typical expatriate. After Nigerian independence, few White people wanted to work in Nigeria. Britain ruled Nigeria indirectly through the three major tribal nations in the country. The Nigerians were self-assured and confident and didn't give deference to the British like the Malawians did. Derrick told me to look him up if I decided to go through Nigeria on my way home. I told him that I would. Then I thought about how Derrick's departure would be a perfect opportunity to place an African in his job as his replacement. However, I could not think of anyone suitable to take the position. Malawi sent loads of people overseas for training, some short term and others for a degree program. Some of my colleagues had been trained overseas, but none had received a degree. I guess it would be hard to fill McKinley's position with an African.

Derrick told me that there was an employee in the office who was an expert puppet maker and was also an illustrator. His name was Henry Chirwa. He told me that he was willing to transfer Chirwa to my office if I wanted and needed him. Of course I said yes. I jumped at any opportunity to add to my staff to increase production in my office.

Derrick introduced me to Henry Chirwa. Henry was an older Malawian, short and somewhat stocky and with a dark complexion. After Derrick left, Henry told me he would like to work for me in Blantyre. He showed me the puppets that he had made. He was actually a pretty good puppet maker. He also showed me some of his illustrations. I told him that I thought we could use a man of his talents. He would continue to work at the same salary he was currently making. He said that he could move and be in the office within a week.

Things were looking up in my office. I was finally getting the staff that I wanted and needed. I had a messenger, my assistant and now an artist.

Going to the Market

We worked a half day on Saturdays. I told Tom that I would stop at the market to pick up food for dinner on Sunday. We still had Sunday meals together. I drove my motorcycle to the market in Blantyre right after work. One could buy just about anything needed in the African market. The market was divided by sex. The women grew their own vegetables and brought them to the market for sale. There were beautiful tomatoes, potatoes, peppers, onions and beans, both fresh and dried. I never knew there were so many colorful varieties of beans. Corn flour was sold for nsima, both fine and coarse. The coarse flour was cheaper in that it was not as refined and was used for ngaiwa. The women also sold all sorts of spices that were piled in mounds on top of tightly woven flat baskets. The men sold carvings, mainly for tourists, but also utilitarian bowls, cups and other housewares.

Only the men operated the meat stalls. I heard that cattle were often marched hundreds of miles south from the northern region, which might explain why the meat was so tough. Each meat vendor had a small stall with hanging carcasses in various stages of dryness. There was no refrigeration, even though a beef or goat carcass would hang until it was sold. There were flies everywhere, but no one seemed to mind. A few vendors might have goats for sale, but there weren't any pigs because of African swine fever. Swine fever must have been bad because the government banned the sale of pigs altogether. Every part of the animal was sold and, I suppose, eaten. Goat heads were a particular delicacy and quickly sold out as soon as the market opened.

On occasion, we found various assortments of insects. When termites swarm, they, as well as grasshoppers and locusts, became plentiful in the market. My messenger once brought a plate of grasshoppers to the office as a morning snack for me. I was really torn as to what I should do. I did not want to insult him by refusing. So I said that I could not eat them without salt. He left the room and soon returned with a saltshaker from which he sprinkled grains of salt over the little grasshopper corpses. I had no choice but to eat them. They had been roasted with their legs intact in a hot pan until they were crispy. When heated at a high temperature, they released their oil, which was why they were cooked without oil. I couldn't say that I disliked the taste. Every bite had a crunch, and I could still taste the grease. I managed to eat them as Joseph stood there with a big grin on his face. I believe that this was just a test to see if I would actually eat them. Not that he was giving me something that he would not eat himself. Malawians find grasshoppers as tasty as they do termites.

While at the market, I decided that we would have beef for dinner. I walked past several vendors looking for the cleanest one with the least number of flies. I stopped at one stall and pointed out the cut that I wanted. The vendor told me that the cut I wanted was not the best because it came attached with bones. He said that I should take the meat from the hindquarters. I tried to explain that rib steaks were very good and tender. He again suggested that I buy a piece from the hip that was solid meat and thus the best buy. I insisted until he finally gave me approximately a pound of meat at two shillings and sixpence. He was pushing the boneless meat, which sold for three shillings a pound. I thought that I would purchase a few potatoes, green beans and tomatoes. That should round out our dinner.

Sometimes Tom and I would go together to purchase a live market chicken. I became "famous" for being able to go to the market, purchase a chicken, tie it to my motorcycle, arrive home, make a fire, heat boiling water, cut the chicken's head off, pick the feathers off the chicken and clean it, cut it up, dredge it in seasoned flour and fry it before it ever got cold. After asking our first houseboy if he could fry chicken and he came into the dining room with a whole fried chicken, I decided that if we were going to have southern fried chicken, I would have to make it myself.

When I returned home from the market, I delivered the food to the cook. On Sunday we had a delicious meal of steak and potatoes with green beans cooked with tomatoes, and Portuguese rosé wine. There was nothing like relaxing on a Sunday after a good meal.

Birthday in Malawi

I celebrated my 24th birthday on August 3. Since it was a Saturday, we had to work a half day before I could begin to celebrate my birthday. I couldn't believe I was nearly a quarter century old. Tom and a few other volunteers in town had agreed to take me out for lunch and beer at our favorite bar in Blantyre. Dick was up for the weekend. Even though he liked his job and surroundings in the Lower Shire, he drove up to Blantyre for the weekend when a feeling of isolation sort of got to him.

We enjoyed a lunch of curried beef, stewed with tomatoes and onions, over rice with a bottle of Carlsberg beer. Carlsberg had recently opened a plant in Malawi. The beer was better than Lion or Castle, but it cost more, so we drank it only on special occasions. Dick proceeded to tell a story of a Malawian who was challenged to drink six beers, one right after the other. He said that the man was able to drink all of the beers without throwing up. Being that it was my birthday, he challenged me to do the same. Dick said that if I won, he would buy the beer, and if I lost, I would have to pay for the six beers. Since I already had one beer with lunch, all I had to do was drink five more. I took up the challenge. Dick asked the waiter to bring over five Lion beers. Lion beer was from Southern Rhodesia. Although I generally boycotted products from Southern Rhodesia as much as possible, I made an exception for Lion beer. Lion beer was pretty close to how American beer tasted but better.

I drank beer number two and three quickly. I belched a couple of times before drinking beer number four. I decided that I would have to wait a few minutes before continuing because I was getting full, having started the contest on a full stomach. They all urged me on. Dick reminded me that if I lost the bet, I would have to pay for the beer. With that encouragement, I started on number five. Somehow, I managed to down the beer, which left number six staring me in the face. By this time, my stomach was extended. I weighed only 160 pounds and had already consumed a couple of quarts of liquid. I slowly picked up the last beer and started to drink. Before barely getting down half the bottle, my stomach started to rumble. I wanted to belch but couldn't. Somebody must have heard my stomach growling because they told me to get up and go to the bathroom. I quickly got up and briskly walked down the corridor toward the restroom. While still in the hallway just before entering the toilet, my stomach exploded. A gush of beer began to rise from my stomach to my mouth. By this time, I was not in control. The beer rushed out like a geyser. Foamy beer mixed with beef curry went all over both sides of the hallway and onto the floor. I proceeded into the toilet where I let out another burst of mixed food and beer. The place was a mess.

I washed my face and returned to the table where my fellow volunteers waited to hear what had happened. Dick said that I owed him for the beer, but I said that I did not. I told him that I drank the beer, and could I help it if the beer refused to stay down? I ordered another beer while we continued to talk. The next time I went to the toilet to pee, a Malawi man remarked about the vomit all down the hallway and how disgusting it was that no one cleaned it up. I agreed and said how could anyone leave such a mess.

Later that evening, with Doug, Dick and Carl in town, Carl Scott brought up a leg of lamb from the farm at Tuchila. We killed one of the chickens we were raising and decided we would have a barbecue as a fitting close to my birthday. We gathered some bricks that were lying around the grounds and put together a cementless barbecue pit. As the platform for the meats, we used one of the grates from the oven in the house. After gathering some firewood from the back of the house, we were all set to barbecue. Carl took over the food preparation. He seasoned and marinated the chicken and lamb. When the fire died down and the coals were white, he gently placed the meat onto the hot grate over the pit. We stood around for a while and then decided that we would go inside and have some beer. Carl went out to check on the meat once and came back. We drank and talked for a while and Carl suggested that I go out and check on the meat this time. When I went outside of the kitchen, I found that all the meat was gone. I called the others. We then began to speculate on what happened. Someone thought a local man might have taken the meat. I said that I doubted that. Tom then reminded me of the hyena I saw when I was riding down the road leading to the house. The hyena was in the middle of the road just before the small wooden bridge. It was as frightened of me as I was of him. It quickly ran off into the bush. I gave it no more thought until now. We all concluded that it must have been a hyena. What other animal could lift a leg of lamb and a whole chicken off a hot fire?

Puppet Theater

My new office and staff were working out fine. Our current major project was to provide puppets, 15 small theaters and agricultural production scripts for all of the rural training centers. I placed Mr. Chirwa in charge of puppet production. Mr. Tembo, who was an excellent carpenter, was transferred temporarily to the Kabula office to make the puppet theaters. He could make anything out of wood and his work was first class. It was Mr. Tembo who helped me secure lumber and poles from the Department of Forestry when I was constructing my house. He was a nice man with an even temperament. I designed the puppet booth for the rural training centers and Mr. Tembo produced them according to specifications. The staff and I worked together on the messages that we incorporated into scripts for the puppet shows to use in teaching local farmers progressive agricultural methods. For some reason, Malawians were attracted to and entertained by puppets and thus would listen carefully to the messages conveyed through the mini theater productions. My theater design was simple. There were three panels with the center panel hinged to the other two sides that allowed for the panels to fold onto each other for easy transport and storage. The center panel had an opening for the stage that was 18" × 24". A cloth on a drawstring in front of the opening acted as the theater curtain that closed at the end of the show. Mr. Tembo was making 15 of these stages, one for each area training center and one for the Tuchila center, which meant that he would be with us for a long time.

Mr. Chirwa had been making the puppets the traditional way with a papier-mâché head with an opening for the index and middle fingers. The body was made from cloth with extensions for fingers that served as the arms. It occurred to me that if the farmers were intrigued by the puppets, why not make them more interesting by designing puppets that allowed the puppeteer to open and close the puppet's mouth. I suggested this design to Mr. Chirwa. Once the paper-mâché head was made, the mouth could be cut and hinged together with gauze that would allow the finger to move the lower jaw. Once Mr. Chirwa got the hang of it, his production of puppets increased dramatically.

Working as a Team

If I had to describe Carl Scott in one word, it was that he was an organizer. He organized the expedition up Mount Mulanje, which I would never forget. Now he was planning a trip to the Luangwa Game Reserve in Zambia. It was one of the largest game reserves in Africa. We were all excited. We were going in early September. I was taking a week off, leaving me with another three weeks for my trip to East Africa.

The office was down to a routine. We all seemed to be getting along well. Mr. Kapanela was a very nice young man who smiled all the time. There was little that would ruffle his feathers. He was now our cook. Being very versatile, he did not mind taking on this added responsibility. The office decided that we would cook our food each day and have a communal meal. Mr. Kapanela volunteered to go to the market and bring back food, which he prepared on our paraffin stove. We all chipped in six pence to purchase the food. I generally contributed one, sometimes two, shillings to make sure Mr. Kapanela had enough money for the needed purchases. Besides, I could not eat in a local restaurant for two shillings, so I did not mind paying a little more than my share. Today, he brought back dried fish, tomatoes, onions and peppers. He sautéed the vegetables in a large pan before adding the fish on top of some of the vegetables. He then added the rest of the vegetables and seasoned the pot with salt and pepper. He let the fish simmer until the dried flesh was reconstituted. He made nsima from the corn flour we kept in the office. I had always hated the smell of dried fish, but when it was cooked, a metamorphosis occurred.

When the fish was done, the metal bowl was placed in the middle of our worktable and we all gathered around to eat. I was a little concerned about eating dry fish because it smelled so bad. My fears were relieved with my first bite of fish that I picked up using a small portion of nsima. It was delicious. In fact, it may have tasted better than the fresh chomba I had at Lake Malawi. Having this communal meal brought us even closer together as a staff. Eating around the table provided a sense of equality. I wanted everyone to feel that we were all in this together, and if our all-Black office was to succeed, it had to be a team effort.

Funeral in Malawi

I participated in the funeral services for our chief accountant, Mr. Bonomi. It was the first time I had attended a Malawi funeral. Mr. Bonomi was a very nice man who could not have been older than 50 or 55. Often, it was difficult to determine the exact age of a Malawian. The men did not look their age, but women often looked older than they were because of the hard work they did all of their lives. Mr. Bonomi was educated in finance and was the highest-ranking Malawian in the regional agricultural office in Blantyre. He was very helpful in getting me settled in my office. Initially,

I was not aware that Mr. Bonomi was ill, but evidently, he had been sick for a long time. Everyone in the office had great respect for him, which explained why the expatriates attended the formal funeral.

Mr. Bonomi lived in Blantyre most of his life. I am not sure where his home village was, but it seemed as if the whole African township turned out for the funeral, which lasted several days. I went to visit the family the evening before the funeral. Many people were gathered outside of his modern-style but modest house in the African township. Women sat on mats on the grounds wailing as they mourned for the dead. I guess that this was a way of connecting with the ancestors. It was interesting that although most Malawians were Christians or Muslims, they were still connected with their traditional African religious practices and customs. Wailing by women was quite common, even in the city. I walked past the women and into the house where the family was gathered. When I reached the door, I said, "Odi" and was invited to enter. I expressed my condolences to his wife and other members of his family. Visitors were expected to leave some form of a gift—money, food, clothing. I left 10 shillings as I departed the house.

The next day was the formal funeral, which was a combination of Christian and traditional religious practices. There was lots of singing and dancing. The Gule Mamkulu dancers, men who belonged to a secret society, performed outside of the house. They were dressed in animal-head costumes that were not as elaborate as they would have been in a traditional village setting. I was told that they performed rites of passage for young men in the village, that these traditions were very old and survived European colonialism by incorporating some Christian traditions into the ceremonies.

The local African cemetery was not far from the township, so the men carried the casket to the burial site. At the funeral, women were separated from the men and sat on the ground, while the male relatives and some dignitaries sat in chairs. Nigel Murphy, Troy David, JW Bower and others were all there. The minister gave a graveside eulogy followed by various people commenting on the life of Mr. Bonomi. Nigel Murphy spoke on behalf of the regional office. He was very eloquent and sincere in his remarks. Mr. Bonomi was truly respected by all.

The Luangwa Game Reserve, Zambia

We traveled to Zambia to visit the Luangwa Game Park in the eastern part of the country. Carl, Tom, John Hunter, Doug and Dick were part of the group. Doug was able to borrow from his cotton extension officer one of the Land Rovers, which comfortably seated six. The Land Rover was a much better choice than all of us riding our motorbikes all the way to the park.

Because we had to work on Saturday, we packed most of our gear the night before so that we would be ready to leave early Saturday afternoon. Since we were late getting started, we decided that we would go as far as Lilongwe where we would spend the night. Lilongwe was the second largest city in Malawi and about 241 miles from Blantyre. After leaving Zomba, most of the roads were dirt. If it had been the rainy season, there was no telling how long it would have taken us. Doug did most of the driving. We made one stop in Dedza for a Fanta soda. Dedza was where my friend Edward Limbani was from and where he wanted me to meet his extended family. That trip was high on my list of things to do. I had not yet spent any time living in a traditional village and I looked forward to the trip.

Christian Missionaries

When we got to Lilongwe, it was nearly six o'clock. We had not made any arrangements to spend the night. Tom said that his hometown church supported an evangelical mission in Lilongwe. He thought the missionaries were from Texas and members of the Pentecostal Methodist Christian Church. The more I learned about missionaries and their work in Africa, the less respect I had for them. Many of my Malawi friends had gone to mission schools for their secondary education. These were residential schools that depended on the churches in the United States and Europe for support. A friend told me about how harsh the teachers were when he was in school. The teachers were all White and demanded total obedience. They did not mind using the paddle on the students. My friend said that once they were in the orchard picking peaches from the trees and were told that they could not pick the fruit from the trees but had to eat the ones that had fallen to the ground. Of course, they were the rotten ones. The good fruit was reserved for use by the missionaries or was sold to bring in additional income. I had personally seen missionaries take a very arrogant attitude toward the people they were supposed to serve. It reminded me of growing up in North Carolina where White people in authority always demanded deference.

We drove around Lilongwe for a while checking out the town. We stopped at the local hotel where Tom inquired about the location of the Pentecostal church and school. Trying to save on expenses, we decided to head to the mission to see if we could get lodging for the night. We passed through the entryway that had a sign saying "Pentecostal Methodist Christian School." We asked a young man where we could find the church minister or headmaster of the school. He said to follow him. We were soon at the home of the Reverend and Mrs. William Johnson. They were tall White people who were obviously middle aged and had just a hint of gray around their temples. We introduced ourselves as Peace Corps volunteers on our way to the game reserve in Zambia. Tom asked if we could spend the night at the mission. We discovered that there were just two of them living in a large ranch-style house that had at least four bedrooms, none of which were extended to us. However, we were invited to spend the night in the garage on the side of the house. We thanked them for their "generosity." The Reverend Johnson pulled his Peugeot station wagon out of the garage and parked it in the driveway giving us plenty of room for our sleeping bags and other gear. No one said a word or complained about the accommodations.

Once we unpacked, we headed back to Lilongwe to get something to eat and drink since the Johnsons had offered neither. We found what looked like a decent place to eat called Madras House. It was clean with a few African and Indian patrons and some Europeans mixed in. We walked in and were seated immediately in the sparsely filled restaurant. We were hungry. We decided that we would have the meal served family style and ordered tandoori chicken, aloo methi (potato and mint), biryani (a mixture of rice, spices and vegetables), dal (lentil) and naan. We danced and drank until nearly midnight before heading back to the mission. As we were walking to the Land Rover, there were a number of large, corrugated boxes on the sidewalk in front of local businesses. Out of the blue, I decided to kick one, and to my surprise a Malawi man emerged from what evidently was his house. I felt terrible and apologized profusely.

Once back at the missionary station, we soon settled on the garage floor for the night. The cement floor was hard, but I think most of us were too tired to notice. The next morning, I walked around to the front of the house and asked if we could use their bathroom to wash up. I knew that such a large rambling house must have at least several bathrooms. Mrs. Johnson, looking somewhat disturbed that we would intrude on her Sunday morning, did not hesitate in saying no to my request. She then suggested that we wash up out back where there was a hose attached to a spigot. I thought to myself, *Here we were, Americans and treated this way by Christian missionaries. If we were treated like this, how were they treating the Africans whom they came here to serve?* The missionaries, as do most White people, had cooks, houseboys, yardmen and nightwatchmen. Those with children had nannies. The Johnsons were living in a four-bedroom brick house with running water, electricity and all of the amenities of an American home. I could imagine them writing to the folks back home about all the suffering they were enduring to spread the word of God among the "heathens." I guess some of these modern-day Christians would not recognize Jesus if they came face to face with him.

We got an early start on our way to Luangwa Game Reserve but had to make a stop at the market in Lilongwe. We purchased fresh supplies for the trip, 40 pounds of beef, which the vendor wrapped in old newspapers, rice, potatoes, flour and an assortment of vegetables and fruits. Our camp at the reserve provided a cook, but we had to provide the food. We thought it best that we wait until the last minute to purchase perishables since we did not have a cooler or ice.

It was still the dry season, so the roads were dusty and the forest dry. We arrived at the park in mid-afternoon. The park was divided into two, southern Luangwa and northern Luangwa. We were in the south end. The park was surrounded by dry woodland that was lush during the rainy season. We immediately noticed the many sausage trees, or Kigelia trees. They had long-looking sausage-like fruit that were often two feet long and could weigh up to 15 pounds. African men liked to compare the fruit on the tree to their own private parts.

As we entered the southern park, we passed a sign that indicated that we were entering the Luangwa Game Reserve, Zambia Department of Natural Resources. The park was dry this time of the year. The Luangwa River transversed the park and at that time of the year, it was shallow, leaving

Our cabin in the Luangwa Game Reserve, Zambia.

many pools where animals congregated. We stopped at the ranger station for information, to check in and secure the location of our cabin in the park. We went directly to the cabin where we found our cook and all-around assistant waiting for us. The cabins were small brown buildings with yellow siding and brown shutters. There was an enclosed porch, a living space, two bedrooms and a bath. I was sure they were designed for European tourists. As Peace Corps volunteers, we found them quite comfortable and luxurious.

Our assistant/cook met us in the yard in front of the cabin. He introduced himself as Frank Ndonga. He was Bantu and was probably related to the Chewa people of Malawi. He spoke a language that was related to Chichewa, but we, or should I say I, did not understand his language beyond his greetings. We told him our names and that we were Peace Corps volunteers. He took charge of our food supplies, taking everything into the camp kitchen where he placed our market meat in a refrigerator with lots of store-bought meat wrapped in cellophane. I was embarrassed when he put our 40 pounds of beef that was wrapped in what was now bloody newspaper in the refrigerator. Frank took everything in stride and it did not seem to bother him. I hoped that the meat had not spoiled during our drive.

We did some independent exploring before dinner. Our official safari was the next morning. We went down to the river where we saw lots of hippos and birds. It was too early for some animals to come in for water, although we saw elephants in the distance. We were told not to go too near the water because dangerous animals also drank from the watering hole. The place was beautiful even in the dry season. There were lots of trees and some foliage near the cabins that were watered by the attendants.

When we got back to camp, it was time for dinner. We washed up and entered a communal dining facility. There were people from all over the world: Britain, Canada, Australia and, of course, South Africa. I felt a little strange that there were no other Black guests and I was the only Black person in the group with the exception of the African servants. Before dinner, the tourists were drinking top brands of liquor while we drank Malawi gin and the Lion beer we had brought with us. Soon, our dinner was on the table. The cook performed a miracle with the food we brought. The large chunk of meat was expertly cut into small steaks that were prepared with sautéed onions and mushrooms. We had sides of french fries and green beans. Our dinner looked like any of the other meals. We were pleased and told our cook how much we enjoyed our meal.

Following dinner, the White tourists got progressively friendlier as they continued to drink their high-end alcoholic beverages. By late evening, even the South Africans were friendly to me. One suggested that I should visit South Africa because of its natural beauty. I said that I could

Chapter Two. My First Year in Malawi

Road through the Luangwa Game Reserve.

not visit a country that practiced segregation. He replied there were many parks where Blacks and Whites could gather without breaking the law. I asked why would I even want to do that knowing how Black people were treated in South Africa. We finished our beers and headed off to bed. We wanted to get a good night's rest because we had to rise before five in the morning to begin our safari at six.

On Safari

By the time we woke up, the rays of the sun were penetrating the bamboo blinds. We were running late. We quickly dressed and joined our group. We were divided into two groups. The first group of tourists had already departed and we were anxious to get going. Lucky was the name of our guide. I couldn't tell if that was his given name or a nickname given to him for having survived the attack of a wild animal. Regardless of how he came by the name, he carried a gun with him. We headed off into the bush in our Peace Corps/Malawi dress. The Europeans were in the traditional safari outfits of khaki shorts and shirts with large pockets on their vests and jackets. Each wore a safari hat.

As soon as we entered the bush, we immediately saw animals. I saw warthogs scurrying through the bush followed by several baby warthogs. They were as ugly in real life as they were in the *National Geographic* magazine. The farther we walked, the more animals appeared. We saw bush bucks, antelopes, and impalas. I was not sure how far we walked, but it was getting hot. There was a peculiar smell in the air, like rotten meat. The farther we went, the stronger the smell. Then suddenly, we came upon an elephant that had been killed for its tusks. The guide said that the kill happened over a month ago and the elephant was left to rot in the hot sun. Imagine several tons of meat rotting in the sun for weeks. The smell was overwhelming and seemed to just hang in the air. We could smell the elephant when we were over a mile away. We traveled another mile before we were able to escape the stink. The guide said that it was unfortunate that the elephant had to die for its tusks. The people who killed the elephant probably only got a few pounds, whereas the people who sold the tusks to ivory dealers were the ones who made all the money. He said that the game wardens did what they could to prevent poaching, but there were too many poachers and too few game wardens.

We continued our safari walking in a circle that included stagnant ponds, as the flow of the Luangwa River had slowed to a trickle. There were lots of egrets and other waterfowl. Water buffalo, giraffes and elephants were not timid as they drank from the ponds. Hyenas made the few kudus and impalas very nervous as they drank from the few available pools that remained. By mid-afternoon, the heat made walking very exhausting. The guide suggested that we call it a day, head back to camp and prepare for an early start tomorrow.

We were all frazzled when we returned to camp. We showered and changed clothes for dinner. I lingered longer than usual in the shower. I was used to bathing from a five-gallon bucket of water, so running water was a real treat. We had steak every day because that was the only meat we had brought with us. Fortunately, we had a very creative and innovative cook who was able to make a variety of dishes from the beef and the assorted vegetables we had purchased at the market in Lilongwe.

After dinner, we relaxed with the other guests as the sun set. It was not long before we all were ready for bed.

The next morning, we were up bright and early. For breakfast, we had tea, toast and peach jam our cook had made from the peaches we had brought. Our guide this morning was named Bronson. When he introduced himself, I could not help but ask him how he came to be named Bronson. He said that he was named after a missionary.

Bronson said that we would be going to the south end of the park today where we should see a variety of animals. We drove for about 10

Chapter Two. My First Year in Malawi 89

miles through a meandering route around the park and saw lots of elephants and black rhinos. When we spotted some water buffalo, we had to stop to take pictures. They were interesting animals with horns that parted down the middle of their heads and descended from the top into curved peaks. The horns looked like the mustaches of old-time barbershop quartet singers.

We passed numerous sausage trees with lots of birds eating the large fruit that had fallen to the ground. Impalas were busy eating the dried grass. We soon spotted a lion sleeping on one of the high tree limbs. When we got to our destination, we found a large pond with lots of animals around it. Bronson parked the Land Rover in the shade, away from the scrutiny of the many predators around the pond. There was a pride of lions sleeping in the shade, maybe five or six females, several baby lions and one large male. Bronson said that the male has to fight other males to maintain control and dominance over his pride. The male lion with his large mane truly looked majestic.

There must have been dozens of hippos in the water, some standing with their heads and backs out of the water, allowing small birds to check them for insects. Every now and then, a hippo would open its huge mouth to yawn, revealing the chasm between those jaws. Bronson pointed toward the crocodiles sunning just offshore. He said that any animals that drank near crocodiles risked being eaten. Two large giraffes approached the water's edge where they spread their long legs, lowered their elegant necks and drank from the pool of water. They drank cautiously because they were vulnerable to attack in such an awkward position. Birds also picked insects off the back and neck of the giraffes as they drank from the pond.

Carl had the foresight to buy flour, which the cook used to make loaves of bread. We had toast earlier, and the cook had prepared and packed sandwiches for our lunch. They were butter or rather canned margarine sandwiches with cucumbers in between the sliced bread, a typical British sandwich. The cook also made a mixed-fruit cocktail of bananas, mangoes, pineapples and pawpaw. It was delicious. I still marvel at how ingenious our cook was. The afternoon passed quickly, and soon we found ourselves heading back to camp. It was a very good day and we took lots of pictures.

I don't think any of us wanted to head back to Malawi and work the next day, but duty called. On the last night at the park, we had dinner and drank the last of the beer that the cook had refrigerated for us. For a change, we had cold beer, a real treat in Africa. I found it amusing that when you were in the African bush and asked for a cold beer, you got a beer that had been sitting in warm water. If you wanted a warm beer, you got a hot beer that had been sitting on the shelf. We inquired about walking down to the water's edge but were advised not to. All sorts of animals would be coming to drink from the pond, so it was best to do our viewing from a distance.

It was hard to believe that our excursion to Zambia was over. It was a very nice break from the routine of work. Now we had to face the long trip back. We decided to leave early enough to make the trip back home in one day. We packed our belongings before going to bed and were ready to leave early the next morning. The cook prepared tea, toast and jam with fruit for our breakfast. We thanked him for such great meals and gave him six pounds, which was for us a lavish tip, even though his services had been included in our accommodation fees.

While driving out of the reserve, we stopped for the occasional animal sightings. As we made a ninety-degree turn around a bend in the road, we almost ran right into a bull elephant. The elephant turned and looked just as startled as we must have looked. It seemed as if the elephant jumped backward with all four feet off the ground. After quickly assessing the situation, the elephant began waving his trunk in the air and flapping his ears and let out a loud elephant roar. He started moving his feet as if he was getting ready to charge. It did not take long for Doug to put the Land Rover in reverse and back up at a high speed. It appeared that the elephant may have been as frightened of us as we were of him. What a way to end a visit to a game reserve! We arrived back in Blantyre in the evening and got ready for bed.

Pork and Flies

Not much was happening in the office the week after we returned. Although I was glad for the short break in Zambia, it was good to be back on the job. On Monday, a man came by the office to see if anyone wanted to buy some pork. It seemed that for the first time in a long while, people were allowed to slaughter their pigs. This man took orders from the staff. I asked for a whole shoulder since the pigs here were small. The pig was slaughtered that evening and brought to the office the next day. I kept the pork shoulder on my shelf in my office all day wrapped in heavy plastic left over from office supplies. By the time I got home, the pig must have been dead for at least 24 hours. The September heat did not help matters. In fact, the heat probably contributed to the further deterioration of the pork. When I unwrapped the meat, it had a green sheen to the outer layer. It did not quite smell right, but I had not had any pork in over a year and I was determined not to let this piece of meat go to waste. I got out my largest pan, cut up the meat and made some homemade barbecue sauce to go over it. To ensure that the chopped pork would be OK, I cooked it for hours on my paraffin stove. When I finally went into the kitchen to check on the meat, there must have been a million green flies outside of my window. My heart sank. There was no question that the meat had spoiled. It was rancid. As I was taking the pot of pork out to dump into the garbage pit I had dung in the backyard, Mr. Katembe's farmhand came up and, through a combination of Chichewa and sign language, asked me if I was throwing away the food in the pot. I said yes, that it was bad meat. He asked if he could have it. I reluctantly gave it to him and hoped that he did not get sick. He looked fine the next day.

When I first built the house, I had some laborers dig this hole in the back that was four feet by four feet and at least four feet deep. I assumed that it would suffice for all of the garbage I would be throwing away. But just as the farmhand asked for my pot of barbecue, anything thrown into the pit was quickly taken by nearby villagers—paper, plastic, old newspapers, bottles, magazines, boxes. What was junk and trash to me had value to those with so little. Much of what we throw away in the West still has utilitarian value in the developing world. I now realized that I could have dug a small pit for what would truly end up as garbage.

Culture Shock

I had been in Malawi for nearly a year, and during that time, I had not experienced the traditional culture shock that the Peace Corps said everyone experienced after being in the country for a month or so. Well, I can honestly say that I did not. I loved being in Africa and being around Africans. I was determined that I would accept Malawians and their ways of doing things. I was eager to learn and to be accepted by my brothers. But culture shock finally descended upon me with a vengeance. Even though it had taken nearly a year for me to experience it, I now knew what culture shock felt like. Sometimes the work could be overwhelming. Maybe I should not say the work because I enjoyed my work; it was more like what it took to get the work done. Although I loved being in Malawi, sometimes I wished I could instill my work ethic into the people I worked with and my other colleagues in the office and in my village. You just couldn't count on getting something done when a Malawian says that it would be done. You always had to add extra time to whatever the task was. Nobody got upset if something was not done on time—it was like, it would eventually get done, so what was the problem? I liked to work on a schedule. If I said that the newsletter would be out on a certain date, I wanted to meet that deadline. Often, I would come into the office on Sundays just to make sure the work stayed on schedule and to make up for what others did not do. This was absolutely driving me crazy. Everybody in the department knew that articles were due by the middle of the month if they were going to appear in next month's newsletter. Yet field staff sent articles anytime during the month with the expectation that they would appear in the next issue. I learned to keep a reserve of articles that were not time sensitive so that I could meet my own deadline for publication. What really bothered me was staff not sending in the assigned feature articles on time.

This attitude was not peculiar to me and my staff. It was true throughout the country. There was such a thing as African time. I guess in Latin America, the term is "mañana," meaning sometime tomorrow or whenever but definitely not a specific time. Until I learned to accept life here as it was, I would always be frustrated. Meanwhile, I was ready for another vacation.

I received a letter from Barbara complaining about how meaningless her work was at IBM. She disliked the fact that White people were pleasant enough in the office and often smiled in your face, but when they see you on the street, it was as if they did not know you. Barbara apologized again for not wanting to come to Africa as I desired. She said that in addition to the need to help her family, she believed that her first obligation was to try to remedy the problems Black people face in America. I could see her point of view since I had always tried to be active in the Civil Rights movement.

My Berea African Classmates

I wrote to my friend Salome Nolega David in Nairobi that I would be on holiday in early November at the end of my first year of duty in Malawi. I told her that I wanted to visit with her and other Kenyans who attended Berea. All the students from Kenya returned home after graduating and were doing well. There was one White Kenyan in Berea when I arrived, David Ashcroft, who was born in Kenya of British parents. He was tall and a great soccer player. Like most young Africans, he learned to play soccer in bare feet. David was a senior when I was a freshman. He and Salome were very good friends. When Salome took me under her wing, I became friends with David too.

Michael Ndungi was also from Kenya and entered Berea our freshman year even though he had had only one year of high school. I thought that he must have been very smart or how else could he have graduated with only one year of high school. Michael and I lived in the same dorm and were friendly enough to each other, but it was Salome who came to be my best friend.

Chapter Two. My First Year in Malawi

Salome Nolega David (left) with my sister, Patricia, at Berea College.

I think that Salome majored in something like home economics at Berea. She was a wonderful cook and introduced me to all types of African dishes. It was through Salome's cooking that I first had my taste of a form of nsima, but it was called ugali in Kenya. I liked it and the relish dishes she prepared for me. We would go on picnics and she would prepare these wonderful lunches. She was so talented. When my sister, Patricia, came to visit me in Berea, Salome had her stay with her in Anna Smith Dormitory. Patricia forgot to bring a dress for church on Easter. Salome purchased materials, took Patricia's measurement and had her dress ready by Sunday morning.

I was very pleased when Salome told me that she would meet me at the airport when we changed planes in Nairobi from British Overseas Airways to East African Airways. I could not have been more pleased when I saw my Berea classmate at the airport. I had promised her then that I would return and spend time with her the first chance I got. So I was waiting to hear back from Salome before completing my vacation plans for East Africa.

New Friends

In the spring of my first year, Tom Barker and I enrolled in a series of lectures on international relations at the University of Malawi. The courses were scheduled to meet on Mondays during the early part of the evening so people leaving work could conveniently attend. The schedule was very convenient for me. I stayed in the office until it was time to leave for class. It was interesting how things work out. I had been stewing in my dislike for expatriates and people generally from South Africa and Southern Rhodesia; then I met the Olivers at the college. They, too, were taking the course on international relations. At the end of one class, they came over and introduced themselves to me. They were from Northern California. Dick taught surveying and engineering at the polytechnic in Blantyre. His wife, Anne, was a stay-at-home mom until she accepted a part-time position keeping records for a local Dutch surgeon. They were some of the nicest people I had ever met. They were by no means typical Americans and they were certainly far from being typical expatriates. Like most Europeans, as the Malawians call all White people, they lived in housing provided by the government or, in this case, the polytechnic. It was a spacious brick home in a White suburban community.

I became friends with the Olivers almost immediately. We seemed to have so much in common. We talked after each class and sometimes went out for a drink or dinner. The Olivers shared my views on the failure of the Malawi government to Africanize. We all understood that our views were not to be broadcast outside of our inner circle lest we were deported for criticizing the government, or should I say, President Banda.

I was invited to their house for dinner on several occasions and met their children who attended the mostly White school for expatriates. Dick told me that their kids were getting a really good education here. He did not like the idea of Malawi children being so limited in the opportunities that they had. They had to pay school fees, $2 a year for the first five grades and $6 for the next three grades. They paid $70 a year for secondary school, which was mainly residential including room and board. That might not seem like a lot of money, but it was in a country where most people were subsistence farmers. Many men go to South Africa to work in the mines or to Southern Rhodesia to work on farms in order to secure enough money to support their families and pay school fees. The higher education system was free. Dick told me that the government actually paid students to go to college.

Anne told me that they were not used to having servants all over the place. They much preferred their privacy. She said that when they arrived last spring, they inherited a gardener, a cook, and a houseman (she refused to call them houseboys). She said that her cook quit shortly after they arrived. She suspected that he was used to working for and being bossed by English expatriates. Anne said that they hired their gardener as their new cook, who surprisingly turned out to be somewhat of a chef. He now took care of meals and did simple housekeeping. They had a wonderful house but lacked the traditional household machines—for example, washer/dryer, dishwasher and vacuum cleaner. Dick had a garden in the back of the house and grew a number of vegetables. The Olivers were good people, and I thoroughly enjoyed their company.

A Terrible Accident

I rode my motorcycle up to Liwonde to work with an extension aid area supervisor. I was interested in getting him to write an article for the newsletter and to learn more about his efforts to get farmers to use fertilizer. He told me that Jack Allison's song "Feteleza Achulukitsa Zokolola" really grabbed the attention of the local farmers. The widely aired song did wonders in helping farmers understand the importance of replenishing the soil if they wanted to improve their crop yield.

On the way back to Blantyre, I had a terrible accident. Travel on unpaved roads was always dangerous, especially on a motorbike. This being the dry season, the roads were extremely sandy. I was traveling about 50 miles an hour when I spotted this man on a bicycle ahead of me. A huge amount of assorted goods were tied to the back of his bike. As soon as the man heard the roar of my bike, he crossed the road in front of me at almost the exact moment as I approached him. Needless to say, I hit the man, knocking him off his bike and flipping me over in front of mine. I landed on my hands, taking off the skin on my palms. I was in terrible pain as I lay on the ground. I was stunned and could not move. I was not sure how long I was there, but I was fortunate that one of our agricultural workers lived nearby and heard the crash. He quickly came to our assistance. He determined that the bicyclist was not hurt and helped him load his bundles on his bike. He loaded my motorcycle on the department's small lorry and took me to his house. After he and his wife surveyed my injuries, they decided that I needed to go to the local infirmary.

They transported me to the next village where I was seen by the local medic. He cleaned up my wounds. My hands were severely damaged with the flesh exposed. He put antiseptic medicine all over my hands and then covered them with cotton. He then applied some sort of medication to the cotton which literally sealed the cotton into the palm of my hands. He then covered them with bandages. I still do not know what the medication was and why it worked so effectively. I was taken back to the house and allowed to rest. I was extremely thirsty and was given cool water from a clay pot covered with a metal plate. After drinking the water and on top of my injury, I came down with a fever. Probably malaria, I thought. I could not remember the last time that I had taken a chloroquine pill, my anti-malaria medication. During the night, my fever spiked. The following day, the ministry in Zomba was notified of my condition. A driver was dispatched to pick me up and take me to the hospital in Zomba.

I was taken to a European hospital in Zomba. The hospital was staffed by White doctors and Black nurses. The nurses had been trained through a partnership with the Germany government. Most of the rooms in the hospital opened onto a veranda, allowing for fresh air to enter the rooms. I was given a hot bath and put in a white gown and given a bed next to the floor-to-ceiling window. As it turned out, I did have malaria and was kept in the hospital for several days until my fever broke. The nurse remarked how well my wounds had been dressed and cared for. I was thankful to all the Malawians who gave me assistance.

The hospital I was admitted to was in marked contrast to the nearby hospital for Africans. At African hospitals, Malawians had to line up for service, which was done on a first-come, first-serve basis. Most of the people just sat in the courtyard waiting their turn to be examined. There were men and women with small children and older adults. Those who were seriously ill were admitted to a large ward that had dozens of beds. The family stayed and cared for their family members, helping them to use the bathroom and feeding them when required. Hospitals for Africans were not on the same scale as those for Europeans, but they were much better in urban areas than in rural communities that lack sufficient medication and

Extension aids staff with local farmers.

other supplies. I was just thankful for the treatment I received both in the bush infirmary and the Zomba hospital. Even though I often complained about the dual and unequal systems for Africans and Europeans, I was willing to be treated in the expatriate hospital, and for this once, I did not complain about the two systems of medical care.

Agriculture Campaigns

The Department of Agriculture initiated a campaign to improve overall agricultural production in Malawi. The campaign was a three-pronged attack: improve farm techniques, control soil erosion and enrich the soil. Staff in the extension aid offices throughout the three regions were called on to support these campaigns through the use of educational visual aids. A serious problem for the staff was that Malawi farmers were generally limited to three types of tools: the hoe, the spade and a machete blade used to cut grass. Farmers cleared their fields each year by a process of slash and burn. Their primary problem had been the failure to restore nutrients back into the soil.

Someone in the Ministry of Agriculture must have heard Jack Allison, the Peace Corps volunteer, sing songs urging mothers to add peanut flour to their baby's cereal or other related songs. Someone in the

Extension aids staff teaching at the Tuchila Training Center.

department contacted him to write a song that would encourage farmers to add fertilizer to their fields. Encouraging farmers to use fertilizer was a major emphasis of our extension office and Jack's song "Feteleza Achulukitsa Zokolola" (Fertilizer increases yield) was doing much to aid us as we encouraged farmers to enrich the soil with fertilizer. To add to the campaign, I had already devoted one issue of our newsletter to promoting soil enrichment and soil conservation.

Puppet Show

Our carpenter completed the first couple of puppet theaters, and Mr. Chirwa created at least a dozen puppets. Nigel Murphy came up with the idea to outfit a covered truck with our puppet show and other AV material and take it around to the annual area agriculture shows. We were assigned a driver, and Mr. Mphiri was to travel with the truck. He also was to sleep inside the truck on a folding cart.

Mr. Mphiri was young, tall, and very fastidious in his habits. He attended a residential high school and excelled in his studies. I was afraid that he had been unduly influenced by his British instructors. He appeared to act more British than the British. He wore a suit jacket, white shirt and tie every day. When Nigel suggested that he not only travel with the truck

Chapter Two. My First Year in Malawi

but also sleep in the back of the vehicle, Mr. Mphiri became upset over the idea of sleeping in a truck. After all, he reasoned, he had a high school education and was above just sleeping anywhere. Although he continued to complain about sleeping in the back of the truck, he did it for the first week. He and the driver went to one of the area training centers and set up the stage on the back end of the truck. Mr. Mphiri put on the show as he was instructed in terms of the particular message the Agriculture Department wanted to convey to the farmers. Some shows were about using fertilizer to increase the farmers' crop production; others were about weeding and planting early in preparation for the annual rains. There were even shows about nutrition aimed at women. We used several of Jack Allison's songs to reinforce the messages we wanted to convey. The audience loved the entertainment since few had radios and no one had television or even knew what that was. The shows were really enhanced by the puppet's ability to move its mouth. I was surprised that others had not thought about that simple innovation to puppet production.

When Mr. Mphiri came back to the office from his first tour, he said that he did not want to travel and sleep in the back of the truck anymore. He did not like the living arrangements and that he had to shower and wash his clothes wherever water was available as he traveled. Nigel came over to talk with Mr. Mphiri and was apparently put off by his attitude. I think that Mr. Mphiri did not give Nigel the due respect he expected from an African. Obviously, they each had different perspectives. Mr. Mphiri assumed that his high school education accorded him certain rights and respect, whereas Nigel assumed that Mr. Mphiri, being young and right out of high school, should have given him deference and respect as his superior. Nigel told him that he did not have a choice: he either traveled with the truck or he was fired.

I felt sorry for Mr. Mphiri, but I did not know what I could do since he refused to carry out his instructions. I was not sure that I would have traveled and lived in the back of a truck myself, but as a young man who needed a job, I thought he could have made the sacrifice. I did not like Nigel's tone and his abrupt firing of Mr. Mphiri, but I did not say anything.

There were now five people working in the office, and as we expanded our workload, we added more staff. I found myself doing more and more administrative work as opposed to the creative aspects of the job like designing and building projects. I liked working on the newsletter, doing photography, and developing my own images. A lot of this work was being transferred to staff; my job had become training Malawians to do the work. At the rate things were going, I would eventually work myself out of a job including as office administrator. Trying to keep myself busy with meaningful and creative work became more difficult.

As I pondered my vacation plans, I could not wait to get to a *real* Black African country. I was sick of the prejudice and discrimination I encountered all the time toward Black Africans. When I was in the Luangwa Game Reserve in Zambia, I wrote in the camp guest book, "The worst thing about being in the game reserve was the racist British, South Africans and Southern Rhodesians, who were the 'wildest animals' in the park." Although it never occurred to me that my comments could be considered anything more than a prank, maybe I should not have expressed myself so vividly about how I felt about the people I had observed during our stay in the park. I understood that I was now in trouble with the Malawi government. Some expatriates from Malawi read my post and informed the police when they returned to Blantyre. I guess that there was a possibility that Banda would expel me for writing down my opinion, even though I considered the whole matter very trivial. Banda seemed to always favor and protect racist Whites. He went so far as to be the first "Black" African leader to recognize South Africa. Of course, he never adhered to the international boycott against South Africa. I did not want to be thrown out of the country, but if I had been deported, I would not have minded being transferred to Kenya. I would hate to leave my African friends in Malawi. After this incident, I was hell bent on speaking out against racism wherever I encountered it.

A Volunteer in Tanzania

Even though I had to work a half day on Saturday, I needed to start planning for my vacation to East Africa. I was very excited about spending nearly a month in Tanzania, Kenya and Uganda, especially having the opportunity to visit Salome. Other volunteers were as excited as I was about having time off in another country.

Michael Adams, our counterpart in Lilongwe, told me that one of his colleagues flew to Dar es Salaam in Tanzania on vacation the previous month and decided to hitchhike across Tanzania back to Lilongwe. Well, he traveled over 1,000 miles to the Malawi northern border with Tanzania. When he got there, he said something smart to the border guard that must have been offensive. The border guard told him that he was missing a stamp from the visa office in Dar es Salaam. He had to hitchhike all the way back to Dar es Salaam to get his passport stamped before he was allowed to cross the border. He was so frustrated that he purchased a plane ticket on East African Airways to Blantyre and then got a Malawi Airlines flight back to Lilongwe. Everybody remarked how terrible this was for the volunteer. However, my attitude was different. I felt like he should have shown more respect being a White man in a Black African country. I felt this was a valuable lesson and I hoped that he learned to be more respectful of people regardless of their status in life.

I could not travel with just anybody in East Africa. I certainly did not want to be with someone who was disrespectful to anyone. So John Hunter and I decided that we would travel together until we got to Nairobi. I planned on staying with my Kenyan classmates. During that time, John planned to go to Mount Kilimanjaro for most of the week. John was much more sensitive to being in Africa than most White people. He really liked being here and had respect for the people and their culture. It's kind of funny seeing him with his Malawi friends. He was so tall and most Malawians were relatively short people. Yet he fit right in with the African community in Zomba.

Getting Ready for East Africa

In preparation for our trip, I did some research on East Africa. When we traveled to Malawi last year, we changed planes in Nairobi for Blantyre, switching to East African Airways. I did not know anything about the airline. I read since that members of the Kenyan parliament were demanding a faster Africanization of the airline's pilots. As members of parliament debated the issue, some said that although they, too, wanted more Kenyan pilots, they did not want to rush the process. They wanted to be sure that the Kenyan pilots were fully trained and experienced before they began flying planes. Well, I completely agreed with that. After all, there were some limits to Africanization. This was never an issue with President Banda. From my experience, all the pilots were Europeans on Malawi Airlines.

East African Airways was not that old. In checking, I found that it was established in the 1940s as a partnership among Kenya, Uganda, Tanganyika and Zanzibar. It was initially operated by the British Overseas Airways Corporation, or BOAC. In 1952 when Princess Elizabeth was visiting East Africa, her father, King George VI, died. She was transported by East African Airways to Entebbe, where she then boarded BOAC for London. East African Airways had the honor of being the first airline to transport the new queen.

Just about all volunteers vacationing in East Africa wanted to climb Mount Kilimanjaro, the tallest mountain in Africa. After my experience on Mount Mulanje, I no longer considered myself a mountain climber. I was satisfied looking at the mountain from a distance. I was more interested in what was happening politically in Tanzania. Ever since I took a course on African history at Berea, I had been fascinated with the continent. I was particularly interested in how various leaders had governed their countries since independence. I thought that in Malawi, Banda had failed the "promise" of its independence, while Tanzania took a new approach to independence and its development. Although I was not a socialist, I thought there was something to be said for Tanzania's Ujamaa socialist policy under Julius Nyerere. I remembered when Nyerere was elected president of the new Republic of Tanganyika in 1962, the year I graduated from high school. African countries were rapidly approaching independence following the independence of Ghana in 1960. The movement for self-determination in Africa certainly had an impact on the Civil Rights movement in the United States. Nyerere, along with Kwame Nkrumah of Ghana, spearheaded the creation of the Organization of African Unity that held so much promise for the continent's development. We eagerly read about these movements in *Jet* and *Ebony* magazines.

Anxious to get a firsthand view of the country to see how it compared to Malawi, I suggested to John that we visit Tanzania first. Dar es Salaam and the whole East African coast held my interest because of its long history and the association of Black Africans with Arabs creating a new creole ethnic group of people called Swahili. I was eager to see what the German occupation in Tanganyika had left in terms of architecture and culture. Maybe they were not there long enough to have a lasting impact because the British soon took over during World War I. I had read so much about Zanzibar, its exotic history and culture, that I could not wait to get there. Like most volunteers, John and I decided that we would not plan any of the details of our trip. We would fly in and out of Dar es Salaam and work out all of the details in between.

Some Notes on Life in Malawi

What a surprise. I was still getting occasional reports about the ramifications of what I had written in the guest book at the Luangwa Game Reserve that was read by some White person, maybe South African, and reported it to the Malawi police, who promised to investigate the situation. Rumor had it that an expatriate police official was pretty upset over the incident, but I had no direct confirmation. Although I did not hear anything official, there was always the possibility of being thrown out of the country. So as soon as I heard the rumors, I went to the immigration office and got a visa for Kenya. I needed to get one anyway for my vacation. I thought it made sense to have one in hand as a precautionary measure.

The president was ever mindful of not doing or saying anything that would offend the South Africans, so of course, he had spies all over. People reported back to him on what he defined as subversive activities and it did not matter if the offender was Malawian, British or American. After Banda recognized South Africa, it seemed like more and more South Africans were coming into the country and taking positions with the government. If the Luangwa park situation did not get me kicked out of the country, I was sure that before my tour of duty was over, I would do or say something that would get me deported. My tolerance for racism and racist acts was lower now than ever. Why should I have to tolerate such behavior? After all, this was supposed to be a Black country. I finished reading the Arusha Declaration in which Julius Nyerere outlined his socialist policies for Tanzania. Sounded awfully good to me compared to the policies of Banda. In the name of development, Banda allowed all sorts of people to come and take over government posts and private operations relating to the country's economic development. I really felt like Malawians were being dominated by South Africans, both economically and politically.

The other day on the street in Blantyre, I ran into Marshall Paul Jones the ambassador, who actually turned his head rather than speak to me. I had been told by other Black volunteers that he had treated them the same way. When I mentioned this to the Peace Corps staff, they all just rationalized it as just the way he was. But was it the way it had to be? After all, he was the U.S. ambassador representing all of us.

Barbara wrote me a lovely letter that just lifted my spirits. I asked Barbara if she wanted me to buy her a dress like the traditional costumes worn by African women. I told her that I was going to buy a costume for myself, and when I got home, we could give African parties in full African regalia. She told me that she went to the Apollo Theater to see James Brown perform. He had just released "I'm Black and I'm Proud." I would have loved to play that record over here for all to hear.

I did something foolish. I went to the Bata bookstore and put down $2.50 on $30 worth of books, mostly on African history. I felt the need to read as much about African history and culture as I could. I purchased a two-volume work on African history and one on the people of Kenya. I decided to study African history as part of my graduate studies. Even so, I would have to pay a price for such extravagance. The Peace Corps figured out just how much money we needed to live like our African counterparts and with nothing much left over. I had spent all of my allowance with the exception of about $9. Since most volunteers spent much of their allowance on food, that was where I had to cut back for the rest of the month. I guess I would need to eat a lot of cabbage and nsima for a while with no money for beer. Thako would also have to make do even though he was still a puppy.

I got a letter from home with $100 in it. Boy, was I happy to get the extra money. A friend just returned from East Africa and told me that he had spent over 150 pounds. I hoped that I could get off cheaper than that since I planned to spend some time with my former Berea classmates while I was in Kenya.

The assistant director of the Peace Corps, Howard Carter, wanted to publish a picture book on Malawi. Knowing that I was in audio-visual aids, he asked me to contribute some of my pictures to the publication. This was one of the times that I agreed to work with the office. I thought it would be nice to see my images in print. I thought I might use one of my images to make my own Christmas cards. I needed to find someone to print them for me. I didn't think I could do that on the office printer.

I was so excited about leaving for East Africa. Since I would be gone for most of the month, there was a tremendous amount of office work that I had to complete. I was sure that both Nigel and Troy would keep an eye on my office while I was away, but I wanted to make sure that everything ran smoothly while I was out of the office. I had a lot to do to catch up on my work, plus I had to plan the work schedule for the entire office in my absence. I decided that I would do the best that I could in getting the office ready for my absence and then not think about it while in East Africa. Since I would not be able to communicate with the staff, this approach would be the best in my opinion.

Government building in Dar es Salaam.

Travel in East Africa

Dar es Salaam

We arrived in Dar es Salaam on November 3. What a beautiful city. John and I left Blantyre on East African Airlines. I noticed that both pilots were African and the flight attendants were also African. I felt like for the first time I would be traveling in an African country that had successfully broken away from its colonial past and was promoting Africa for Africans, a marked contrast to Banda's policies in Malawi.

Although we did not plan our trip in detail, we did make reservations at the Safari Hotel in downtown Dar es Salaam through our travel agent in Blantyre. The hotel was located in the old section of the city with many buildings designed and built by the Germans, so it was not difficult to determine their age. Other buildings were built and occupied by East Indians. The architecture of some buildings showed a marked influence of the Arabs through the Swahili people. Then there were those buildings constructed by the British during the colonial period. Many of them looked like buildings in Malawi.

Our hotel was across the street from a similar hotel called the Palace. Both were constructed around the turn of the century. The Safari Hotel was what I called "colonial comfortable." The lobby was staid with

The Palace Hotel, Dar es Salaam.

overstuffed leather chairs and sofas. We entered the lobby through double doors that remained open during the day. The registration desk was in front of us as we entered. We were assigned rooms on the fifth, or top, floor. I had a nice view of the surrounding neighborhood and I liked the wide windows that allowed fresh air to flow into the room. There was a ceiling fan that spun slowly and a single light bulb beneath the fan. A double bed was located in the center of the room against the wall with end tables and lamps on both sides. There was a side chair and a writing or eating table next to the window. Although there was a sink in the room, hotel guests had to share a toilet and shower at the end of the hall. It appeared to me that each floor had about six rooms. John and I settled in our respective rooms and agreed to meet downstairs for dinner.

At 7:00 p.m., we were in the lobby asking for recommendations for restaurants. The desk clerk recommended only European restaurants since John had asked. I wondered what he would have recommended if I had made the inquiry instead. We agreed that we would walk around before finally settling on where to eat.

We wandered into an Indian neighborhood—we could tell by the strong smell of curry or Indian seasoning wafting in the air. I was a little surprised at the number of Indians in East Africa. They were shopkeepers just as they were in Malawi.

A warm gentle breeze blew in the evening air, so we selected a restaurant that had outdoor seating. It seemed that most of the buildings from the colonial era had verandas that could accommodate six or seven tables with chairs. We went inside and asked the maître d' to seat us outside. We quickly ordered beers. This time, we tried Kilimanjaro, an East African lager. It was good for a change that we did not have to depend on either Lion or Castle beer from South Africa or Southern Rhodesia. It was kind of ironic how I avoided buying South African products as much as possible, only to develop a habit of drinking Lion beer. We enjoyed a beer while relaxing before we ordered dinner. I had curried chicken, a vegetable medley and naan. John had the tandoori chicken with chickpeas and rice. We both ordered another beer. We talked about what we would do tomorrow. After dinner, we each retired to our rooms for the night.

Time passed quickly. We tried to get in as much sightseeing as we could over three days. We walked everywhere. The first day, we walked up to the Kivukoni fish market, which was huge. It was located on Kivukoni Road. I think we went north and then branched out on Kivukono Road which hugged the harbor. The harbor in Dar es Salaam was a natural harbor surrounded by land on three sides with an opening to the Indian Ocean. There were a lot of ships coming in and out of the harbor all day long. There were many boats docked just below the fish market. I

Chapter Two. My First Year in Malawi 107

I'm at the harbor, Dar es Salaam.

was fascinated by these boats since they had such a long history associated with East African coastal trade. We decided to walk around the market to see the various types of seafood available. There were small and gigantic shrimps, all sizes of squid, octopus, crabs, clams and any other variety of fish desired. Even though the market had a distinct smell, the fish for sale was usually caught and brought to the market early in the same day. There was no refrigeration as in the Blantyre market where fresh fish was seldom sold. Here, the fresh fish were stacked on top of the vendors' tables where they remained until sold. There were rows and rows of tables piled high with many varieties of seafood. The tables extended well beyond the covered market. There were many vendors who sold not only seafood but vegetables, trinkets, carvings, baskets, cooking pots, pans and plates as well as cooking and eating utensils.

We had become accustomed to eating in small Malawi restaurants, so we decided to have lunch at one of the numerous African food vendors selling traditional African food. Other East Indian vendors were selling a variety of Indian dishes. I walked around several African vendors before settling on the pilau, a mixture of rice, fish and various seasonings all cooked in one pot. I ordered a plate that came with a generous helping of a tomato, onion and chili sauce. As in Malawi, the food was traditionally eaten with one's hands. The vendor provided a pot of water (but no soap) in which everyone washed their hands. After cleaning my hands, I purchased

Waterfront, Dar es Salaam.

some chapati, a form of flatbread that I used like I would nsima. The food was delicious. I thought I would try the chicken or goat pilau next time.

After we ate, we walked down to the waterfront to watch the ships sail into the harbor. There were numerous boats of all sizes. My mind wandered back to the nineteenth century and earlier when Arabs controlled the slave trade. Arabs raided the interior but also depended on African middlemen from whom they purchased slaves. We often think about slavery primarily being on the west coast of Africa, but there was an active slave trade on the east coast that carried slaves into the Near East and as far away as India. I heard that the Swahili people, a mixture of Bantu Africans and Arabs, were active middlemen on the trade. The Swahili traders had a long history of being active traders along the coast of East Africa so that the language was now spoken throughout the eastern part of the continent.

Once we made the decision to travel to Mombasa via Zanzibar, we walked down to the dock where there were harbor offices and asked the clerk if there were any ships going to Zanzibar. We were lucky. There was a freighter that also carried passengers that made stops in Zanzibar and Mombasa before heading on to India. The price was 50 shillings for third class. We said that we would take it. The clerk said that Europeans were not allowed to travel third class, but he could book us cabins for 80 shillings each. Only Africans and Indians were allowed in the "hole," or third class, which was one large compartment with no formal provisions for sleeping and eating. People generally brought their own sleeping blankets and food, which they cooked on charcoal stoves. The people in the third class also had to clean up after themselves and wash their own clothes.

There was still so much to do and see in Dar es Salaam before we left. We walked all over the city. One day was spent doing what I call educational tourism. We walked by the State House or Ikulu, where President Julius Nyerere lived and worked. I hoped that I would get a glimpse of him either coming or going, but we were not so lucky. The State House was built by the Germans in the 1890s but had to be rebuilt by the British after it was burned. The British completed the State House in 1922. It was an imposing white building. It was too bad that the public was not allowed to go inside, but we could read about the history on the plaque outside and tour the exterior of the site.

Next, we walked down to the National Museum and House of Culture, which according to the museum guide, was first opened in the 1940s. I was fascinated by the many fossils turned over to the museum by Louis Leakey. Leakey had been digging for fossils for many years from the Olduvai Gorge. I had read about some of his finds when I was a student at Berea taking a class in geology. The guide at the museum said that the team of Louis and Mary Leakey had worked in Olduvai Gorge and had discovered fossils going back millions of years that were linked to early man. The case and diorama labels said that the two paleoanthropologists had discovered *Homo habilis* and *Homo erectus*. The Leakeys believed in Charles Darwin's theory that man originated in Africa and set about to prove it. The Leakeys became my heroes. There were other museum exhibitions about the tribal heritage of various groups of Bantu peoples in Tanzania. I particularly liked examining their crafts and musical instruments. There was also an exhibition on the slave trade that had existed for centuries on the East African coast. Malawi, too, has an illustrious history before and after its "discovery" by Livingstone but has no appropriate place to house its national history.

That was more than enough educational tourism for us. We spent the next and final day going out to the Makonde "urban" village. The village was composed of a group of wood carvers who specialized in carving wonderful creations from ebony wood. The people were originally from northern Mozambique and southern Tanzania. I guess if we had more time, we could have actually traveled to one of their original villages to purchase art. I immediately fell in love with the sculptures they created. Much of their work was abstract and influenced by "evil spirits." I really liked the family tree sculptures that were like totem poles with each member of the family depicted. Some of the artwork looked like it was designed for the tourist market as was the case in Malawi, where nearly all of the crafts were made for tourists. One of the carvers told me that he made smaller pieces because tourists bought them. The larger, artistic pieces did not sell as well because they took longer to make and thus were more expensive. I purchased a couple of statues of a man sitting and a totem family sculpture that was about 18 inches tall. I had all my purchases shipped back to my regional agricultural office in Blantyre. John and I both were trying to travel as light as we could. We each had one suitcase out of which we had to live for the next three weeks.

On our last night in Dar es Salaam, we decided to go to a nightclub. We found one within walking distance of our hotel. We had dinner and then walked to the club. It was called the Harambee Club and featured a band from Congo. We loved the music. We stood at the bar trying various East African beers. After a while, we started dancing with some of the bar girls. As in Malawi, no respectable African women would be caught in a bar. So we knew that they were there to service the men. I'm afraid that I drank too much and ended up in one of the back rooms with a bar girl. I never did get her name. I don't remember too much after that. John and I made it back to the hotel and got a few hours of sleep before we headed out to the wharf.

Zanzibar

The next morning, I had a headache and I hoped nothing else. There was a lively commerce along the East African coast, with numerous ships traveling from Beira in Mozambique up the coast to Mombasa before heading east to Bombay and other ports in India. We were fortunate to gain passage on one of these ships. We checked our bags at the dock to be delivered to our rooms and walked up the gang plank to the top level of the ship. We saw several East Indians walking from the dock straight into the bowels of the ship. The ship had a few first-class cabins, but always mindful of our budget, we had purchased second-class tickets. There were about 20 small second-class rooms. Each room had a single bed that doubled as a sitting area. There was a small bathroom with a shower, toilet and washbowl. I guess it was comfortable compared to being in the ship's hole. The second-class passengers dined in the same dining room as the first-class passengers and the captain of the ship. Although Africans could purchase any accommodations they could afford, for all practical purposes, as in Malawi, there existed economic segregation.

The ship looked more like a freighter than an ocean liner. The passengers seemed secondary to the ship's cargo. We later learned that the hole was pretty foul. What the ticket agent told me about the hole turned out to be true. People were jammed into a large area with little or no privacy. Everyone shared the bathroom. If you wanted to wash your clothes, you had to tie them to a rope, throw them over the side of the ship and let the ship drag them through the water. When I looked behind us, I could see clothes being dragged by the ship and could smell the smoke and aroma from people cooking their meals. The ship had a large deck with lifeboats on either side. I doubt that it had enough lifeboats for all of the people in the hole.

The ship left shortly after we boarded, getting us into Zanzibar well before noon. When the ship docked in Zanzibar, the ship's crew unloaded cargo and then took on new cargo bound for India. We had nearly the whole day traveling around the island once we were allowed to go ashore. It seemed as if Zanzibar was still in a state of revolution and had not welcomed back tourists. We went ashore with a group of Indians and did not have any difficulty once we got to town.

Our day was filled with wonder. As we left the dock area, we were in what was called the Old Stone Town because most of the buildings were made of stone, or rather coral that turned to stone. The buildings were substantially different from those found in Dar es Salaam and definitely different from those in Malawi. People in Malawi did not have a history of building with stone. Buildings in Zanzibar seemed to be a mixture of African, Arab, Indian and maybe Persian influence. The streets were very narrow with most unable to accommodate automobile traffic. The whole area seemed rather bleak and dismal. The city had certainly seen better days with many of the buildings either run-down or in various states of disrepair. The natural coral had a reddish color marked by dark stains from weathering. On either side of the narrow streets were homes, shops and a few bazaars and mosques. The most remarkable thing about the buildings were the wooden doors that were rich with carvings and bas-reliefs and studded with bronze. John and I took turns taking each other's pictures in front of the many doors, some of which were arched on top while others were rectangular.

There were not a lot of tourists on the island, but there were several policemen and soldiers. I did not expect to see a military presence four years after the revolution when the sultan was overthrown and the Afro-Shirazi Party established a socialist government. I read that over 20,000 Arabs and Indians were killed during the revolution. I guess the military troops explained why we encountered so few tourists. The party's headquarters was in the House of Wonder, which was the home of the sultan before he was overthrown. The house was a square three-story building with verandas on all three levels. The verandas were supported by dozens of columns. There was a clock tower on the roof facing the front of the building. Even in disrepair, the house was a magnificent building located on the waterfront. The house was located near the Old Fort with its very high, daunting walls. The fort, shaped in a square, was built by the Omani Arabs to protect the island against European invasions.

One of the reasons Livingstone settled in Malawi was to put an end to the African slave trade. I was very interested in anything relating to slavery. We walked over to the Anglican cathedral of Christ Church on Mkunazini Road, where the largest slave trading center was located. When I asked the local priest about the history of the church, he said that the church was built on the site of the slave trade as a monument to those who died and as part of the effort to end the slave trade.

By afternoon, it was getting hot and very humid, and we were getting tired and hungry. We decided to look for the open-air market. The market in Zanzibar resembled the market in Blantyre and most of the other African markets we encountered. There were lots of fruits and vegetables and plenty of vendors who prepared street food for local consumption. We ordered something like an Italian pizza. We watched as the vendor prepared our dish made from unleavened dough filled with meat, veggies, egg and cheese and fried in ghee. In addition to the Zanzibar pizza, I purchased two samosas, which I had come to love. We walked over to the park and sat in the shade as we enjoyed our lunch. The park had not been kept up very well, but it was still beautiful with lush green flowering trees and sidewalks lined with palm trees. The shrubberies were overgrown but still managed to provide lovely red blooms.

We walked back over to the market to buy a beer, not trusting the many fruit drinks that were for sale. I wanted to learn more about the Arab slave trade, so we walked over to the Tippu Tib House that once belonged to an Afro-Arab slave trader by the same name. I had read about the house in one of the books I had purchased on African history. The house was not open for visitation. I had read that those Arab traders had made their way up through Tanganyika as far as Congo seeking slaves. Once captured or secured through trade, they returned to the coast with the enslaved often carrying ivory and other commodities. The Tippu Tib House was once very lavish and suitable for the wealth he had accumulated from the slave trade and the plantation he owned. As for the slaves, they were housed in mostly an underground building in 15 small cells holding up to 75 people in a room with no windows and toilets. I guess this experience prepared the slaves for what was to come.

As evening approached, we walked down the road bordering on the waterfront. We could see a few large merchant ships, but the harbor was dominated by dhows of every size. It had been a long day, and I looked forward to a hot shower and a nice meal on board. John and I agreed to meet for dinner at seven.

I changed into my long pants and knit shirt. John wore a white shirt. That was our usual dinner attire. There were some Europeans in first class and a dozen or more Europeans and Indians in second class with us in the dining room. We met a young White couple who were traveling around the world visiting as many countries as they could in their once-in-a-lifetime adventure. They were from California and decided to take a year off from graduate school. They were fascinated by our Peace Corps experiences as we talked over dinner.

That evening, the chef served oxtail. I had never had oxtail before and loved it the minute I tasted it. It must have been sautéed for a long time because it was so tender and came with this wonderful sauce with potatoes on the side.

After walking around the deck, I smoked a cigarette and turned in for the night.

Mombasa

Our ship, while docked in Zanzibar, loaded cargo bound for Mombasa and India. It must have been well after 2:00 p.m. before everything was on board and we were ready to sail for Mombasa. Even though the distance to Mombasa was less than 150 miles, we did not arrive until morning.

When I woke up the next morning, I looked out of my window to see Kilindini Harbor, which I gathered was the main port for Mombasa. The ship steward told us that Kilindini was Swahili for "deep water." I looked forward to visiting this exotic and historic port that was Kenya's oldest city and second largest in size. I read that the history of the city went back centuries and had been controlled by Africans, the Portuguese, Arabs and finally the British. Unlike land-locked Malawi, the east coast of Kenya had a long history of trade between the interior of East Africa and India and China. I suppose that this helped to explain the large number of Indians as well as Arabs living in the city. Again, I was interested in knowing more about the city's involvement in the slave trade as well as its trade in spices, gold and ivory. If it had not been for the international intervention in the ivory trade, the elephant population would have been wiped out. Britain was the last country to control Mombasa and ruled there until the capital was moved to Nairobi. With Nairobi being nearly a mile high, I am sure the British found the climate there more to their liking. The mild climate also helped to explain the large settlement of the British in Nairobi. Climate like in Nairobi and Blantyre had a lot in common including large settlements of British. Mombasa is located on an island connected by ferries and a bridge. It looked as if this city of a quarter of a million people was expanding into the countryside. I was anxious to see this historic city.

This ancient city of Mombasa was just beautiful as we entered the harbor. The area along the coast was pretty close to sea level and there were no high-rise buildings, so the city was fairly parallel to the horizon. The closer we got to the old city of Mombasa, the prettier it became. After the ship docked, the Peace Corps volunteers and a few other travelers left the ship while it loaded additional cargo and passengers going to India.

When we disembarked, the dock did not seem particularly welcoming. It seemed as if there were no passenger ships docking here or at least there were few in the harbor the day we arrived; there were just mainly a lot of ships with freight being loaded and unloaded. The train from Kampala ends its journey here in Mombasa. I am not sure what Kenya was exporting, but it seemed that it was getting a lot of freight from other countries. There were a number of taxis waiting for pickups. We chose the first driver who approached us.

"Habari gani," I said, which was about all I knew of Ki-Swahili. I then reverted to English and the driver understood and replied in somewhat broken English. I indicated that we wanted to go to Old Town and needed to find a clean but cheap hotel. "No problem" was the reply as he loaded our luggage. We drove on to the island of Mombasa, which was where the old town was located. We passed by many interesting buildings, which we would no doubt explore later. When we arrived at the hotel, it was painted white with blue trim, something I noticed about a lot of buildings in Mombasa; blue and white evidently were the favorite colors of the local inhabitants.

We got out of the taxi, paid the fare and entered the hotel. I was not impressed. The lobby was lit by single bulbs hanging from the ceiling. The furniture was left over from its better colonial days. Several chairs were positioned around the room. There was an elaborate carved table, overstuffed sofa and chair against the wall opposite the registration desk. The hotel registration was located behind a semicircle counter that had iron bars from the top of the desk to the ceiling. The metal bars were painted light green to give an air of "friendliness." We were each assigned a room. We paid the equivalent of $3 a day and were given our keys. The desk attendant warned us to lock our rooms at all times, even when we went to the restroom at the end of the hall. I guess that the hotel was patterned after inexpensive British hotels that provided a basin in the room itself with the actual toilet and shower at the end of the hall. He also said that there were restaurants all around the hotel but none inside. He said that in the evening, the hotel bar was available for beer and other drinks.

There was no elevator. My room, on the second level, faced the street.

Chapter Two. My First Year in Malawi

There was a window with curtains, one bed with mosquito netting, a chair and a desk. There was no closet, but there was a rack to hang clothes and a dresser with three drawers. One single light bulb emerged from the bottom of a ceiling fan, which provided the only means of air circulation since there was no breeze coming through the window. I chose not to unpack my suitcase. The sheets were clean, but I dared not look under the mattress. The hotel reminded me of the Zomba Inn. I just hoped that the ceiling would not collapse while we were there. We agreed to meet in the lobby and start our Mombasa adventure.

Mombasa was a lot like Zanzibar city. It was old, but the narrow streets were not so narrow as to prevent a small car from driving down them. The buildings, when painted at all, were sienna orange or white with blue trim. John wanted to go to Nyali beach, but I suggested that we save the beach for the next day and head out to Fort Jesus. The fort was built by King Philip I of Portugal between 1593 and 1596 as an outpost on the Indian Ocean. It was now a national park.

We headed out walking even though several Africans asked if we needed a taxi. We figured that the best way to see a city was on foot. Plus, on a limited budget, we saved on transportation costs. Finding the fort was not hard. It was a large and prominent feature of the city's waterfront. The fort was looking its age. There were several restored buildings in the interior of the fort. There was signage that described when the fort was constructed, by whom and the various governments that controlled it over the years.

From there, we went to get some street food. Although the money we got from the Peace Corps for our vacation was reasonable, it was not enough to live in luxury, even in Africa. We saved money where we could. There were plenty of street vendors selling fresh fruits and vegetables as well as prepared food from food carts and charcoal grills. While we were trying to decide what to eat, we purchased a bag of cassava chips sprinkled with red chili pepper. I had learned to really like hot pepper since arriving in Africa. I figured that nothing could be hotter than the pepper we ate at the home of the Indian mayor of Lilongwe. We eventually lucked out on a street vendor grilling meat on skewers. I asked what it was, and the vendor said that it was called mishkaki. He said that I could have either chicken or beef. Both were served with a tamarind sauce. I selected the beef and John selected the chicken. We sat under a shade tree and enjoyed our late lunch.

Next on our agenda was a visit to Mamba Village, billed as the largest crocodile sanctuary in the world. We caught a taxi for the 20-minute ride out there. It was impressive with more than 100 crocodiles in all stages of development, from the large, so-called maneaters to medium size down to newly hatched baby crocodiles. The introductory movie provided the visitor with an overview of the life cycle of the crocodile.

There was also a snake farm, or serpentarium. Although I hate snakes, I didn't mind seeing them in an enclosure and at a distance. We viewed all sorts of African snakes including the green and black mamba, two of the deadliest in Africa, so I had been told. I thought about the time that some friends of Dick Caldwell wanted me to deliver a green mamba to their colleague in Blantyre. Since I had the Mini Moke, I agreed. Everything was fine until I took a turn too fast and ended up running up an embankment and nearly turning over the vehicle. Fortunately, the snake did not escape, but if it had escaped and bitten me, I would have been a goner, with no one around to help me. I learned a lot about the green mamba or eastern green mamba that inhabited Malawi and the coastal regions of East Africa. The green mamba liked to live in trees and wait for their prey. The exhibit label confirmed the fact of their toxicity. A severe snake bite leads to swelling and difficulty breathing, and eventually the venom can cause irregular heartbeat and death. I thought back to the time that I tried to scare Doug MacDonald with the snake I found in the house. I guess he could have had a heart attack from fright.

We hurried back to the crocodile farm to see the five o'clock feeding. The attendants titillated the crowd that had gathered to watch by holding a large chunk of meat on a long pole over the crocodile pit. We watched the large and small crocodiles scramble for position to see who could reach the pole and grab the prize. I had seen crocs fight over food before in movies but never in person. It was a sight to behold. The attendants then distributed food throughout the pen, and the crocodiles all scrambled to grab what they could before all the meat was eaten by their pen mates. It was fascinating.

All of that fighting over food must have made us hungry. We decided to grab a bite in the onsite restaurant. We chose to sit in the open-air area of the restaurant. The first thing we ordered was a round of Tusker beer, the local brew distributed throughout the three countries of East Africa. These beers came in what I call regular bottles and supersize or 24 oz bottles. We ordered the larger bottles to avoid having to keep ordering more. The menu offered a variety of exotic meats from crocodile, of course, to zebra and ostrich. Zebra was a little too exotic for me, so I ordered the crocodile bites and we agreed to share an ostrich burger. The food was good. My taste for the strange and exotic had grown since living in Malawi. I could eat anything after eating grasshoppers and termites. I thought the crocodile meat tasted something like tough chicken; the ostrich had a taste of its own but was still good, if somewhat stringy. We walked around for a while before heading back to the hotel.

We asked the taxi driver to drive to the entrance of the modern city where the four large elephant tusks crossed over the road to form a large

Chapter Two. My First Year in Malawi

M for Mombasa. The tusks crossed over the main four-lane thoroughfare divided by a three-foot-wide medium. The avenue was quite nice with tropical flowers planted all the way down the center of the road. Our taxi driver explained that the tusks were made from aluminum and were erected in honor of the 1952 visit by Queen Elizabeth II. They had become a hallmark of the city. I thought originally that they might have been erected in recognition of the efforts to eliminate the trade in elephant tusks that was having a severe impact on the elephant population. We decided to get out of the taxi and walk back to the hotel. As we approached our hotel, we heard loud music coming from a neighborhood bar and decided to stop for a beer and enjoy the local entertainment.

The bar was dark with small tables sparsely interspersed throughout the room. At the end of the room was a slightly elevated stage with a band, and to the right of the stage was a bar. We chose to sit at the bar, which gave us an unobstructed view of the band. I asked the bartender what type of music the band was playing. He said that it was a blend of African and Arab. He thought the music originated in Zanzibar which then spread throughout East Africa. I could hear the Arab influence, but it was also distinctly African. I liked the beat of the drums that gave almost a samba/Caribbean rhythm to the music. Both John and I loved dancing with the bar girls, a habit we had picked up early on. There was something about African music that really appealed to me. I also enjoyed looking at the women dancers. After a couple of beers, we were ready to leave for the hotel.

We got a late start on our last full day in Mombasa. We wore our swim trunks underneath our trousers in preparation for spending most of the day at the beach. But first, we wanted to walk to the market to look for souvenirs. I purchased some locally made cloth because I figured it would be easy to carry the rest of the journey through Kenya and Uganda. We stopped for lunch. I wanted to eat lightly to save my appetite for a seafood dinner, so I purchased some mishkaki, beef on a skewer, with some naan. I thought I was becoming a real connoisseur of international cuisine.

By the time we finished eating and browsing, it was mid-afternoon. We headed down to Nyali beach to spend the rest of the day there. As we approached the beach, we followed a wide sandy path that led to the water. On the right side of the path was a sign that read, "Help us keep our beach clean, do not litter." Either people could not read or they did not care. There was trash all over the place. Someone had tried to pile some of the trash into heaps, but this did not help since the piles were left uncollected. I found it very interesting that African villages were very clean, constantly being swept with straw brooms. But for some reason, Africans were oblivious to waste on city streets, especially in market areas. Although the beaches on Lake Malawi were much cleaner, there were no real resorts on Lake Malawi compared to development on the East African coast. We continued our walk until we came upon a shady area with picnic tables, benches, and lots of palm trees. It was an ideal spot. We took off our outer clothes and headed into the warm, calm, blue water. We swam, waded, and walked the beach looking for shells.

The sun was hot, but by this time, I was already two shades darker than when I left Malawi. Even in Malawi, I had grown darker from the sun. I thought that it would not be long before I looked as dark as an African. Somehow, maybe subconsciously, I was trying to become darker so that I would look more like I belonged. I even got my hair cut short by local barbers. You could find barbers anywhere, along the side of the road, in the market or under a shade tree. I generally stopped for a haircut whenever I felt like my hair was getting too long. I was not picky about a barber. Anyone would do. I just stopped along the roadside or in a park to sit under a tree while someone cut my hair with what sometimes turned out to be dull clippers. At any rate, it did not matter. I was wearing my hair cut very close, quite different from when I first came to the country.

Toward the end of the day, we dried off and dusted off the sand and put our clothes back on. By this time, the swim trunks had dried. We walked over to one of the beach resort hotels where we planned to have dinner and a few beers. There was poolside dining that offered a view of the ocean. It was perfect. After a couple of beers, the waiter came over to see if we were ready to order. We decided to splurge and order lots of tapas: North African chicken wings marinated in a variety of spices, fried calamari in olive oil and wine with caramelized onions, fresh pan-fried octopus with Swahili coconut sauce, rice and veggie tempura. What a relaxing evening and closure to a wonderful Mombasa holiday. I know we busted the budget, but who cared when the food was so good in an idyllic environment? We walked back to the hotel and immediately went to our rooms and retired after an exhausting but exhilarating day.

Nairobi

We were up and out of the hotel for a last look around town and a good meal. We had to check out of the hotel by noon, so we checked our bags with the desk clerk until it was time to leave for the train station. We arrived at the station about an hour early, purchased our tickets and proceeded to wait for the time to board. The train was nowhere to be seen. In fact, it was hours before the train arrived and hours before we actually left the station. Having been in Malawi for a year now, I learned to live by African time, so it no longer created the anxiety I had when I first arrived on

Chapter Two. My First Year in Malawi

Train from Mombasa to Nairobi, East African Railroad.

the continent. The station itself looked as if it was a relic from the colonial past. Although there was no official segregation, first-class ticket holders, usually Europeans, were separated from the Africans by virtue of their higher priced tickets. We waited outside with our African compatriots. The wait seemed longer in that it was so hot and muggy. There were three classes of tickets on the Kenya rail system: first class with private compartment usually occupied by Europeans, second-class compartments used by middle-class to well-to-do African and Indians and third-class, general coach seating preferred by most Africans because the tickets were inexpensive. I never had the opportunity to travel by rail in Malawi. I guess I could have traveled to Beira along the Trans-Zambezia Railway but I never ventured beyond the border towns in Mozambique.

We purchased second-class tickets and were told to bring our own insect repellents, toilet paper and drinking water. When the train finally arrived, we boarded and soon found our compartment. The compartment had two padded benches that could be converted into two beds. Overhead were bunk beds that could be pulled out at night. We shared our compartment with an Indian man and his son. The Indian man had packed a lunch or dinner for him and his son. When he opened the lunch, it was full of aromatic Indian spiced foods. He reached into his container and gave his son a samosa and one to me. He shared everything with his son and with me but did not offer John any food. I was convinced that he thought that I was Indian or of Indian descent. This was not the first time that I was mistaken for an Indian or Arab. It did not bother the man in the least that I did not have an Indian accent or speak any Indian language. It was as if he could see that I was one of them, and that was all that mattered.

The trip from Mombasa to Nairobi took 14 hours. Besides looking at the scenery and wildlife, there was very little to do. The train must have been the slowest train in existence. The compartment was hot. There was a fan, but it did not seem to help. We finally opened our window to let in some fresh air, but all we got was fresh, hot, humid air. Since I could not communicate with my compartment mates, I either daydreamed or looked out of the window at the scenery and the occasional animals in the distance. The farther we got from Mombasa, the more animals we saw. We went through the Tsavo National Park where there were lots of animals. I was told that when the rail system was being built in the 1890s, well over 100 Africans and Indians had been killed by lions. That whole project took years and at great expense, both in lives and labor. So far on this trip, I had seen impalas, giraffes, ostriches, zebras, and even a few elephants.

Because the train did not leave on time, we had no idea when it would arrive. Michael, Harriet and Salome were meeting me at the station. I assumed that they would know to keep checking on the train's arrival time in Nairobi. The rail system was still using the old narrow-gauge tracks, which meant that the train could travel only so fast. The train would eventually travel from an elevation of 59 feet in Mombasa to 5,453 by the time we reached Nairobi, a distance of over 300 miles. There were about eight or 10 stops between Mombasa and Nairobi. The scenery was beautiful. As we headed west, there was a slow rise in the elevation; the vegetation changed from tropical to more steppe-like low-lying scrubs. The ground was a reddish dirt brown and dry this time of the year. There was an occasional village with traditional mud huts and thatched roofs. As the train passed, villagers, especially children, stopped whatever they were doing to watch the train go by. The areas through which we passed were sparsely populated until we reached towns such as Mtito, Andei, Kibwezi and Emali. None of these towns meant anything to me. We stopped and a few people boarded and a few got off. The majority of people stayed on the train to continue their journey to Nairobi. Most of the stops involved loading and unloading goods.

The conductor came in around 12:00 p.m. to turn down the beds. The compartment had four beds, two upper and two lower. John took the upper, I the lower, the Indian man the lower and his son the upper. We were told at the station to keep our windows shut and the doors locked

Salome Nolega David in front of her Nairobi home.

when we were in the compartment and when we were out to the diner or using the bathroom. We felt the need to keep the windows opened for air circulation. The compartment had a sink where we could wash our hands and brush our teeth. The train was due to arrive the next morning in Nairobi.

I was elated to see Michael, Harriet and Salome at the train station when we arrived in Nairobi. They knew to keep calling for updates on the arrival of the train from Mombasa so that they would not have to wait for long, as the train was usually not on time. There were also the two volunteers John was to meet for their trip to the Serengeti National Park in Tanzania. We had agreed to meet back in Nairobi in a week before we traveled to Uganda. I introduced everyone to my classmates from Berea College. We said our goodbyes and then Michael drove me to his house. On the way, he gave me a tour of Nairobi and was proud of the growth of the city over the last 10 years, especially since independence. It was the first large city I had visited since arriving in Africa. The city was beautifully laid out with high-rise buildings, wide thoroughfares divided by mediums planted with a variety of tropical plants and trees. Harriet said that her favorite shrubs were the royal poinciana with their bright red blooms and the purple azaleas. I must hand it to the British; they created some excellent parks both in Malawi and throughout East Africa. The plants added an exotic flavor to the cultural environment created by Europeans, Indians and Africans. It was truly cosmopolitan. What also struck me about the city was how clean it was. No trash to be seen anywhere. There were lots of Indian stores selling all sorts of goods. There were many curio shops catering to tourists. I was dumbstruck at all of the modern buildings and the skyline of Nairobi.

I had never seen so many cars in an African city. Those who did not have cars used public transportation, which was probably as efficient as anywhere in Africa. The buses were modern and attractive looking. There were roundabouts and African police in wool uniforms directing traffic. I never understood why African governments did not have their uniforms made in their home country. They, including Malawi, continued to buy uniforms from Britain who used fabric more suitable for a colder climate. But there Kenyan police officers were, directing traffic in Nairobi in the heat wearing wool shirts.

In addition to the many curio shops, there were several travel agencies such as Safari Tour Ltd. or Jambo Tours Ltd. It was obvious that tourism was big business in Nairobi. There were a few people selling street food, but not as many as you would find in other African towns. A number of people, especially women, still carried large bundles the traditional way—on top of their heads.

Nairobi was an international hub for lots of businesses in addition to the tourist trade. I saw on top of an office building a BOAC billboard advertising non-stop flights to London. There were lots of hotels and new ones such as the round Hilton Hotel building, which was still under construction. The Hotel Intercontinental was one of the recently built impressive structures dotting the Nairobi skyline. Salome suggested that I go there with her later in the week for some type of international conference. We passed by the University of East Africa at Nairobi. Originally, there was just the Makerere College of the University of East Africa at Kampala, Uganda, that served the higher education needs of the three colonies. But after independence, it was not long before each country wanted to have its own campus. The university here was very modern and impressive. The Malawi education program from elementary school to university was severely limited compared to what was available to those Africans living in East Africa.

My first day in Nairobi left me awestruck by how modern and large the city was. I think my Berea classmates wanted to impress me in case I had the usual misconceptions about Africa being a primitive continent that people in the West often had. Even though there were still large numbers of British expatriates who remained in the country after independence, there was no question that this was an African country despite the large Indian population.

Salome was the first Kenyan to graduate from Berea. When Salome returned to Kenya, we kept in touch by writing letters. She soon landed a job in the Department of Education. Before long, she was promoted to headmistress at the former colonial school for girls that had been restricted to Europeans. Expatriates had the option of sending their teenagers to boarding schools in the United Kingdom at the expense of the colonial governments. Those teenagers who chose to remain in Kenya could attend the prestigious school for girls in Kenya headed by my friend Salome. I assumed that the pay was very good. She had her own house with servants. It was the house that the British headmistress occupied before independence.

Michael Ndungi was in my class and graduated from Berea in 1966. He also had a good job in the Ministry of Agriculture. He was not yet a senior official in the department and therefore did not have a large house but a smaller one that he shared with his wife, Harriet. Nevertheless, he wanted me to stay with them at least one night before he had to leave town on business. He also wanted to entertain me and show me a side of Nairobi I would not see on my own. Michael was very proud of his Kenyan heritage, especially his Kikuyu ancestry. He was always very political and, being a Kikuyu, was active in the ruling political party. Jomo Kenyatta was the president and head of the Kenya African National Union. Salome was a Luo from the Lake Victoria region of the country. I liked Michael because he was a firm believer in African rule and had many questions about and criticism of Banda's rule in Malawi. Michael did much to educate me and other Black students in Berea about the history of colonialism in Africa and the struggles for independence.

Michael took me to one of the largest African markets in Kenya. We talked as we wandered through the bustling streets. It was good to catch up with Michael on what he had been doing since returning to Kenya. The African market was in a large settlement of Africans just outside of Nairobi proper. Michael said that the government tried to provide housing in the townships, but there were just too many Kenyans seeking jobs in the city for the housing market to keep up with the needs. It seemed that everyone wanted to live in the city, but even with city wages, many could not afford to pay the rental prices for private decent places to live. They therefore ended up living in shantytowns or makeshift housing that was overcrowded and often without city services. I was glad that the Malawi government limited access to urban life. It provided housing for civil servants. Others had to live outside of urban areas in rural villages. Whereas the roads were paved leading into these areas in Nairobi, there were few paved roads within some of the townships. It was beginning to look like the Africa I knew in Malawi, with the exception that there were many more cars and motorbikes on the streets. The houses in the townships were not substantial but did have metal roofs. I was not sure about toilet facilities and running water. Unlike the streets in the center of Nairobi that were kept clean, the roads in the township were littered with trash and waste.

There was a large centralized market that served the residents of the area. Michael took me to the center of the market that sold food. Unlike what I had observed in other countries, people in Kenya like to eat lots of meat and Michael was no exception. After walking around getting a sense of the place, Michael took me to a meat market that had beef hanging by their hoofs. Customers would go up to the butcher and ask or point to the piece of beef they wanted. The butcher would grill or give the meat to his wife to grill. The meat was served either on a skewer or grilled whole. Once done, the butcher chopped the meat into bite-size pieces and gave it to the customer wrapped in paper. Michael ordered a pound of beef for each of us. It was a lot of meat. A pound of meat would have served a family of four or more people in Malawi for several days.

Once we got our "nyama ngombe," we walked through the market looking at the variety of goods being sold from food to clothes to metal pots and pans. There was one stall with old tires that craftsmen turned into trendy sandals with treads. Another was selling cloth from large reams. Circling around, we ended up back in the food area. You could buy just about anything you wanted to eat. There were the traditional tomatoes, onions, peppers of all varieties, coconuts, pineapples, pawpaws, mangoes, bananas and various fruits and vegetables. There were vendors selling prepared food, most of which was served with ugali. I think I like ugali much better than nsima because, like ngaiwa, it was less refined.

I really enjoyed the day and visiting with my friend Michael. He drove me back to his house where I said goodbye to Harriet, thanked her for her hospitality and collected my suitcase. Michael said that he would be back in Nairobi before I left for Malawi. We said goodbye for now and he dropped me off at Salome's house.

Salome had a very nice home with three large bedrooms, two baths, a formal living and dining area and an indoor kitchen with all of the modern conveniences. There was a very spacious patio to the side of the house surrounded by tropical greenery and flowering shrubs. Her house was larger than Michael's and reflected her higher status within the Department of Education. Her house was the most affluent African home I ever visited. I did not know any Malawian who lived so well.

Salome had a cook who prepared some very delicious meals. The second day of my visit, Salome invited two of her close friends over for dinner. She introduced me to Tom and Susan Anderson, a British couple, who were active in the Society of Friends, or Quakers. Salome had introduced me to the Friends meeting group in Berea. I had actively participated in their meetings as well as the Fellowship of Reconciliation while a student. Both groups were actively involved in the Civil Rights and the anti-war movements. The British couple arrived in Kenya well before independence. They decided to stay, as Tom was the leader in the local Friends meeting. The evening was very pleasant and gave me an opportunity to meet some people who were genuinely interested in helping Africans advance without prejudice, discrimination and imposing their own values on them. We had roast beef, potatoes, broccoli and homemade bread for dinner. Salome made the bread. She majored in what we called home economics in high school.

Salome evidently was big in the Department of Education and among Kenyans generally. The next day, she drove us to a private club that once served only expatriates. During colonial days, the only way Africans could enter the club was through employment in one of the service trades. How things had changed in such a short time. Membership was still composed primarily of expatriates, but a number of notable African businessmen and politicians were now members. It was a favorite place for these politicians and businessmen to hang out. I was not sure why Salome joined, but she was a member and was recognized as we walked through the lobby on our way to the restaurant for lunch. The lobby reminded me of old films

University College building in Nairobi.

of Africa where expatriates still ruled. The club was furnished with handsome leather overstuffed chairs and sofas arranged in groups to encourage conversation. There were also isolated chairs where you could sit in solitude, enjoying a good cigar while having a midday drink of gin and tonic.

We entered the dining room where we were seated at a table with linen, fine silverware and stemmed crystal glassware. It was a far cry from what I had been used to for the last year. Several people came over to greet Salome. One man, probably a newly rich businessman, ignored me altogether even after Salome introduced me to him. I guess he felt like I was a nobody and he would not waste his time talking to me. It was during this time that I wished I had brought a jacket so I would not look so informal in my khaki pants and sports shirt. Regardless, we had a lovely meal of quail, wild rice and a vegetable medley. Salome ordered a bottle of wine, an enjoyable departure from my usual beer.

After lunch, we walked over to the University of Nairobi and toured the grounds. The university was part of the University of East Africa. I was so impressed that I decided that I wanted to come back to Nairobi to live, and maybe if I earned another degree, I could teach at the university.

We ended the evening going to an international conference called the Afro-American Dialogue located at the Hotel Intercontinental. Salome told me that many of her friends who were Quakers would be there and I would like them. She said that Quakers had been in western Kenya for a long time. I guess this was why she felt so comfortable around the small group of Quakers at Berea. She said that there would probably be members of the diplomatic community at the reception as well.

When we entered, the lobby was filled with all sorts of important people. I could tell by their dress and demeanor. I had on my best shirt and slacks but still did not fit in with my informal attire. There were dignitaries from all over Africa, Europe and the United States. There were ministers and heads of state. President Jomo Kenyatta had just left before we arrived. The editor of *Newsweek* and many others attended the conference. I made some small talk with a couple of people and then walked over to get a beer. I noticed in the corner of the room a man sitting by himself on the stairs leading up to the second floor. I walked over and introduced myself. He said that his name was Bayard Rustin and that he was from the States. He seemed friendly enough, especially after I introduced myself as being an American and a member of the Peace Corps. We talked about affairs back home and the killing of Martin Luther King, Jr. He said that he had worked with King behind the scenes organizing the March on Washington. He said that he was devastated by Dr. King's assassination. We talked about the war in Vietnam. I told him how I was against the war and had participated in a demonstration in New York City in August 1964. I told him that the demonstration occurred when I was on an American Friends Service Project in Philadelphia and was in New York for the weekend. My friends and I heard that the May 2nd Movement had planned a demonstration at Duffy Square and decided that we would participate. While demonstrating peacefully, we were ordered to disperse, and when we refused, we were attacked by the New York mounted police. Two mounted policemen rode into the crowd of mostly college-aged students, sending one young man to the ground. One of the horses stepped on his hip. We were horrified. The next day, the story appeared on the front page of the *New York Times*, and our picture appeared on the front page of the *New York Herald Tribune*.

Mr. Rustin and I talked about the Harlem riots that occurred the summer of 1964. I said that my friends and I drove through Harlem and the entire area was covered by armed military men. I had never experienced anything like that in my life. Bayard said that he remembered the riots well and the killing of a young Black teenager by a police officer. Although I wanted to talk more and get to know this interesting man, Salome said that it was time to leave. We were going to travel to Kisumu to visit her mother the next day. I bade goodbye to Bayard Rustin and wished him well.

Kisumu

We drove 211 miles from Nairobi to Kisumu, an up-and-coming town on Lake Victoria. It may have been the third largest town in Kenya after Mombasa, but I am not sure. Our trip was leisurely as we were not in a hurry, plus I wanted to see as much of the countryside as possible. Salome had not only learned how to drive since leaving Berea but also had purchased a car. We took turns driving. The roads were very nice and, above all, paved, which I couldn't say about many of Malawi's roads. It was a beautiful time of the year to be heading northwest, and of course, the increased elevation lowered the temperature making the days very pleasant with cool nights. The grass was green and there were many fields dotted with small, thatched houses made in the traditional way. We also saw large tea and coffee plantations, some stretching as far as the eye could see. Salome said that Europeans took as much as four million acres of land from the African inhabitants and turned the land into these great tea plantations. We traveled across the Great Rift Valley that extended from Jordan to Mozambique. We saw baboons playing with their babies along the road. As we neared small towns, wild animals gave way to cattle that seemed to roam freely. Every time we stopped in a small town, we were inundated by people wanting to sell us goods. We gave in and purchased a variety of vegetables, which we took to Salome's mother.

After seven or eight hours of travel on paved roads, we reached Kisumu where we decided to stay at one of the local hotels before we headed out to the village. I immediately liked Kisumu. It still had the old colonial architecture reflected in the older buildings. There was no indication of White control here. It was an African city with few Europeans visible.

We checked into a somewhat refurbished hotel that was clean and comfortable but definitely not modern. Salome wanted me to meet some of her friends and colleagues after we went to our rooms to refresh for dinner.

After showering and dressing for dinner, we headed out to a small bar restaurant not far from the hotel. There were two Kenyans waiting for us. They were Salome's former classmates. The man was a politician, and his wife was a teacher. Salome introduced me to Mr. and Mrs. Rodney (Brenda) Mutoka. Both their parents went to schools run by the Quakers, so I guess that explained their English first names. Salome was of course named after the biblical queen Salome, but her middle name was Nolega. She took the name David when she came to America, which was her father's name. I learned that Rodney was a member of parliament, and his wife was a local schoolteacher trained in Kenya. I suppose Salome was able to get the position as school principal because she had an American bachelor's degree.

When I arrived on the continent, I knew very little African history, but fortunately I have been able to do a lot of reading on my own. I was very anxious to learn more about the Luo people, Lake Victoria, and the Nile, and Rodney was a willing teacher. He said that the Luo people came from the north, but Europeans did not consider that African history existed until John Speke came down the Nile and discovered Lake Victoria, which he named after his English queen in 1858. The lake covered more than 23,000 square miles and was the second largest in the world next to one of our great lakes in the States, he explained. He told me that the lake was the source of the Nile and bordered Uganda, Tanzania and Kenya. We talked for a long time, and finally the waiter came to take our order. Mr. Rodney Mutoka suggested that we attend the agricultural fair tomorrow. I told him that I would like that since I worked as a Peace Corps volunteer in agriculture.

We ordered Tusker beer while we talked and thought about what we would have for dinner. Salome suggested that we let her order for the table. Salome used to cook for me as a Berea student and I liked everything she made. We had so much fun in the basement of the Anna Smith Dormitory. Salome would play African music and we would dance while the food finished cooking. So I was anxious to taste African food in her homeland. She ordered grilled tilapia sautéed in a tomato sauce, red kidney beans in coconut milk, local greens with sides of ugali and rice. We talked about Kenyan politics and life since independence. It was a satisfying feeling to be around my people with no White people in sight.

Back at the hotel, we retired early in anticipation of another busy day.

The next day, we were up early. I met Salome downstairs for breakfast, which to my surprise was a traditional British breakfast of fried eggs, bacon, toast with orange marmalade and a fried tomato. We both had Kenyan coffee with its robust flavor. As we were finishing our breakfast, Rodney and Brenda joined us for coffee. They agreed to take us, or rather me, on a sightseeing trip before we went to the agricultural fair. We first drove to the lake where there were numerous people gathered at the market to purchase fresh fish. Fishermen had brought in their haul for the morning and were busy laying out their catch on tables in the market areas. Others were cleaning their fish and putting them on tables to dry in the sun. Some were smoking their fish, which gave off a distinct aroma. Still others were mending their nets in preparation for fishing the next day. After walking around the lakefront and market, it was time to leave for the agricultural show.

The agricultural show was larger than anything that I had experienced in Malawi. First, there were many people dressed in their traditional clothes with beautiful feathers in their hair. I asked why some were carrying shields, and Rodney said that they would be performing traditional dances as part of the day's entertainment. There were lots and lots of people. This must have been a regional production for so many people to be in attendance. People brought their prized cattle, sheep, goats and chickens for judging. Evidently, the government had introduced new strains of animals to mix with their traditional herds to improve the quality of animal stock. New vegetable seeds produced a variety of crops that had higher yields than traditional vegetables grown in the villages. Salome said that while these crops were more productive, they did not necessarily taste better than the vegetables grown by villages. She said that I would notice the difference when I tasted her mother's cooking.

There were many vendors selling food—grilled vegetables and pies but mainly grilled beef and goat. We had a light lunch before walking to the edge of the fair to watch a game of young Kenyan boys playing soccer barefoot. Boys learned to play soccer at a young age before they received their first pair of shoes. Many would become quite agile in their ability to control the ball with their bare feet.

Following the game, we went back to our hotel to gather our belongings and check out. We bade goodbye to Rodney and Brenda and headed out to Salome's village. The village was much more prosperous than any in Malawi. There were many more houses constructed in the western style out of brick with corrugated roofs. In front of her mother's traditional thatched house, Salome had built her mother a modern three-bedroom house with electricity and running water. It was very nicely furnished. I was surprised to learn that her mother would not live in the house but preferred to stay in her traditional home where she cooked food in clay pots outside on an open fire.

After getting settled, we walked around back and entered the house where her mother lived. Salome introduced me to her mother who was named Tisa because she was the ninth child born in her family. I started to call her Mrs. David, but Salome told me to call her Mama Tisa. Mama Tisa was a small, dark-skinned woman like Salome. She wore a traditional wrap around her waist and was barefoot. Mama Tisa approached me on her knees, a tradition that older women practiced when being introduced to prominent males. Not that I was prominent in any way, but I did have a college degree, something greatly admired and respected by Africans. I was always embarrassed to see frail old women on their knees like that, but I accepted it as part of their traditions and as a show of respect. My guess was Mama Tisa was in her early seventies, but it was hard to tell just how old African women were.

Mama Tisa did not speak much English, so Salome translated for us. She told her mother about our friendship in Berea and about my family. Before Salome graduated from college, I had invited her to go home with me to Morganton, North Carolina, for the Christmas holiday. We rode the Trailways bus as far as Asheville, where my parents picked us up, and then we drove 50 miles to Morganton.

Since we lived in a small three-bedroom house, Mother arranged for Miss Hester Carson, our neighbor, to let Salome stay with her in her guest bedroom. The Carsons lived in a brick house, one house down and across the street from where we lived. Salome would have her meals with us during the day and sleep at the Carsons' at night. Salome was a hit in the small, segregated community of Morganton. She was welcomed to St. Stephen's Episcopal Church where we attended Christmas service. Even though Salome went to a Quaker school, she was also very familiar with the Anglican Church and felt at home at St. Stephen's. I think the visit with my family made Salome even more anxious for me to visit with her mother and get to know her home village.

That evening, Mama Tisa fixed a delicious home-cooked meal. She had killed a chicken earlier in the day in my honor. Her chickens roamed freely in her yard, which accounted for the marvelous taste. I had never had a chicken with so much flavor. She cooked the chicken in a clay pot on an open fire with coconut milk and onions. Salome said that the dish was called kuku na nazi. We had sukuma wiki, which she knew I would

Chapter Two. My First Year in Malawi

Salome in front of Lake Nakuru.

like because it was basically a collard greens dish that I was used to eating growing up in the southern United States. We also had irio, a dish of green peas and potato mashed together. Of course, we had to have ugali. I was glad that Salome had made ugali for me in college because by the time I came to Africa, I was accustomed to some traditional African foods. The meal was delicious. I lavished Mama Tisa with praise for cooking such a wonderful meal.

Salome said that she had to get back to Nairobi because she had a lot to do in preparation for Kenya's Independence Day celebration. I hated to leave the Luo village. I had been treated like one of the family and thoroughly enjoyed my time with Mama Tisa and Salome's friends. We had a leisurely drive from Kisumu back to Nairobi.

Salome wanted me to see Lake Nakuru because it was famous for its pink flamingos. The lake is in the Great Rift Valley, surrounded by low-lying mountain ridges with the lake situated on the valley floor. Lake Nakuru is a shallow, soda lake. Salome said that the flamingos ate insect larvae, which gave them their beautiful pink color. The lake and surrounding grassland was absolutely beautiful. To make the setting even more ideal, the lake was about a mile above sea level giving the area surrounding it a moderate climate. I can easily see why the British settlers were attracted to this area. The climate was ideal, and the vegetation was lush. From the lake, we drove to the equator where Salome and I took turns taking each other's picture below the sign marking the spot where the equator crosses Kenya. When we got out of the car, Salome was wearing her trench coat and I had to put on my sweater. It was so cold. I had always thought of the equator as being hot and humid, but standing there, halfway between the North and South Poles, and discovering it at this high elevation and cold was a marvelous experience that I will not forget.

On my last day in Nairobi, Salome and I visited the Nairobi National Museum and Snake Park. I had read about the work of the Leakeys in East Africa, but I did not imagine that I would ever be in the museum where the Leakeys volunteered as curators and were instrumental in setting up the museum exhibitions on Kenya's pre-history and cultural history. As a budding Africanist, I was pleased to learn that early man developed in East Africa nearly two million years ago. The world was indebted to the work of the Leakeys, especially Mary Leakey, for their work at Olduvai Gorge and adding to our knowledge of early African and world history. I think that the Leakey family was an inspiring example of what other expatriates could have done if they had made a commitment to the people and the country rather than exploiting the people and its natural resources. Salome told me the museum was formed early in the twentieth century by the East African and Ugandan Historical Society. When the society developed it into a true museum, it was named for Sir Robert Corydon, a former colonial governor. During this time, it was an all–White museum until the

I'm shown here at the equator in Kenya.

Leakeys "allowed" Africans to visit. After independence, the museum was renamed the Nairobi National Museum.

I was also interested in Snake Park adjacent to the museum. I had a fearful fascination with African snakes. In the park, there were snakes enclosed in glass cages and others in open pits. The snakes included cobras, puff adders, mambas, and the large African rock python. Ever since I had that accident while transporting a green mamba to Blantyre, I had kept my distance from snakes. I was staring at a black mamba in the snake pit as it climbed up on the naked branches of a dead tree and worked itself out on a single limb. Some White tourists tried to feed the snake by extending what looked like pieces of apple in their hands to the snake. The snake went as far as it could on the limb and raised its body and took a leap toward the tourists. They all screamed and jumped back from the edge of the glass railing surrounding the pit. I also thought the snake had jumped over the railing, but it fell and landed back on the floor of the pit. I, like the other tourists, was truly shaken by the mamba's failed leap.

I wanted very much to remain in Kenya to be part of the Independence Day celebrations on December 12. I remembered how excited Michael Ndungi, Harry Mbui, Salome and the other Kenyan students were when Kenya became independent from Great Britain. Although I was glad for them, I did not appreciate the importance of December 12 to these students. I was never clear on Jomo Kenyatta's involvement with

Dancers in Nairobi.

the Mau Mau, but Michael told me that he was not involved and that the British colonial authorities had used him as a scapegoat. Kenyatta had been arrested, tried and sent to prison for seven years and then held under house arrest for another two. When the Kenya African National Union Party was formed, they elected Kenyatta as its first president. Now President Kenyatta was viewed as one of Africa's most prominent political leaders.

Although I would not be in Nairobi for the actual independence celebration, I was able to see some early pre-celebration and rehearsal activities at the stadium. When we arrived, people were already gathering for the march into the stadium. There were various tribes represented in their ethnic dress. African women were very devoted to their national leaders and Kenyan women were no exception. Many wore the colors of the national flag, red, black and green. Others wore beaded costumes with elaborate headdresses. There were several groups of men with their traditional spears and shields, all gathered to rehearse their performance for the president. Then there were the military men dressed in their green uniforms with red hats looking very smart as they marched into the stadium.

In preparation for the entrance of the president, the women were to follow Mzee (elder) Jomo Kenyatta's caravan undulating in shrill voices, "lalalalalala," or something like that. Mzee spoke Swahili, much different from our President Banda, who spoke only English. I was a little surprised to see a number of White people at the rehearsal. Salome told me that the White settlers, as they were called, expected to be expelled from the country. Instead, they were pleasantly surprised at how well they had been received by the president and his administration. They initially feared that the president might retaliate against them based on the way they fought and killed Africans during their struggle for independence.

John Hunter and his friends had returned from visiting Mount Kilimanjaro. We decided to visit the Nairobi Game Reserve just outside of the city before heading for Uganda. The whole of East Africa was rich in wild animals unlike Malawi where most of the animals had long disappeared. Nowhere else in the world could you find all sorts of wild animals from lions to zebras to giraffes to monkeys to hippos all within a short drive from the city. We made our reservations for the half-day tour and were picked up at a hotel in downtown Nairobi. We joined a group with a Kenyan guide, four other people, one British couple and a couple from Germany.

It did not take long to drive to the park. We spent the first few hours leisurely driving through the park with the roof of our Land Rover open so that we could stand and take pictures of the animals. I was not aware that lions, tigers and leopards could live so close to humans in an urban environment. Obviously, the government has restricted human development on the outskirts of the city. We saw plenty of giraffes and antelopes of various types and sizes. I guess that I should have learned the difference between these types of animals because they were distinct; however, I could tell the difference between a buffalo and a wildebeest. I had my new Canon camera with me and I took lots of pictures.

We pulled into a rest area for a bathroom break and a chance to get some coffee or tea. The guide then told us that we were going to take the walking tour along the trail that paralleled the stream. He said that we could expect to see lots of animals because many use the stream as their source of water. When we got to the area where the stream broadened into a small pond, there were lots and lots of tourists, all of whom were White of different nationalities. There were several hippos swimming in the pool. There were birds everywhere waiting for the tourists to leave them some food. I noticed a group of monkeys in the trees above us. They seemed more used to having people around them than we were used to having monkeys around us. One lady from Europe decided to load her camera with fresh film. She pulled out a roll of Kodak film that was encased in bright aluminum foil. Suddenly, a monkey jumped out of one of the trees, over to where the woman was standing and grabbed the film and foil out of her hands, then scampered back into the tree above. She was terrified. However, the monkey only wanted the bright foil that was glistening in the sunlight. It attracted the monkey's attention and curiosity. I was startled initially and then thought how amusing the whole situation was. We continued along the trail watching for all types of exotic birds and other wildlife. It was the adventure of a lifetime, very convenient for tourists who might be in Nairobi for business and didn't have the time to travel to a park like Serengeti, which was some distance out from Nairobi.

Uganda

I found it difficult to say goodbye to all my Kenyan friends, especially Salome, because I really enjoyed our visit, although I looked forward to returning to Nairobi and seeing my friends again before departing for Blantyre. Following our trip to the Nairobi Game Reserve, John and I left Kenya for Uganda by bus, which was the first time I had traveled on a bus in Africa. In Malawi, I either rode my motorbike or hitched a ride with someone. The bus was packed even though it was early in the morning. We decided to take an early morning bus so that we could enjoy the scenery between Nairobi and Kampala. Many people prefer to make the long trip at night so that they could sleep. We were the only non–Africans on the bus that was packed with Kenyans and Ugandans. The top of the bus was loaded with suitcases and all types of sacks filled with clothes, household items and vegetables.

The landscape was absolutely beautiful between Nairobi and Kampala, the capital of Uganda. The landscape changed from savannah to lush forest with many banana trees dotting the landscape. There were a few small villages along the main highway between the two countries. There were numerous vendors on the streets and in small shops selling anything and everything to those driving by. We made several stops along the way including Limuru and Nakuru. These towns are located in the Great Rift Valley. Both are White settlements and in what is known as the White highlands. The area has very rich soil, coupled with a moderate climate, making this land ideal for growing coffee and tea, which explains the large settlement of British in the area. The coffee and tea plantations are still visible along the road. The whole area reminded me of the Shire Highlands and Mulanje where Whites settled and had both coffee and tea plantations. Not much had changed in the short time since independence, but I understood that more Kenyans were growing these cash crops.

The bus made many stops to allow people to get off and others to get on. In the towns, there were restroom facilities from modern ones in Nakuru to primitive latrines in smaller communities. It was not unusual for people, especially men to walk a few feet away from others and urinate alongside the road. That was a common practice in Malawi too. I suppose with so few facilities, people had to go where they could. We picked up some bananas on one of the stops and a couple of orange Fantas to quench our thirst. We did not have to worry about having to wash the bananas. We continued the practice of not drinking the water when outside of the city. No one wanted to get diarrhea on the journey. During one stop, an elderly lady got on the bus and sat in front of me. Every 20 or 30 minutes, she had to cough and then spit out the window. The problem was that my window was open and I was unable to close it. Some of her spit landed several times right in my face!

When we got to the border crossing at Busia, Kenya, we all had to get off the bus and go through customs. We had our passport, visa, and yellow fever certificate, so we did not anticipate any problems. Generally, Kenyan citizens were allowed to cross the border by merely showing their identification cards. The same was true for Ugandans traveling to Kenya. I was allowed to pass without a problem. However, the Ugandan border patrol asked John to identify his luggage. The border guard had the luggage removed from the top of the bus and placed on the sidewalk. John then had to open the bag and empty his belongings on the side of the road. The customs officer then rummaged through John's belongings; heaven only knew what he was looking for. I am convinced that John was singled out for special inspection because he was White. Although John was a friend and fellow Peace Corps volunteer, I could not help the feeling of righteous justice when I saw a White person discriminated against because of his color. I could see that John was very irritated. I didn't say anything, but I thought it was a good experience for John to know what it felt like to be discriminated against because of the color of his skin.

We arrived in Uganda mid-afternoon. We caught a cab over to the Speke Hotel. Although not a luxurious hotel, it was decent and just above our spending limit, but we decided to stay at a nice, centrally located hotel since this would be the end of our stay in East Africa before heading back to Malawi.

The Speke Hotel was in the central area of Kampala on Nile Avenue. It was named after John Speke, the English explorer who made several trips to the interior of Africa to try to locate the origins of the Nile. He was the first European to see Lake Nyanza, among its many local African names, which he then renamed Lake Victoria, after Queen Victoria. Of course, bodies of water, as all things in Africa before the arrival of Europeans, had African names. The name Lake Victoria stuck even after the surrounding countries became independent. I guess since several countries bordered on the lake, it would have been hard for all of them to agree on a name.

I was glad to get to my room. The trip from Nairobi was not an easy journey with all the stops, the overcrowded conditions and spit blowing in my face. The first thing I did was to wash my face and to shower. The train trip from Mombasa was much more pleasurable even though it was a long trip time-wise. My room was pleasant but basic. I could not afford a room with a veranda or even one with a window facing the courtyard. Instead, I ended up with a small room at the back of the hotel. I did not complain because it was a good deal for the price.

Once refreshed, we met in the lobby to begin our sightseeing tour of the city. At first, we just walked randomly around. We ended up in the Nakasero Market, one of the oldest African markets in the country. It was huge with every sort of fruit and vegetable one could want. The produce was generally sold in the open air while shoes, clothes, and other goods were sold in a covered building. After walking through the market, we headed to one of the food vendors. Ever mindful of dysentery, we decided to get some grilled meat. We soon saw a vendor selling nyama ya mbuzi, or goat meat on a skewer. I had fallen in love with goat meat and would eat it every chance I got. We bought Fanta to wash the food down and continued our excursion.

Tourism was big business in Uganda because of the lovely climate, beautiful scenery, wildlife, Lake Victoria and Murchison Falls. Everyone wanted to travel to the headwaters of the Nile. Consequently, there were

Headwaters of the Nile River, Lake Victoria.

lots of items for sale to tourists. I was tempted to buy several items but did not want to be bogged down carrying any more luggage or bags than I had to. So we just strolled through the marketplace with vendors trying to entice us to buy their wares.

We were impressed with the way the Ugandan ladies dressed. Their national dress looked like it was derived from another century. The dresses were long, very colorful with puff sleeves and a sash tied around the waist. I had asked the lady at the hotel front desk about the dress and she told me that the national costume was based on Buganda traditional dress that was made from bark cloth. She said that some people believed that the dress was introduced by the White missionaries who thought that it was indecent for women to show their breasts, so they had Indian seamstresses make full-length dresses with puff sleeves. At any rate, the style had been adopted by most people and was always worn on special occasions. You see women dressed in these costumes in restaurants, churches, and so forth. I think she said that they were called Gomesi. Malawi women did not have a national dress beyond tying a large piece of cloth around their waist.

We continued to walk around for a while and then headed back to the hotel. We spent some time in the hotel bar drinking East African beers. Although European beer was widely available, it was more expensive. So we ordered Bell and Nile beers, which we could get for a shilling. We saw a local African restaurant as we were walking back to the hotel and decided to check it out for dinner. It was a small place, very plain. One might even say it was austere. We really didn't care about the decor if the food was good, cheap and allowed us to stay on budget. I ordered goat meat stewed until very tender with tomatoes and onions. Tomatoes and onions seemed to be used throughout Africa in making stews. I had a choice of matooke or posho with my meal. Since posho was a lot like ugali in Kenya and nsima in Malawi, I decided to try matooke, which was made from boiled green bananas mashed into a paste. The bananas were not sweet, so Ugandans eat it like ugali or rice with their meals. It was a taste that I could have gotten used to, but I much preferred ugali.

During our last night in Uganda, we made plans to head back via bus to Nairobi and then to Dar es Salaam where we would catch an East African Airways flight to Blantyre. I now thought that it was a mistake to get round trip tickets to Dar es Salaam because we had to make the long trip back to that city by road.

We saw a lot during our trip to Uganda, including a day in Entebbe, the old colonial capital before independence. One morning, we hired a taxi for the day to drive us to Entebbe and around the area for sightseeing. The outstanding thing about Entebbe was that it was the headwater of Lake Victoria. The lake was beautiful and huge. I never thought I would see the source of the Nile. John suggested that we return home via Uganda so that we could get a boat and travel from the headwaters of the Nile through Sudan and into Egypt until we got to Cairo and the delta. It sounded like a good idea; I said I would consider it.

When we returned to Kampala, we took a tour of Makerere University, which was a lovely old college. One sign on campus indicated that

Makerere University, Kampala.

the college started as a technical school in 1922 and then became Uganda Technical College. In 1935, it was expanded into higher education and, eventually in 1949, became University College affiliated with University College London. Finally in 1963, it became part of the University of East Africa. The grounds were well maintained and manicured perfectly. The buildings, especially the main building, were very impressive.

Our driver had been so helpful and informative that we asked him to take us around the city of Kampala for a fixed price. The driver told us his name was Batjargal, which meant "happiness." He was a member of the Baganda people, who were the majority of the population of Uganda. I asked Batjargal if we could visit the Kabaka Palace. Kabaka was the king of the Baganda people. Batjargal explained the palace was closed when Sir Edward Frederick Mutesa was overthrown by President Milton Obote in 1966, just two years before. I think people in the West had expected a lot from Obote as he led his country to independence in 1962 and became the country's first president.

Following our tour, our driver took us back to the hotel where we prepared to leave the next day for Nairobi.

Back to Malawi

We took a bus back to Nairobi where we stayed with my Kenyan friends who were very generous in providing accommodations. All my Kenyan friends got together and gave us a going-away party which was

I'm on the shore of Lake Victoria, Uganda.

very nice. Mike had collected enough money that allowed me to change my ticket and to fly directly from Nairobi back to Blantyre rather than having to take the bus to Dar es Salaam. We had an uneventful trip home from the airport in Nairobi where we flew on East African Airways to Blantyre. The time spent in East Africa would stay with me for a lifetime. I was glad that we did not plan our trip down to the last details. We were able to explore and take advantage of opportunities as they arose.

Chapter Three

Second Year in Malawi

Back to Work

    I had been busy since returning to Malawi, catching up on work in the office with little time for anything else. As I began my last year in Malawi, I had to give some thought to the transition from being head of the extension aids office to securing a Malawian as my replacement. This had always been a high priority for me. I thought I might run into some difficulty with the regional extension aid officer as well as the head of the A/V aid office in Zomba. People gave lip service to the idea of indigenous supervisors, but didn't always follow through on their promises. I planned to keep the pressure up if this was ever going to happen.

    Another group of Peace Corps volunteers arrived in Blantyre this month. True to form, they were another all–White group. The White liberals had again descended on the continent to save the poor natives. I supposed that I was being unfair, but I wondered why more Blacks were not part of these groups. You could count on one hand the number of Black volunteers in Malawi. I guess that most of us did not have the luxury of giving up two years of our lives to be a volunteer. I knew that my own father thought that after I graduated from college I should get a good job and make some money. I feared that that attitude was common for recent Black graduates, unlike middle- to upper-class Whites. Many of us did not have the luxury to work for free. Barbara told me that she wanted to get a good job to repay her mother for the support she had provided her and her sisters while they were in college. Certainly, I thought that my dad saw going to college as an investment and did not see the value of working for "nothing" for two years as a volunteer. Dad never went to college, but he was determined that all of us received an education beyond high school. My interest in missionary work was the key to why I was here. Christmas was fast approaching and I was invited to spend the holidays with some of my Malawi friends.

Notes on the Peace Corps

Unlike most volunteers, I tried to avoid the Peace Corps office and staff as much as possible. I had never gone to Todd Mayes's Saturday pancake breakfasts. It wasn't because I disliked Todd and his family—I found that he was a very good director. I decided not to attend his breakfasts because I felt like being in Blantyre, it was too easy to be involved with the Peace Corps rather than Malawians whom we came here to serve, to get to know them and have them get to know us. I decided early on to just stay away from the Peace Corps office unless there was an emergency or some health problems. Then I would take advantage of Peace Corps services.

The Peace Corps had asked me to allow them to do a story on me, my office and home for a brochure or some kind of promotional piece to attract more Blacks into the service. I never said that I would not do it, but I procrastinated for so long that it was too late for my involvement. They seemed to want to highlight the few Black volunteers they had in Malawi. I feared that some of us Black volunteers had been nasty toward the staff, but that never seemed to matter because they were all liberals and just seemed to take such behavior in stride and continue business as usual.

I was getting tired of having to provide accommodations for volunteers who came into Blantyre. It would be something else if they would give me a little something for their food, but that never happened. I remembered once making a big spaghetti dinner with three loaves of homemade french bread for six volunteers. The meal was enjoyed by all, but not a shilling was contributed toward the purchase of the food, much of which I had to buy from the European market.

Tom and I got along much better now that we had separate houses. Tom stayed in the plantation house when I moved out. We bought two sheep together. We planned to raise one and kill the other for New Year's. Since arriving in Malawi, there was not much I could not do from buying live chickens in the market and bringing them home and killing them to buying and raising sheep for slaughter. I still had trouble dealing with snakes. I once found one in the house and my stupid dog didn't even bother to try to catch it or to try to kill it. I finally managed to coach it into a shoebox and take it far outside the house for release.

Holidays

About a week ago, I mailed my Christmas letter to various friends and family with personal notes on the back. It was one of the few letters that I typed and then mimeographed. I used an aerogram for writing most of my letters, the cheapest way to mail letters. I had already started trying to catch up on my work. I seemed to work harder than the other volunteers who easily fell into the African way of doing things, but I had set out goals for myself. I wanted to develop my visual aid office into a first-rate facility run by people of color. I wanted to train young Africans to run the office efficiently and to train a Malawian to become the new visual aid officer in preparation for my departure. I wanted to promote Africanization of the southern regional office as much as I could.

It now rained steadily and heavily as we were in the rainy season. The roads during the dry season were packed and sturdy, except in areas that were very sandy. When the rains came, the unpaved roads turned into mud. No matter how careful we drove our motorcycles, we all knew there would be an accident before the rainy season was over. I remembered Howard Carter telling us that the accident rate for volunteers on motorcycles was 100 percent. Even though I believed him, I was certain that I could beat those odds until I rode onto a gravel-covered driveway, hit my brake and immediately turned the bike over. After experiencing my first accident, I anticipated that I would have more before the rainy season was over. When the rains came, so did the mosquitoes. They were everywhere but particularly bad at night. Thank goodness for the mosquito nets provided by the Peace Corps.

The dog I, or rather Tom and I together, acquired had grown since I returned from East Africa. Poor Thako broke his foot and we had to take him to the vet to have a cast put on it. Everson took care of him while I was gone. The cast had come off. I was pleased that Thako still remembered me and was as glad to see me as I was to see him.

Christmas was coming in a couple of days, and I was grateful that Mark Chiphwanya and his wife had invited me to their home for the holidays. As a single person, I had always managed to become friends with people who enjoyed good food and could cook. The Chiphwanyas and I had become the best of friends.

My office put on a Christmas puppet show for children in the local hospital (African section). I was able to raise a few pounds to buy the children some candy. The show was very nice and the children enjoyed it. With no television, things like puppet shows were very entertaining.

Barbara told me in her last letter that she had been sick. I was sure she felt lonely at this time of the year not going home for the holidays. I also informed her that I had been sick to my stomach for the last couple of days. I sent her some nice African carvings for Christmas.

Boxing Day is a holiday tradition originating in Great Britain when the poor and those in service were given alms and gifts. Malawi followed so many of the practices and customs developed in the United Kingdom that I was not surprised to learn that Malawians also celebrated Boxing Day. I was glad for the holiday because it gave me time to catch up on my rest.

My second Christmas holiday in Malawi was just wonderful. Mark Chiphwanya invited me to spend the day with his family in his home village. Mark had turned out to be one of my best friends. He finished high school and went on to the University of Malawi for his undergraduate degree where he majored in administration. I guess it was some form of business administration. At any rate, he joined the Department of Agriculture as a regional officer. It was not long before he was sent stateside for graduate study. I believe he said at Cornell University in agriculture. The one thing I noticed about people who got ahead in government offices run by expatriates was that the more "Western" they look in physical appearance, the greater their opportunities. Mark was average height for a Malawian, handsome with Western features. But in his case, he was smart and knew what he was doing. I did not observe that he had any encounters with European supervisors. Mark expected me to know more Chichewa than I knew. He was always trying to speak to me in the language. I seemed to have a barrier to learning all foreign languages, not just Chichewa. So we started off with a few sayings, "Moni. Muli bwinji. Ndili bwino," and a few more common phrases before I had to revert to English. Mark would sometimes look annoyed at me, but he would eventually revert to English.

Mark was married to Beatrice, a very attractive woman. Beatrice had taken a two-year course in what we at home called home economics. She was teaching in secondary school when they got married. I think Beatrice was about 10 years younger than Mark. She was one of the most beautiful Malawi women I had met. I wonder if I thought this because she too had "Western" features rather than the typical Bantu features like most Malawi women. They had two children, and considering the couple's looks, it was no wonder that they had two handsome boys, aged two and three. Because of their education, I doubted that they would have a lot of children.

Mark and Beatrice invited me over for dinner on several occasions. On one occasion, I brought Agnes Banda with me. Agnes had attended nursing school in Germany. She quickly learned German and successfully completed her course of study and became a registered nurse. I always marveled at how adaptable Africans were. They could go to any country, learn the language and successfully complete their college education. Agnes worked in the European hospital in Blantyre and lived in the apartment complex reserved for single nurses. All of the women who had been educated overseas were much more liberal in their behavior and didn't mind trying new things. For instance, unlike a traditional Malawi woman, Agnes had no problem riding on the back of my motorcycle.

This Christmas, I was alone in joining the Chiphwanyas in their home village for the holidays. The Chiphwanyas lived in a European-style home in Blantyre because of Mark's status as a district officer. However, he had a second home that he'd built in his village some years ago and he stayed in that house when visiting his mother. The house had electricity and running water, both unusual in a village.

The Chiphwanyas had been at home all week, but I arrived by motorcycle on Wednesday, the 25th, around noon. The house was furnished very comfortably. I was welcomed by Mark. Beatrice came from the kitchen to greet me. I was seated in the living room by the time Mark's mother entered the house. She got down on her knees and more or less crawled over to shake my hand. We exchanged greetings in Chichewa. The children were playing in the yard when Beatrice called out to them to come in and greet me. Malawians were very polite and believed in these social graces. After we exchanged greetings, I gave the boys the soccer ball that I bought for them for Christmas. I presented Mrs. Chiphwanya with a wooden bowl that I had my carpenter at the office make from mahogany wood. The carpenter was stationed on Kubula Hill while he made the puppet theaters for the rural training centers. While working out of the office, I also got him to make me a Bao game also out of mahogany. He was really an expert carpenter and both the bowl and Bao game were examples of his craftsmanship. I was always surprised at how skilled the African artisans were using a small axe and simple carving tools.

The house was decorated modestly for the Christmas season. There was a small Christmas tree on the table and a wreath on the door. Mark's mother and Beatrice were busy in the kitchen preparing the food for dinner with some of the cooking done outside on an open fire. Mark had a goat killed for the holiday. I was not sure if he knew that goat was one of my favorite meats.

While we waited for dinner, Mark and I talked in the living room about what had been happening in the States. Although there was no TV, everyone had a radio or at least access to a radio. Malawi radio carried BBC news, so we kept up to date on what was happening in the world. Everyone was shocked when Dr. Martin Luther King, Jr., was assassinated followed a few months later by the murder of Robert Kennedy. Dr. King was a worldwide hero and people also thought a lot of the Kennedys. The killing of King and Kennedy did tremendous damage to American foreign policy. It was difficult for Mark and others in Malawi to understand why anyone would kill either man. We talked about the riots that followed. Mark was appalled with how America treated its Black citizens. Mark said that he did not encounter a lot of discrimination in New York State while in school, but he was aware of what was happening in the South.

Mark was in the States when the Freedom Riders were traveling South and being beaten for just trying to enter a bus station reserved for Whites. Mark understood prejudice and discrimination because Malawians faced the same under British colonial rule, but Malawians did not experience the beatings and murders experienced by Black people in the States. I often told Mark how much I disliked how expatriates treated Malawians. He said that things were improving especially in the central and northern regions of the country where President Banda had been able to Africanize the government at a faster rate than in the South. I think that was because expatriates preferred to live in the southern region, especially Blantyre, Zomba and the tea-producing areas near Mount Mulanje. Mark said that if the American government realized the reaction of people around the world to how badly Black people were treated, the government would be more proactive in trying to solve its racial problem. Mark asked how the United States could promote democracy abroad when it denied democracy to its own citizens. Africans saw the irony between what America said regarding equality as a nation and what we did. I completely agreed with Mark's assessment of America's racial problems.

Beatrice came in to say that Mark and I had spent enough time talking about politics and that it was now time for dinner and that we should wash our hands. I thought to myself how hungry I was and that I was getting better at eating with my hands. Beatrice would often serve rice with her meals, but today she was serving nsima. I told her once that I liked ngaiwa, the coarse grain. I guess she thought that I would look down on her for serving what many viewed as peasant food. It was interesting that the more refined the grain, the more status it had and the less nutrients it offered.

Beatrice said she knew that I was used to having either turkey or ham for Christmas dinner, but today I would share something special with her family. Mark had one of the young goats killed, which made me hungry just thinking about eating curried goat. I was surprised to learn that we would be eating the lungs and intestines of the goat. Beatrice said that once the goat was killed, the small intestines were cleaned thoroughly. They were used to wrap around the small pieces of goat lung and were sautéed until tender. She said that we were also having roasted chicken, several dishes made with greens, onions and tomatoes and, of course, nsima. We all sat down to eat, and I was pleasantly surprised at how good the goat lungs tasted. I think I ate more of that dish than anything else.

As we talked, Beatrice asked me about my family, and if my parents were still living. I said that they were. I told her that my father was a furniture factory worker until he became disabled. He then took a janitorial job at a state home for disabled children. My mother was a school dietitian until the work was too much for her. She then got a job working with disabled children at a state-supported school. They were both still working because they were in their fifties and too young to retire. Beatrice remarked that it was good that we had a retirement system that provided for our elderly. I said that most Black folks were not that fortunate and had to live on Social Security, which did not provide a lot of financial support. Beatrice said that the only social security system they had in Malawi, and most of Africa, was what children provided for their parents. That was why people had so many children. She said women had a lot of children because some would not survive childhood. So if a woman had seven or eight children, that was considered a safety net for their old age. Mark said that was why it had been so difficult to do family planning in Malawi. People just would not listen to recommendations to limit their families when the government did not provide an alternative form of support for their old age.

We talked well into the evening when I said that I would have to get ready to leave for home. It had been a good holiday and I enjoyed spending it with my wonderful friends.

A New Year, 1969

A whole year had passed since I arrived in Malawi. It was hard to believe that I had less than a year left on my tour of duty.

The Rainy Season

Rain, rain and more rain! There was flooding in the river valleys in the southern part of the country. I was fortunate that my house was on high ground, but that did not eliminate the many problems caused by the rain. My house was located on a hill that was ever so slightly inclined toward the house. When it rained, water naturally flowed toward the house. I dug a trench in front of the house to allow the water to go to either side, but when we had heavy downpours, the water flowed over the trench and into my house. I just opened the front door and allowed the water to continue out the back door. Problem solved. But the roads were a more serious problem. Sometimes roads were impassable because of streams flowing freely across them. Once when I was traveling with a group of agriculture staff members in the Lower Shire Valley, our Land Rover got stuck in the mud. We were there for more than four hours. Later that day, we came across a bridge that had been flooded with at least one foot of water flowing across it. Crossing the bridge was necessary for us to get home, so we took a chance. For a moment, I thought the car would stall, but it didn't, and we made it across. I realized what a mistake that was, but fortunately we made it.

On a daily basis, the worst for me was getting home. Once I left the main highway, I had another mile of road leading to my home at Mpemba. I had to cross a small bridge over what usually was a trickle of water, but during the rainy season, the water was often as high as the bridge and sometimes over it. We had been isolated a couple of times because the bridge was impassable. For most of the month, I had not been able to open my front door because it had swollen and jammed due to the high humidity.

During the rainy season, the roads were generally muddy all over the region with the exception of roads in Blantyre and the road to Zomba and Limbe. Otherwise, most of the roads I had to travel were dirt roads that were sandy during the dry season and very muddy during the rainy season.

Being a Peace Corps Volunteer

I worried about how my motorcycle would hold up since it already had 15,000 miles—not that I drove that many miles myself. It must have had at least half that amount when the cycle was assigned to me. The Peace Corps mechanic was still mad at me for allowing the oil to drain out of the engine and the motor to lock. I was not sure how the engine of the cycle got cracked, which caused the oil to leak. At any rate, while I was driving in Mulanje, my engine froze and locked. I had to put the gears in neutral and push the bike to the nearest outpost where I called the regional agriculture office to get transportation to Blantyre. By the time I delivered the cycle to the Peace Corps warehouse, Robert Johnson, the mechanic, was furious that I had not taken better care of my bike. I think that he believed all of us volunteers were pampered and didn't appreciate what we had. Robert reluctantly assigned me another motorcycle, but he was not happy.

I was notified by the Peace Corps office that our second annual conference would take place just outside of Blantyre at a retreat generally used by expatriates but was now open for use by all, including Africans. I attended one conference, which was OK, but now I felt it would be a waste of my time. I already told the staff that I would not be participating. Howard, our assistant director, was pretty sensitive and I liked him and his wife a lot. He has asked me to write the cross-cultural programs for the next agricultural group coming in. I was honored that he asked me and would begin thinking about what I was going to put in it. I thought I would eventually go up to the lake at our hostel there for an extended weekend. This would give me the opportunity for some downtime to think about Howard's request.

The work at the office accelerated soon enough. We were getting a new offset press. It would greatly improve the quality of our production of extension aids materials. Sometimes I wished I had one of the field jobs. From what I had witnessed in the field, there was not a lot of pressure to get things done. The volunteers in the field generally followed Malawi or African time. Things would get done when they got done. No timetables here. However, I'm not sure that I would have the same sense of accomplishment working in the field as I had working in the extension aids office. I didn't like being an administrator because it involved having to deal with so many personnel issues. Once I got used to all of the inconveniences of working in a developing country and accepted Malawi time as my modus operandi, my anxiety decreased substantially.

With 10 months to go until my term was completed, I was setting some goals for myself for the rest of the year. I planned to continue training staff, and I may have been optimistic, but I still looked forward to getting a Malawian who would take over when I left. I had to get training on how to operate the offset press. I hoped that I would get a new staff person who could take the training with me rather than me taking the training and then training my staff.

I thought about applying to the University of Chicago where I could study under John Hope Franklin. I had planned to go to graduate school after college. While working for the Hyde Park YMCA in Michigan, I arranged to go to Chicago to meet with Dr. Franklin. When I finally arrived at the end of the summer, he had gone to Europe and asked Richard Wade if he would interview me. I had also thought about studying under C. Vann Woodson at Yale. Other options included the University of Wisconsin, the University of California and of course the University of North Carolina. All these schools had good programs or faculty in African American history. Alternatively, I thought about a job in another host country as a Peace Corps employee. In spite of my feelings toward the Peace Corps initially, being a volunteer had been a good experience for me. I also appreciated the support I received when needed. I planned to finish collecting African artifacts to send home for family and friends. I certainly did not want to have to travel with loads of stuff. So my plan was to ship home what I had collected. Depending on when the package was mailed, I might actually beat the box home because I would be shipping everything by surface mail.

I sent a brief letter home telling my parents how disappointed I was that I had not heard from anyone during the holidays, not even a Christmas card. Although I enjoyed Christmas with my Malawi friends, I still felt bad that I did not receive anything from home. I had not received a letter since early December. When I did not hear from home for a long time,

I thought that something might be wrong and then I began to worry. Barbara was very thoughtful. She sent me money to buy myself something for Christmas. She was very kind in that way.

The government added another hour to our workday. It wouldn't be a problem for me since I put in more hours than required anyway.

Raising Farm Animals

Some time ago, Tom and I decided that we would raise some chickens. The Agricultural Department had started a breeding program to encourage farmers to mate their new breeds with their village chickens to improve their stock. Tom and I purchased 10 chickens to raise to serve as examples for the local villagers and as food for us. We lost two chicks when we were invaded by the soldier ants. We had also purchased two goats to raise for food since we both became very fond of goat meat. After the incident with the hyena, I suggested to Tom that he keep the chickens and goats in the spare bedroom in his house. To my surprise, he agreed. So each morning, he let the chickens and goats out to roam in the yard and in the evening he put them back into the house. One day, I happened to investigate the bedroom and found the place filthy with chicken and goat droppings. Tom did not seem to mind and neither did I.

Over time, we killed all of the chickens and ate them. The goats were another matter. When it came time to kill the goats, we captured one and proceeded to cut its throat with what turned out to be a dull knife. The goat started screaming for dear life. It must have been pretty painful because I even felt sorry for the goat. The other goat broke loose and started running for its life. Everson, our neighbor, the agricultural driver and everyone else chased the goat throughout the yard, across the field, up and down a nearby hill until finally Everson caught it by its hind legs and brought it back to the house. Our neighbor went to his house and brought back a machete and promptly chopped off the heads of both goats. We hung the goats and skinned and dressed them, something neither of us had done before. We shared some of the meat with our friends and neighbors, wrapped two legs and froze them in our freezer and barbecued the rest for the expanded dinner party.

One of the older employees of the department asked that we save the heads for him. We placed the two heads on a shelf outside of the carriage house. There they stayed until Monday morning when the driver returned to collect his heads. I was sure that they were good and ripe by then.

Since returning from East Africa, I had really become an Afrophile. I loved being in East Africa and could easily live there. I told Barbara how much I loved the continent, how I wanted to major in African history and return probably to Kenya to teach. Her response was disappointing. She told me that Black people in the States were in as much need as Africans and that she wanted to devote her life to helping our people. She explained that she just could not identify with Africans and African culture beyond an intellectual level. Although I was committed to the Civil Rights movement, I now saw myself living in Africa, where I would be among the majority. It felt great not being a minority for once. Even though I loved the people of Malawi, this country was going to have to change a lot for me to want to live here. Banda was so pro–White to the detriment of African advancement and African nationalism. East Africa was such an eye-opener for me.

Snakes and Pot

I found another snake in the house. I hated snakes but maybe not as much as Doug MacDonald. At any rate, I had difficulty getting the snake out of the house, and again, Thako was no help at all. It poured every day in January. Roads were in terrible shape. It was hard for me to ride my cycle and stay upright. I got mud all over my clothes, and when passing a car or lorry, I had to be especially careful because they spewed liquid mud all over the place. I had a tent-shaped canvas cape that I wore to keep me somewhat dry.

Barbara told me in her latest letter that she was thinking about getting an Afro. I thought that that would be neat. I told her that she should have the cloth I sent made into an African dress and really look like a high-fashion African model. I hinted in my letter that she would really be hip if she was smoking a little pot. Of course, I could not write that in a letter because of the Peace Corps rules against smoking pot. Many volunteers I knew smoked. They even brought me some on occasion. The first time I had pot here, the stuff was so mild that you had to roll your cigarette the size of a large cigar to get even mildly home.

I was in trouble with the Peace Corps again. Todd Mayes had left as our director. He was a good guy and very committed to the Peace Corps programs. He was replaced by Ed Marsh who appeared to be right off a Midwest farm. Many thought that he was gregarious, but I thought that he was crude. My first issue with Ed was when he decided to give up his suburban house and move into the African community. These township houses were small by Western standards but quite large by Malawi standards. They were designed for middle-class administrators either in government or the private sector. The houses had a living room, kitchen, and two to three bedrooms depending on the size of the family. When Ed decided that he and his wife would move into the African community

Chapter Three. Second Year in Malawi

housing, he asked for and received permission to move into a duplex where they tore down the walls separating the two units and combined them into one large house. Although I'm sure he was trying to identify with the host-country nationals, what that move meant to me was they ended up denying housing to not just one but two Malawi families. This colored my relationship with him. There were things about him that I just didn't like.

Soon after Ed arrived and took over as director, someone reported to him that some volunteers were smoking pot. I am not sure if an investigation was done, but Ed ended up ordering them to be sent home. My friend Dick was one of the volunteers sent home. Dick was in our group and was our cotton representative in the Lower Shire. He lived in a small trailer and was totally dedicated to his work, spoke Chichewa and was a part of the community in which he lived. He was the epitome of what the Peace Corps wanted its volunteers to be. Unfortunately for Dick, he started smoking pot with other locals in the community. To me, it was no more than sharing local homemade beer with Malawians that I often have done. When I thought about what Dick stood for as a volunteer and what Ed represented as the Peace Corps director, I became furious. I thought that it was totally unfair for Ed to send Dick and the other volunteers home, especially on such short notice. My first thought was to organize fellow volunteers, beginning with my group, to protest Ed's action and attempt to get him to reverse his decision. Drawing from my experiences with direct action tactics and sit-ins in the States, I suggested that we compile and present a series of demands and reforms that we wanted the Peace Corps to make and take over the Peace Corps office until our demands were met. I thought that we should demand that the volunteers who were sent home be reinstated, or we would resign en masse. To my surprise, no one would join me. I believe my fellow volunteers thought that I was too radical and did not want to get involved. I was terribly disappointed and began to feel that I could not depend on my fellow volunteers to do what was right. These were the kind of milquetoast liberals no one could depend on when the going got rough. People liked to complain and bitch about every little thing, but when it came to making meaningful change, they were nowhere to be found. I felt that if no one was willing to take risks, then why should I, as a Black volunteer, take the risks alone. After all was said and done, Dick was a White volunteer. Yet, regardless of race, how could I be quiet? Dick was a friend. I decided that I would have to take a principled stand. I would put into writing just how I felt about the situation. The following is a copy of the letter I sent to the director of the Peace Corps office:

12 February 1969

Dear Mr. E. Marsh,

There are certain things that must be spoken if one is to remain true to oneself and one's friends. Thus I find myself writing you this letter, not with the expectation of getting results but out of an urgency derived from the loss of a friendship. As an addendum, I will discuss a few of the problems with the Peace Corps as an organization as I see them and what I think can be done to correct them. Please keep in mind as you read this letter that it is not a personal attack on you or your staff, for I have no strong feelings toward any of you either way. Please accept the following as suggestions or just food for thought. Sorry to have to admit that if I had my way, these would not come to you in the form of suggestions but as demands to be backed up by threats of mass resignations. Unfortunately, there were few volunteers interested in forcing (sorry to have to use that word, but institutions as part of the establishment never make meaningful change without some sort of coercion) real change at the risk of upsetting their neat little lives. (As a means of interjection, I think it is sad that volunteers do not see enough wrong with the status quo to vocalize their concerns to you, much less demand that some real changes be made.) Thus, we find a situation where many volunteers speak of their discontent with staff and Peace Corps policy, but no one is interested enough to do anything about it. So even though there are many volunteers who feel that they would like to see the directorship changed, rest assured that their apathy will leave you secure in your job.

    I don't believe that the staff really has the interest of the volunteers at heart. Being Black myself, I had never felt that the Peace Corps would offer me any meaningful support, the organization being what it is and Malawi being the country that it is. The corps is extremely unresponsive to volunteer concerns. The volunteer not only must suffer the capricious actions of individual staff members, but also they must bend to the whimsical inclinations of the staff's personal morals or what have you. Now let's begin with a fact. At least 80% of the volunteers in Malawi smoke pot and this can be verified by asking any volunteer to give you an estimate of the number. Certainly, the staff does not live in a vacuum and must be aware of this. This being the case, I and other volunteers fail to see how Dick Caldwell and the Clarkes can be punished for what is tacitly accepted by the staff. This seems to be an example of arbitrary "justice" to enforce, without warning a directive against smoking pot that heretofore has not been enforced. Dick is one of the best volunteers in the country. But the organization being what it is, you, no doubt, never took this into consideration. In this case and in future cases involving discipline, I think that a committee of volunteers should be established to determine what actions, if any, are necessitated. Arbitrary action meted out by an older generation is the sort of thing young people in the States are trying to destroy. It is time that our organization stopped deciding what is best for us. Just look at the mess your generation has created from World War II to the present. Some of us realize the propensity for repeating the same mistakes. Certainly, the protests over the war in Vietnam concerns the basic issue of not having the people involved making the decisions. It is far more tolerable for us to suffer for our own mistakes than to suffer at the hands of someone making the mistakes for us. Certainly, your generation has created a world for us that we neither want nor will tolerate. Peace Corps is an organization I thought would honor the principles of self-determination, but your actions certainly do not verify this notion. Certainly, your actions concerning Dick were grounded in the system you found here when you

Chapter Three. Second Year in Malawi

came, so what I am doing is not only questioning your action but the system itself. I fail to see why or how an organization based in Washington, thousands of miles from here and other Peace Corps countries, can direct the policies of those countries. I suggest to you that this committee of volunteers, mentioned above, be permitted to screen all directives from Washington and the Blantyre office to evaluate their effectiveness and applicability to the Malawi situation and individual volunteer situation.

Some Peace Corps staff take the attitude that the organization was established for their benefit and it should serve them first and volunteers second. Above and beyond this, the organization requires that each volunteer undergo rigorous screening before he or she is allowed to assume duties in a country. The same should be applied to staff. There is no reason why a staff person, upon being selected by Peace Corps Washington, should be automatically confirmed in his position. The volunteers should have some say as to the suitability of the staff in relation to his job, to the volunteers themselves and to the host-country nationals. As there is no stigma against de-selection of volunteers, staff should also take the viewpoint that no stigma should be attached to them if, after a trial period, volunteers find them to be unsuitable for this type of service.

There should not be another group of Peace Corps volunteers to come to Malawi without the approval of the group they are to replace. No formal action should be taken until this approval has been received from the volunteers. The foundation, as a guide for staff, for any new group should be supplied by volunteers and then detailed, worked out by the staff.

These are my thoughts to you to be disposed of as you see fit. I don't expect you to accept them with open arms, for if experience is worth anything, you will probably react in a hostile manner, which is your right. I hesitate to add but will for your own enlightened knowledge that you are resented by a large number of volunteers. Whether the removal of Dick and the Clarkes is enough to exacerbate this resentment, I do not know. I do know that some enlightened policies should soon be coming from the Peace Corps office.

Signed,

John E. Fleming

I sent the letter to Ed at the Peace Corps office via my messenger. Ed's reaction was immediate and furious. He called me on the phone and demanded that I come down to the office. By the time I got to the office, he had lost all self-control. He ranted and raved for over a half hour. Initially, I did not say anything. I kept my cool and just listened. I took up for Dick as best I could. With Dick and the other volunteers having left the country and after the director and I had talked for a while, Ed finally said that he may have been hasty in rushing them home but that he was following the Peace Corps policy of no tolerance for drugs. I told him that I did not think that pot was a drug, but we just differed on that interpretation. He did agree that in future situations, he would give a volunteer a fair hearing before rushing to judgment. When I left, I knew that I had destroyed any relationship that I might have had with Ed. But that was OK. I had very little contact with the office anyway, so I would barely notice any ill will Ed would harbor toward me.

I decided not to take a vacation this year but instead take a four-day weekend on the lake. Since the Department of Agriculture owned the property, it would not cost me anything except gas to get there by motorcycle and food. I always bought the local vegetables and of course the beloved chambo fish. I heard that there were over 700 species of fish in the lake, but I liked chambo the best. This was what I call a really cheap but very pleasant weekend.

Thoughts on Modesty

Will the rain never end? I went to work in the rain and returned home in the rain. There was nothing to do in the evening but listen to the rain fall on the metal roof. The visit to the lake with Tom and Doug went well. We bought lots of beer, smoked a little weed and ate lots of fresh fish. We bathed and swam in the lake early in the morning and relaxed under the palm and pawpaw trees during the heat of the day. It gave me a chance to rest and catch up on some of my reading. Sometimes I walked along the lakeshore and saw women washing their dishes and clothes. On occasion, men would undress and bathe in the lake. Women were much more modest than men. I never saw a woman bathe. Even though they were very modest by Western standards, Malawi women often do not cover their breasts. Going bare breasted was a practice that the various religious denominations had tried to discourage. They wanted these women to conform to Western standards of morality or modesty. Women here saw their breasts as part of their bodies to feed and nourish their babies. We in the West have made breasts sex objects. Sometimes in the presence of Europeans, a woman covered her breasts, especially if she saw a European man staring at her.

Our New Offset Press

As soon as I returned from the lake, I knew that I had a lot of work before me. We had just received an offset press so that our work would be more efficient and our publications looked more professional. I estimated that our workload would triple in the future. I had my first class on how to use an offset press at the headquarters in Zomba. I didn't think that I could run a press based on what I learned there. It was a good thing that the Rhodesian salesman was willing to work with me to teach me how to operate the press. I had Mr. Ntungama participate in the remaining lessons since he would be the operator of the offset press. I was surprised at how nice the salesman was considering that he was originally from South Africa. I suppose that people would be nice and less racist when they were in a Black-majority country. I just knew that he was willing to work with us so that we produced the best-quality publications we could. I wanted this office to shine and to show the expatriates that Africans could produce publications at the highest level. I was as much a product of my upbringing as anyone else. My high school math teacher, Mr. McIntosh, told us constantly that to succeed in the future with White people, we had to be better in order to be considered as "good" as White people. This was reinforced throughout the years I attended our segregated Olive Hill High School. All our teachers were aware of how difficult it would be for us to be successful in a segregated America. We were told that it did not matter if you were a professional or a janitor, we should always be the best at whatever we do. I tried to follow this advice all of my life. So I applied this philosophy to my work in Malawi.

Thoughts on Race and Race Relations

Richard Nixon had now settled in as president. Who would have thought this would happen so soon after the presidencies of John Kennedy and Lyndon Johnson? I was suspicious of Johnson as a southerner. I think Johnson's civil rights record, even with being a southerner, made him a good president, but he allowed the war in Vietnam to bring down his administration.

The Black Power movement had just been getting underway when I joined the Peace Corps. The Democratic Convention was torn apart by mass demonstrations. I guess all of this contributed to an atmosphere that led to the election of Nixon. It had been very hard for me and the few other Black Peace Corps volunteers here to have to deal with apartheid spilling over into Malawi and then having to deal with a conservative Republican elected as president at home. We needed a president who had a vision for the future in which all people were treated equally. I had always been opposed to the Vietnam War and all wars on principle. The Black Power movement was making me rethink my position on the use of nonviolent protest. Would I fight on the side of the Black Panthers if a race war broke out in the United States? What would I do if there were a race war in South Africa? I felt that Nixon would intervene on behalf of the Whites in South Africa if a race war broke out there. In my last letter to Barbara, I reflected on our history of oppression and so much was now happening in terms of race and race relations that I was unwilling to take any shit from any White people either in this country or back home.

Mike Clark wrote me a letter letting me know that he was living in Tennessee and seeking conscientious objector status. I didn't know that Mike was a pacifist when we were at Berea, but times changed. He certainly was one of the organizers of Berea's involvement with the march from Selma to Montgomery. I got the impression that his family might have disowned him for his involvement in that movement, which made me admire him even more for his stand. I seemed to be questioning my own position on non-violence in terms of Black–White relations. We, as Black people, were expected to forgive and forget, but how much and how many times must we forgive? Were we to overlook all the atrocities that have been heaped on us all of these centuries? The more I read about what was happening in the States in terms of race relations, the angrier I got.

The Peace Corps office staff seemed a little upset when I refused for a second time to attend the annual in-country Peace Corps conference. They begged my other Black counterpart to attend to give a semblance of an integrated conference, but he also refused. So they were left with an all–White conference. They needed at least one of us to add some color to the event. White people avoided integration all of these years and were now pleading with us to integrate. It sort of reminded me of my first year at Berea. If a Black student tried to integrate a table of White students sitting in a dining room or at a snack bar, the Whites would get up en masse and move. It became a running joke with the Black students. If we entered a room where there were no vacant tables, one of us would just go up and sit down at a table with White students. Immediately, everyone would get up and free the table for the remaining Black students to sit down. Now that some of us prefer to be around our own people in our own institutions, they beg us to integrate.

I had been reading Eldridge Cleaver and felt like I needed to go home right away and become part of the movement. I really had to think about my future and the work that I wanted to do and the work that needed to be done in the States.

On Becoming Malawian

I got another letter from Barbara in which she had given me some sound advice. She knew how hard I had been working. I explained to her that as much as I liked being in Malawi, there was something about the culture here that was different from the culture back home. Her advice was to slow down and adjust to the way things were done here and not try to impose my values on people from a different culture. Although I thought Barbara's response was sensible, it was easier said than done. I was raised by a father who had three jobs to support his family. He taught me the value of work, which was reinforced by the work study program at Berea College. Even though I knew that some of the Western values were foreign to my colleagues, it was my goal to instill some of these work habits in them before I left. I was proud of my work, and I wanted my staff to be proud of our work. A couple of my staff members didn't particularly care if their work was finished on time, while I believed in producing a good product and getting it done on time. I knew that people always talked about "African time," meaning that it would get done when it got done. I tried to be a good role model by working hard, coming in early and leaving late, but sometimes I thought that my staff viewed me as a crazy Westerner.

Now that I had been accepted in my village area, people just dropped by and stayed and stayed. They just sat there being "company." I didn't seem to have a lot of privacy or time to call my own. At first, this really bothered me, but I had come to accept the practice as part of living here. I really liked, in theory, the idea that my home was their home and they were free to come and go as they pleased.

Getting Married

When I received Barbara's letter indicating that she wanted to get married when I returned to the States, I could hardly believe my eyes. Barbara had been my confidante and I had burdened her with all my issues. I was now surprised that she agreed to formally get married. It made me the happiest man in the world. I was so excited. I immediately wrote to my parents to let them know the good news. I told my aunt Lucille. I was sure she would be happy to know that I was marrying a good Catholic girl; I needed to ask Barbara if she was still a practicing Catholic. Now I had to rethink all of my plans for graduate school. Barbara thought that we ought to consider Howard University in Washington, D.C. I had not thought about Howard, but it was a fine, historically Black university located in a majority Black city. This was something to really think about. My sister was in D.C., and I had a number of cousins in the area. It might not be such a bad idea. If I had to face readjustments to American culture, it might as well be in a majority Black city.

For now, I needed to concentrate on my work here. There was so much to do and to accomplish before I left Malawi. I thought my years as a Berea College student provided me with a good work ethic. Afterall, we all had to manage working, going to class and studying, which meant that we had to be organized. I now arrived at work at 7:00 a.m. and stayed until 6:00 p.m. As I looked to the fall, I realized that my time was getting short. On top of everything else, I had agreed to do the cross-cultural studies program for the next group of volunteers arriving in the country. The project would give me a little extra money in addition to my $1,200 readjustment allowance I would have when I got home. I was now looking forward to getting home. That was not to say that I was not enjoying my work and living in Malawi, but I would have been here for two years by fall. The rains kept coming and not letting up. Sometimes it rained so hard that I undressed and took a shower in the downpour. The rain had not kept the mosquitoes at bay; in fact, they were worse than ever. I was either seeing mosquitoes in the office or tsetse flies. I thought some of them carried sleeping sickness, but I was not sure which ones. I knew firsthand from experience that the mosquitoes here carried malaria.

Missionaries, Fish and Coconut Cake

I went to Fort Johnston on a short holiday by myself. I told Barbara in my last letter about the mission there and how I almost was assigned there by the Anglican Church. I was really glad that that did not work out. I would have hated working with missionaries. After I wrote that statement, I thought how strange it sounded. I came to Africa for the experience of working here and to decide if I wanted to be a missionary. Unconsciously, I guess I had made the decision that I did not want to be a missionary after all. It was a decision that evolved over time. I even wondered if the good that missionaries did was outweighed by the bad. After all, they opened the doors for the slave trade and the colonization and exploitation of Africa and Africans.

I thought that I had made the right choice in becoming a Peace Corps volunteer. As it was, I was free to go and come as I pleased within reason. I thought my work was making a small difference. The holidays at the agricultural station on the lake were just what I needed. I had the available days to take off by not taking a vacation my second year. It cost me about $2 for the three days that I was there. I took some cheese, bread and coffee and bought the local chambo fish. I purchased a big fish for about 12 cents. I picked all the fruit I needed from the local trees surrounding the huts. I collected ripe coconuts, oranges, grapefruits, lemons and pawpaws. Where else in the world could you have a three-day vacation for $2?

I liked to entertain, especially as I refined my cooking skills. I invited six people over for lunch at the plantation house so I could use the wood-burning stove with the oven. I started cooking on Wednesday. Using Fannie Farmer's cookbook and remembering how my grandmother and Aunt Annie made their Christmas cake, I made a three-layer coconut cake with white double-boiler icing. I also cooked a roast, barbecued a chicken and baked lots of whole-wheat bread. It was not convenient to have to go down to Tom's house to use the oven for the baking. I got up at 5:00 a.m. to make sure everything was perfect. The dinner went well and everyone seemed to have enjoyed themselves, but I was exhausted.

Chapter Three. Second Year in Malawi

Living and Working as a Volunteer

My mail finally came through, or at least my family had started writing more. I knew my parents were anxious for me to come home. I had not told them yet that I planned to travel in Africa and Europe on my way home. And, of course, I would be spending some time with Barbara in New York.

Office work was going well. Even with a larger staff, we were still eating our lunches together in the office. It certainly helped me save money. We all contributed equally, but I gave our messenger a little more so he could buy maize flour for the nsima and dried fish with tomatoes and onions. Mr. Kapanela did all the market shopping and the cooking, so he did not have to contribute to the fund. We all ate from a communal table. Every now and then, I would join another volunteer at a local English café that specialized in hamburgers. They were the traditional English hamburgers that were half meat and half cereal. Add the hamburger bun and you ended up with mostly grain. I much preferred the samosas, which were the best I had ever had. They cost only three cents each, so I usually had three for lunch.

Easter had come and gone with nothing special happening here. The rains had finally let up, and the weather was very pleasant before we had to face the cold season in the summer. Volunteers felt free to stay with us at Mpemba whenever they were in town. I suppose it was not a problem to house and feed volunteers from my group. After all, they were my friends. Tom and I each kept track of what we paid for food each month and then we settled up at the end of the month. I guess that volunteers must have thought that we were running a free hotel. Providing room was not a problem, but feeding these folks on our meager Peace Corps allowance was a little much. We needed to let the Peace Corps volunteers know that in the future, no more freebies.

I had planned to go up to the lake for a few days but had to make an unexpected field trip to Zomba. I had to drive 50 miles in pouring rain. It was always dangerous to ride a motorcycle to Zomba where the highway has only one lane of tarmac. Some Malawians driving cars seemed to feel that they were entitled to the whole road. In such cases, I had no choice but to leave the tarmac and get on the dirt part. Moving from paved to dirt road was dangerous and was more of a problem when it was raining. I was thankful that I made it safely. I generally stayed at John Hunter's house in the African township and shared the cost of food when necessary. There were lots of bars around with good West African highlife music and songs from the Congo. John was at least six feet three inches and he just loved to dance. After a few beers, John and his Malawi friends and I ended up on the dance floor with the local bar girls.

After spending two days of work in Zomba, I was called back to the office because of the workload. I was pleased with the progress of staff training and the work we were putting out. We were completing our most ambitious project to date, an 80-page cotton manual for the department. I guess our reputation was getting around because the regional health office asked us to produce 30,000 copies of a health handout. Even though I liked to stay busy, I didn't want to overwork. I remembered how I pushed myself at Berea to get out in three years and ended up a nervous wreck. I finally had to seek the counsel of our resident dorm director, professor of philosophy and former missionary George Noss. I always remembered how Dr. Noss got out of bed and made me a raw egg milkshake and took time late at night to counsel me and reassure me until I had calmed down. Now that I was in Africa and didn't have anyone here to counsel me and to look after my mental health, I had to do it myself, which meant not overworking to the point where I was mentally exhausted.

The week before, I got a chance to see Philibert Tsiranana, president of Madagascar, who was visiting President Banda. I happened to be traveling when I ran into the president's motorcade. Of course, all traffic had to stop, including those of us on motorbikes and bicycles. The weather could not have been better for a state visit. I didn't really know much about Madagascar other than that it was off the coast of East Africa. I thought that President Tsiranana might have been conservative like Banda. Banda was very pragmatic and did not mind cozying up to the White leaders of South Africa and Southern Rhodesia. But it was only a matter of time before even these countries gained their independence too, and when that happened, what would Banda do then?

Of all the staff at the Peace Corps office, I liked Howard Carter the best. A couple of months ago, Howard asked me to write a narrative about volunteer cross-cultural experiences here in Malawi. I wrote the following essay for him to explain my feelings about being a Peace Corps volunteer in this post-colonial country.

"On Being a Volunteer in Malawi" (copy of the essay I sent Howard Carter, deputy director of the Malawi Peace Corps, 1969)

> Upon first being selected to participate in the Agricultural Training Programs for Malawi, I was forced to think seriously as to my role in a country that was billed as a country controlled by racists with an orientation to South Africa. Yet there was a strong desire to come to Malawi, the country being one of the poorest on the continent, the need here for volunteers being the greatest. I, being dichotomized from the beginning, had continued an inner debate as to whether I could continue in the country, all things considered, where I had to be constantly on my guard as to how I would react to situations that might get me deported.

Chapter Three. Second Year in Malawi 163

I have now been in Malawi for over 16 months. When I arrived, I felt a mixture of emotions as a Black man emanating from the expatriates' behavior and attitudes I encountered. The reaction of the expatriates in the Regional Office was "let's wait and see what this man can do." My fellow officers did not do all that they could have to help me establish the Extension Aids Officers. I was given a small room which was scarcely suitable for an office much less any sort of working space. Socially I was "accepted" along with the other volunteers, but as soon as we indicated that we did not come to Malawi to have Europeans completely monopolize our social lives, this particular unpleasant social pressure dropped. Being sensitive to racial behavior, I found myself in a position of having to stand up for Malawians when treated inhumanely by expatriates and then found that some of the expatriates were treating me the same way. But they found that I would not tolerate their insinuations and sneers. I was outspoken and found myself in a few disagreements. Not during any of these times did I hesitate to hide my feelings from Malawians in the office.

As I gradually learned what was expected of me and what my particular duties were, my work greatly improved and as a result, I received the respect of the expatriate officers. As a result I was automatically placed in a position of influence compared to their attitudes and behavior toward Malawians. The Volunteers in the Regional Office tended to show by example that all people should be treated equally. For instance, when we came to the country, we were invited by some expatriates to participate in various social functions. Most of these groups were "snow White" which tended to make me not want to attend. All social functions I sponsored initially were 95% Black. On a few occasions, I invited some expatriates. Thus, a situation was created where Africans and Europeans were placed in a social environment. Some were not at ease at first, but as soon as they saw how comfortable others were, they relaxed. It was my opinion that Volunteers in the Department bridged the gap between Africans and expatriates. Today, one can find expatriates inviting Africans to parties and other social gatherings.

We, as Volunteers, never missed an occasion where we, no matter how indirectly, indicated our feeling toward Africanization. This has not created a situation where the expatriates were leaving en masse, but in at least two situations, it has spurred two men into thinking about the subject and reflecting upon how long they should remain here.

I had very strong feelings on Africanization and indicated that my job should not be replaced by a Volunteer, nor should it be replaced by an expatriate. I wrote into my job description that part of my job would be to train Malawians in the office and recruit a diploma student to become Extension Aids Officer. This will be the first time an African has held an Officer's post in the Southern Regional headquarters. This was an uphill struggle all the way but a significant breakthrough. The Southern Region has traditionally been the last stronghold of Europeans.

My relationships on the job and socially had been almost exclusively with Malawians. In the office we work together on a first name basis, this being something new since most expatriates require "Mr." before their names. Most people had come to consider me as their friend and thus we were able to converse with each other as if we were two Africans talking. There was a free exchange of ideas which more often than not included political discussions. Certainly, the very least that can be said of these discussions, was that the Malawians I know were more politically conscious and were aware that everything said by the government should not be taken as the "gospel" truth. My favorite ploy was to introduce Malawians to certain books in my library and let our discussion begin from there. This was not to say that I had actively participated in politics, but only to say that my friends had been made aware of what's happening in this country, Southern Africa, Africa, and the world at large. Certainly, they were now able to appreciate what was happening here in Malawi with an added sense of what's happening in the world.

I think that the most important contribution that I was making was letting Malawians see that I treat all people the same, from a Minister to a laborer, from expatriate government officials to fellow Peace Corps volunteers. In no way should a greater amount of respect be given to a person solely because his skin happens to be White, while at the same time African laborers should be respected and not treated as some expatriates do.

No matter how insensitive the worst volunteer might be, Malawians know that the volunteer was different, and they appreciate this difference. If there was anything that Malawians needed, it was self-assurance. Volunteers in Agriculture have come a long way in creating an atmosphere in our department of equality and respect.

Some Inner Thoughts

As I traveled in the field, I had lots of time to think and reflect. I wrote to Barbara before leaving. Since she was a psychology major, I wrote her a long letter hoping that she could help me understand my periodic feelings of depression. Periods of depression had occurred throughout most of my short adult life. When I was a student at Berea, I would feel depressed but usually had no remedies or people to talk with. Whenever this happened, I would sleep a lot, and when I could not sleep, I would take a sleeping pill. After graduating from college, I would use alcohol to mask my feelings of depression, which would last a few days. Now that I was in Malawi, I continued to use alcohol for the same purpose. I couldn't afford to buy European gin, so I drank the Malawi gin made from corn mush. Farmers sold this mush to the Malawi Distilleries Ltd. It was far cheaper to buy, about $1 for a pint. I really didn't like the taste, but it relieved my anxiety. About once a month, I went through a period of being down, low; I guess it was a form of depression. I didn't like being around people when I was feeling low. I found that I had a short temper and often got angry for no reason. And then these feelings would leave as quickly as they came upon me. I was generally happier and often felt elated after the depression episode passed. I guess that this was something that I had to live with. I did not feel comfortable talking to the Peace Corps doctor or anyone else about this. I wanted to share my feelings with Barbara because we planned to be married and she needed to know how I felt sometimes.

With my bout of depression over, everything seemed right in this little corner of Africa. I had decided that I had given all that I could to office work and sensed that it was in good shape. I had come to understand that Western values, which I had tried to instill in the office staff, would eventually come to Africa, for better or worse. There were many good aspects of African life here: communal living, sharing, no one starving, and so forth. The people were so wonderful, cheerful, and genuine. Western work habits would come in time. I thought that I had planted a seed that would grow and flourish as it was watered and nurtured by others once I left the country. I realized my limitations. I could not change the world or even change my little section of it sitting on Kabula Hill. I thought that I have had an impact and felt good about what I had accomplished so far. It was a feeling that now allowed me to be more relaxed about work. I looked forward to enjoying my work more and not feeling so anxious about what I could not change.

Malaria Again

I had a cold for the last two weeks but had kept working. And then I came down with another case of malaria. I was sure I was taking my chloroquine tablets given to us by the Peace Corps doctor. I must not have taken them the week I went down to the Lower Shire Valley where mosquitoes were terrible, especially at night. By the end of the week, I had become terribly sick. I had a temperature of 104 degrees. I did not know how I came down with a case of dysentery. I was home alone all weekend; I didn't even see Tom or anyone else. He must have been traveling. I was too sick to fix anything to eat even if I had felt like eating. There was a cold drizzling rain that fell all weekend. I was going to the toilet day and night. I was either throwing up or having a bowel movement in my toilet, which was no more than a hole in the cement floor. When I had the house constructed, I had the builder dig a large hole, cover it with a concrete floor with a hole in the center and then brick up the exterior. The entrance did not have a door but an inner partition, which kept me hidden from anyone passing by. It was a mistake to put a thatched roof on the top because during a recent heavy rainstorm, it collapsed. I wished I had taken the time to have it replaced. Now I had to continually go to the bathroom in bone-chilling rain without a roof. On Saturday while stooping over the hole, I looked in front of me and saw a small green snake wedged between two bricks. We made a mutual agreement: if you don't bother me, I won't bother you. We both went about our business.

Somehow, I managed to get through the weekend. By Sunday night, my diarrhea had ended, and my temperature slowly began to drop. I don't think that I had ever felt so sick, so alone and so helpless. On Monday morning, I got up enough energy to ride my bike into Blantyre to the Peace Corps office to see the doctor. When I entered the office, the staff gasped. The secretary said, "What in hell happened to you?" I just said that I had been sick. It did not take long for the doctor to see me. He said, based on my medical records, I had lost 15 pounds. That was a lot for me since I weighed only 160 pounds when I entered the Peace Corps. He took my temperature and said that it was still 100 degrees. The doctor gave me medication to control my diarrhea and liquids for my dehydration. He said that I would have to stay off my feet for the rest of the week. He also gave me some sleeping pills to help me sleep at night. After this horrific weekend, I took the doctor's advice and got some rest.

I was slowly recovering and getting my strength back. While I had not been to work, I had been thinking about the future. Last week, Howard had asked me to extend my tour of duty for another year. The extension aids headquarters in Zomba also asked me to stay on for another year. Initially, I said no but agreed to think about it. In spite of staying at a distance from the Peace Corps office, I was still one of the few Black volunteers in the country. I guess that counted for something. After being so sick, I thought that I was ready to go home. There is nothing like being ill and alone to make you homesick. An extension would have kept me from Barbara, and I was more anxious than ever to get home to her. I was already thinking about looking for a job in New York so we could be together. I had no idea how I would adjust to life in such a large city, but I was so excited about getting married. I had already asked my best friend, Ken Cox, to serve as my best man, so I guess I was committed.

I was feeling pretty good now. My appetite had returned and I felt well enough to cook and eat the steaks that Tom purchased from the European market. As I recovered from my illness, I had thought a lot about life here. I was pleased that the office work was going well, even if the workload was increasing. I heard that I was getting my African replacement in July, which gave me a few months to work with him and to slack off from work for a change. I might even get to take some more time off. The Peace Corps office arranged for our termination conference to take place in a game reserve on top of a plateau in the north later this summer. I was trying to bone up on my French in anticipation of visiting francophone African countries and, of course, going to France itself on the way home. There was a lot to do.

I ordered a new 35 mm Canon camera from Hong Kong for my trip home. I wanted to take as many pictures as I could to document my journey. I had been using the office camera for both business and personal use.

By afternoon, a shipment of 135 reams of paper arrived at the office and had to be unloaded and stored. We had been asked to produce 60,000 copies of a tuberculosis handout for the Ministry of Health. Now that we had the new press, we were getting more and more work. I planned to go to the movies tonight to see *North by Northwest*. Even though I had already seen the movie, I was going again just for the relaxation because I had not been to the movies since arriving in the country. The weather would be cold on the way home.

Taking a Half Day Off

I took off from work and came home at noon to get some rest. I wasn't getting a lot of rest these days with so much work at the office. Since we got the offset press, we still had to do our regular work of producing brochures, pamphlets, etc., for the training centers and field staff. The *Southern Advisor* turned out to be a very popular newsletter in the department. Now all the field staff were interested in getting an article in print. That was good, but it still was a lot of work for me. I had to read every article, edit them, type the final draft and burn the plates for the offset press. I was thankful to have Mr. Ntungama in training to help in the production process.

Our office finished printing an 85-page cotton manual. I thought Tom and Doug made a real contribution to this project. I was sure they were pleased. As our reputation grew, other departments were asking us to print materials for them. Our next major project was to publish a 50-page book for the Veterinary Department. The future of the office looked brighter. I understood from Nigel Murphy that they thought they had found someone to replace me as regional extension aid officer. I could hardly explain how much of a struggle this had been. I suppose if I had not insisted on a Malawian replacing me, it might not have happened.

I was thinking more and more about the future. Dad and Mom wanted me to come home or at least go to school closer to home. I was still waiting to hear from various universities where I had submitted applications for admissions. I was thinking more and more about working when I got home and postponing starting school until the fall of 1970. I had experience working for the Kentucky Human Rights Commission. With my publishing work here, I thought I would apply for a position with the New York City Civil Rights Commission in their publication section.

There was a big wedding in the village near my house. It was a two-day celebration. The daughter of a local Malawi merchant was married. The merchant not only owned a number of small stores, but he also had a large lorry and other trucks used in his business. I was not sure exactly all of the things that he did, but from all outward appearances, he was well-off. He had a large house in a compound with large grain storage bins, mainly corn. He had smaller houses surrounding his home where his staff and servants resided. The wedding was held in the local church and the celebration was at his house near here. I was invited and went to the celebration. There was a lot of local beer and gin at the celebration. People did traditional dances with musical instruments. I thought the drums played non-stop for nearly two days. I had gotten used to drum beating at night, so none of this bothered me even after I left the party and went home to bed.

I forgot to send my sister a birthday greeting. I would now have to write her a letter and explain that I just forgot it was her birthday coming up. We were only 11 months apart. Come July 2, we would be the same age for a month. Boy, did Patricia take advantage of that fact when we were growing up. She always liked to tell people we were the same age. As a little boy, I hated that. It was as if she was saying that she was as old and as smart as I was. I did not want to hear that. I think because we were nearly the same age, we were always close and could tell each other anything. I was sorry I missed sending her a card.

Thinking of Home

I got a nice letter from Barbara today. She was concerned about my health and work habits. She strongly suggested that I change my ways. Although I realized that she was right and that I did need to slow down, I probably should not have mentioned to her in such detail about how sick I had been last month. I promised that I would try to slow down, but it takes a while to change human behavior. I was so looking forward to having my replacement on board. There was so much I would like to do and see in Malawi before leaving. I was also reading more and more books on African and African American history. I continued to work on my French lessons. After my long illnesses, I had a new lease on life and a new outlook. I was beginning to enjoy just living in Malawi. Although it was still cold, I was much better off than the average person here. People braved this cold in nothing more than a T-shirt, pants and often no shoes. So I could not complain. I did not have heat in my little house, but at least I had a tight shelter to keep out the cold.

Liz Hunter Visits Her Brother John

John asked me up to Zomba to meet his sister Elizabeth Hunter shortly after she arrived in Malawi. Liz was his younger sister. She had been in Malawi for several weeks. I thought that she must have just graduated from high school. She looked so much younger than John. John said that their parents gave her this trip as a graduation present. It was hard for me to believe that as young as she was, she was allowed to travel thousands of miles by herself. I thought John must have painted a rosy picture of his living conditions. It was obvious that the siblings were very fond of each other. Liz was a very nice young lady and, from what I could tell, had fit into John's living arrangements very well, even without going through Peace Corps cultural training. She had no difficulty eating the food, even nsima. The fortunate thing was that John lived in a township that had toilets, running water and electricity, which made all the difference in the world to a person who was new to the country and culture.

Liz socialized well with people and adjusted to John's lifestyle. She even tried to learn the language, and given time, I was sure she would have been speaking Chichewa fluently. She enjoyed going to the local bars and dancing to the music played by a local Zomba band. Liz turned out to be a good dancer, catching on to African rhythm very quickly. We enjoyed dancing together. She was a lot of fun to be around. However, I thought that she had a crush on me. I had come to like Liz a lot, but I thought that she was too young for me. I had to be careful not to lead her on.

Car Crash

Barbara was working on making sure that my applications were complete to the University of Wisconsin, University of Chicago, University of North Carolina and Howard University. It was complicated trying to get all those applications in with transcripts and references working halfway around the world. I had asked James Holloway, my Berea College philosophy teacher, to serve as one of my references. Dr. Holloway was another of my professors who influenced my thinking in the area of religion and philosophy. When you were in school, you listened to lectures, had class discussions, read and wrote papers not knowing how all the time you were not only absorbing what you were learning but also developing your own philosophy that would stay with you for the rest of your life.

I was involved in another car crash with the Mini Moke. I was not hurt, but there was damage to both the car I drove and the car that hit me. Since I was not at fault, there were no charges against me. I was beginning to feel like a jinx having had so many accidents either in the car or on my motorbike. I didn't believe the Peace Corps officer when he told us that the accident rate for volunteers driving motorcycles was 100 percent. I now believed him but hoped that I was not getting paranoid about it.

I was exploring the possibility of moving into the African township to bring me closer to town. I was tired of living out in the bush with no running water or electricity. It had really been a hardship this winter traveling to and from town in the cold and then living without heat. It really got bad when the chiperone set in. The chiperone was this constant light rain that occurred when the clouds or cold mist descended onto the Blantyre plateau.

I was beginning to wonder if I would have a cold all summer, which was winter here. I didn't seem to be able to kick the one that had been lingering for what seemed like months. I was fortunate that I had a small house because I had no way of heating it. So the warmth given off by my body was the only heat I had in the house. It was also well insulated, which helped. There was a big snowstorm this month in South Africa. I didn't think we would have any snow here, but the temperature might fall into the 40s.

We had four months left on our tour of duty. The Peace Corps was planning a termination conference in August. I guess I would have to participate in that since I had boycotted the other conferences.

Greek Encounter

I met some friends for beer at their house. We then decided to go out to the local bar where I met the other Black Peace Corps volunteer, Ronald Cox. We thought we would check out the local Greek nightclub, La Cabaña. I had not been there before. I tended to stay away from places that charge a lot of money for food and drinks. It was a pretty nice place owned by this heavy-set Greek woman. We sat at the bar and talked for a while about what we planned to do when we got home. I said that I planned to marry my college sweetheart who now lived in New York and worked for IBM. I said that she just got an apartment in anticipation of my return and that I planned to work in the city until I was ready to attend graduate school. Ronald told me that he also planned to get a job teaching in an inner-city school. We both agreed that in spite of all the things we had had to endure, the Peace Corps had been a mostly positive experience for us and that Malawi had truly impacted our lives. We were very much interested in being more involved in improving conditions for Blacks back home. I told him that the only thing I felt qualified to do was work for the New York City Civil Rights Commission since I had experience in this area.

Our conversation was interrupted several times by the Greek owner yelling obscenities at her Malawi employees. She kept telling this one employee how stupid he was. Well, I got fed up with her behavior and had had just enough to drink to ask her why the hell did she think that she could talk to her workers like that. I said that she was acting like a bitch and told her off. That's when the fireworks started. She directed her venom toward me. We traded barbs, and I told her that she needed to go back to where she came from. She told me that she would get me thrown out of the country. Everybody in the club listened to us argue. Finally, my friend dragged me out of the club. As we were leaving, we laughed at the lady and thought she would not have lasted long in a true African country.

I heard that my letter to the Peace Corps magazine criticizing Peace Corps Washington for not being more forceful in taking a stand against apartheid in South African was published. I gave the office credit for publishing a letter critical of its operation. I guess I was going back to my radical ways in anticipation of returning home to the States.

We started celebrating Malawi's independence. We had one more day to party because the celebration lasted for five days. Last weekend, I gave a small party at the house, just a few friends for dinner and wine. The next day, I went to visit my friends, the Chiphwanyas, at their second home in Mark's village near Balaka, about 50 miles away. They had turned out to be my best friends in Malawi.

Reflections on Malawi

Being in Africa has been a wonderful experience despite all of the trials and tribulations. I just wished that Barbara could have been with me at least part of the time and that I could have shared my experiences with my family in Morganton. Nevertheless, I had already started gathering items to send home. I purchased hand carvings and African cloth, anything that I thought they would enjoy and would provide them with a sense of the culture here.

I made so many friends. I was constantly being invited out by someone. Last weekend, I didn't think I spent more than three hours at home except for sleeping. Recently, the weather has been perfect, not too cold for this winter season. The rains have let up and next month we would be getting ready for the dry season. This coming week, I was going to Dedza, on the Mozambique border, to visit the family of my good friend and colleague Mr. Limbani.

I did not go to the Independence Day celebrations in Blantyre as I did last year when I had stood for hours. This year, I tried to get VIP tickets but to no avail. So, during the celebration of the republic, I went down to Ngabu for three days, and while in the Lower Shire Valley, I went to see President Banda install a paramount chief. From what I gathered, during colonial days, the British used chiefs and paramount chiefs to govern indirectly in rural areas. Each village had a headman; groups of headmen were under a chief and several chiefs were under a paramount chief. Evidently, Banda did not disturb the status quo even as he imposed his own rule and administration on the country. Of course, for the ceremony Banda was impeccably dressed in his three-piece suit and overcoat (no matter how hot the weather, he dressed very formally) and his traditional bowler hat and sunglasses. Cecilia Kadzamira, the official hostess of the president, was, as usual, by his side. Banda never married, so he had Ms. Kadzamira to serve as his official hostess. Of course, many of us thought that she was his mistress, but no one would dare say that in public.

The paramount chief exercised a lot of power, but his authority was limited by what the president would tolerate. The chief wore a traditional dress, which contrasted with the president's Western attire. There were many traditional dancers and musicians who performed during the ceremony. The event was important because Banda as the president bestowed power on the chief during the installation. There were other government officials present as well as some from the diplomatic corps. I managed to take some good pictures of the president.

Overall, I was pleased with how things were going in the office. My staff members were now familiar with their jobs and required less supervision than before. Instead of being hands-on all the time, I was now able to devote more of my time to general administration. I really looked forward to having my replacement on board. I understood that he would be reporting for duty next week. I had insisted from the very beginning that my replacement be an African. By the time I left, the entire office would be Malawians. I saw this as a major accomplishment considering that the government was so slow to Africanize, especially in the southern region.

I continued to stay busy but had to spend some time looking for a job in the States. I really needed to have a job if I was going to get married. The pay range for the jobs that I had applied for was $9,000–$13,000. That would be pretty good since when I left the States, I was making only $4,800. I was also thinking that if I was accepted at Howard University, Barbara and I could settle down in Washington, D.C., a majority Black city.

As for the jobs, I applied for a couple of new positions, one as coordinator of foreign student programs at New York University. I think I would like to work with foreign students, having lived and worked overseas. The other was a position as assistant administrative director of a project on the Bowery. Having been away from the States during such a critical period in American history, I wanted to work in the social service area. I had no idea if I had a chance at any of these jobs, but I told my father that I thought my years of service in the Peace Corps would be a plus for my résumé. I had no idea what my local draft board would do when I got out of the Peace Corps. There was the distinct possibility that I could be drafted to do alternative service. This would have an impact on all of the plans I had been making, especially going back to school.

The Southern Advisor

I was pleased with how the *Southern Advisor* had turned out. We were now in our second year of production or volume 2. The July issue began volume 2, number 6 and was dedicated to Malawi Independence. We had a picture of the Independence Arch over the highway leading into Blantyre as a symbol of independence from Great Britain in 1964. The newsletter was designed to serve the needs of the extension staff in the southern region. It went from a small, crude mimeographed newsletter of a couple hundred copies to a sophisticated newsletter produced on an offset press with a circulation of 800 copies per month. It was a real task pulling this off. I remember when I did everything for the newsletter from securing and/or writing the stories, typing, editing, etc., to collating, stapling and finally distributing. The office was fully staffed now. Mr. Ntungama was now in charge of the newsletter, from the typing and initial editing of the articles to overseeing final production. Mr. Chirwa produced illustrations and helped with layout. After learning how to run the offset press, I then taught Mr. Ntungama how to operate it. I was still in the process of teaching him how to develop negatives and print pictures. He became very efficient and creative in the use of the camera in providing images for the newsletter. I was still doing the final editing. I will pass this responsibility on to the new administrator when he arrives.

Troy David wrote "Extension Office Notes" for the field staff as the training officer for the region. He used his column to encourage staff to think through their needs and to plan their work in advance. This was important if they, in turn, were to help the farmers plan in their farm production. Already Troy was encouraging farmers to preserve enough of their groundnut seeds for next year's planting.

Our July issue featured a letter from the permanent secretary, Mr. R.J. Dare, who was retiring this year. He used his letter to the field staff to recap the progress the Ministry of Agriculture had made under his administration. He was particularly pleased with the Lilongwe land development project and the cattle marketing network he had established to market the half million cattle produced throughout the country.

I think he would be remembered for his reforestation programs in which millions of trees were planted to ensure the production of wood for future generations. Since there was no widespread access to electricity, gas or other forms of fuels in Malawi, people had cut down trees for firewood for generations. Secretary Dare's reforestation programs were much needed throughout Malawi.

A feature that I included in the newsletter was called "Do You Know?" which served as a filler for space while providing interesting tidbits of information. I had always depended on the field staff to provide most, if not all, of the articles. As the field staff started sending in information about their families and villages, I added a section called "Bits and Pieces" that included promotions, new births, birthdays, marriages, etc. The agricultural field staff and teachers in the training centers had taken the newsletter very seriously and took pride in the articles they wrote from rice production in the Lower Shire Valley to tea and coffee production in the Mulanje and Thyolo districts. Malawi was slowly moving from large tea plantations to small tea holders. Therefore, the work of our field staff was increasingly important, especially working among small tea farmers in the Mulanje district. News and information from the Tuchila Farm Institute always generated attention. People were interested in knowing what training was scheduled as well as what opportunities for training in the future were available.

Women played a central role in farming in the country and occupied many of the training slots at the institute. I added a section to the newsletter called "Women at Tuchila," which covered such broad areas as home economics and new farming techniques. The articles were now written by Mrs. A.S. Kundecha, wife of one of our area supervisors.

In one issue, we decided to feature the work of Doug MacDonald from the cotton extension office. Doug wrote *The Cotton Manual, a Field Work Guide to Modern Cotton Growing for Agriculture Extension Workers in the Southern Region*. I was very pleased that my office produced the manual for the cotton office. I thought that the extension staff ought to know more about Doug and his work, so we did an article on his fieldwork, especially his work in instructing farmers on the best techniques for cotton production.

Another big program of the department was the national radio programs and listening groups established throughout the country. Not many people in villages could afford their own radios, so the department gave some staff members the responsibility for establishing and coordinating radio listening groups in their areas. The programs were produced in the national extension aids office in Zomba by Simplex Mkandawire, who headed the public relations and communications division. We also included an essay contest for staff where the Times Bookstore in Blantyre provided a one-pound gift certificate to the winner. Although it required some additional work for the staff, the essay contest encouraged them to think about their work in new and creative ways as well as encouraging them to improve their writing skills. The winning essay was published in the newsletter.

The "Down Your Way" section provided an opportunity for staff to let other staff members know what current projects were underway in their areas. "Health and Child Care" served the needs of the ladies in the department who worked with women in the villages to help improve home health care for their children. When Jack Allison recorded his song "Ufa Wa Mtedza" (the peanut flour song), the staff used the song to encourage village women to improve the nutrition of their children by adding groundnut flour to their children's porridge.

I was most proud of the fact that Malawians had been trained to produce the newsletter with little supervision from me. It was my intention from the beginning to work myself out of a job. The problem was that I liked what I was doing when I did not have a staff or a small number of staff. I liked being the photographer developing photos for the newsletter. I even enjoyed editing but not so much the typing and retyping of the newsletter each month. Now I was stuck with mostly administrative work while the staff got to do the creative jobs. I was looking forward to getting my replacement, and then I truly would have worked myself out of a job. My final goal regarding the newsletter was to produce a newsletter cover in color. I thought that this would be the first time this would have been done at the regional level. It would really be significant coming out of an all–African office staff. I needed to secure enough coated paper to produce the color issue. I had about four more months or four more issues to accomplish this.

Trip to Dedza

When the regional agricultural office decided to redevelop Mpemba, the former tobacco plantation, the first thing they did was build houses for area supervisors. Mr. Limbani was a senior area supervisor and lived in one of the larger houses constructed for staff. He was older than I was but looked quite young. He finished the equivalent of our high school and then went to polytechnic for a while before the Ministry of Agriculture sent him to the United States for a certificate in farm administration. He was a student in the graduate programs at North Carolina A&T College. I think having attended school in my home state of North Carolina gave us one more thing in common. Edward was sharp and destined to go far in the department. He was already a senior area supervisor. I suspect that he would one day become a regional officer.

Edward and I became friends immediately. He was one of the first Malawians to invite me into his home to share a meal. Mrs. Limbani included okra among the dishes she prepared but did not expect me to eat it. Okra was considered women's food because it was so slimy. I told Mrs. Limbani that I was from the South where we all ate okra. She added pumpkin leaves to the okra that made it really slimy. So when I was offered some of the cooked okra, I tried to dip it with a spoon, but it kept sliding off the spoon. Finally, I tried pouring it from the bowl and it would not stop running. I ended up cutting it with a knife to stop the flow of slime. Everybody laughed when they saw my plate full of slimy okra. Needless to say, that okra was not easy to pick up using my hand and the nsima. I thought my attempt at eating okra endeared me to Mrs. Limbani. I was always welcomed into her home.

I was extremely honored when Mr. Limbani invited me to visit his family in their home village outside of Dedza. I don't know why I did not ride my bike. Maybe because it was the dry season and the roads were extremely dusty and hard to navigate on a bike. At any rate, I set out on Friday for a trip that was less than 100 miles. I got a ride with a fellow officer from the regional office as far as Zomba.

I was traveling on Malawi 1, the main highway from Blantyre to Dedza. I was confident that it would not take me long hitchhiking, but I was wrong. I must have sat on the road for hours before this black Mercedes stopped and the occupant asked me if I needed a ride. The car was driven by a Malawi driver with a member of the Malawi parliament in the back. I got in the back with the member of parliament. He said that his name was Mr. Banda, unrelated to the president. Mr. Banda asked me if I was a Peace Corps volunteer. I told him that I was and that I worked for the Ministry of Agriculture in Blantyre and that this was my second year in Malawi. He said that I would have to pay him five shillings for the ride. I was really surprised that he wanted to charge me for the ride. Of course this cooled my attitude toward government politicians. Here I was, volunteering to help his people and he charged me for riding with him. It was not as if he had to go out of his way.

I rode with Mr. Banda as far as Balaka, which was his destination. I continued hitchhiking or at least attempting to catch a ride. Again, I was left sitting on the side of a very dusty road in the hot afternoon sun. It must have been close to 6:00 p.m. before a lorry stopped to give me a lift. I was told I could ride in the back with sacks of who knows what piled on the bed. At least I was riding. The driver made a couple of stops before I arrived at the Catholic mission. I got off and thanked the driver.

Getting to my friend's village was another matter. Now it was getting dark, and I had no idea where I was going. I decided to stop at the

White fathers' Catholic mission to inquire about directions or lodging for the night. I knocked on the door of this impressive brick building, and a White priest with a French accent answered the door. I explained my predicament to the priest. I said that I had no idea how to get to my friend's village, especially now that it was night. I asked the priest if I could spend the night there. I was immediately told that I could not. Neither could he provide directions. I was really getting desperate and a little panicky. I inquired about the possibility of sleeping on his porch or even in the church. But the answer was an emphatic *no*.

I went over to the secondary school and knocked on the door of one of the houses provided for teachers. As it turned out, the house was occupied by British volunteers, the United Kingdom's answer to the American Peace Corps. The volunteers were all female teachers and knew the surrounding areas. They were kind enough to provide me with directions to Mr. Limbani's village and loaned me a torch, or flashlight, since it was now dark. I had a little more confidence, but I still had over a mile to travel in the dark with no lights except the light from my borrowed torch. I was ever so grateful for this act of kindness.

I followed the road from the mission that eventually narrowed into what appeared to me like a deep, dark jungle. There was no moonlight, and the vegetation was so thick that I could not even see stars in the night sky. The British volunteers told me that I would have to travel about a mile once the road ended. They did not explain that this would be through a dense jungle. I was terrified to venture into the bush alone, but what was I to do but follow the path? My imagination ran wild with fear that I might encounter a lion or some other wild animal. I could see the headlines now: "American volunteer devoured by a wild lion." I was even more afraid of snakes than a big feline. There were many more snakes in Malawi than man-eating lions. I was thankful for the torch. At least I could see a few feet in front of me and managed not to stumble and fall. I still cannot describe in words the terror and loneliness I felt that night. After traveling for what felt like forever, I saw the flicker of light in the distance. I finally saw the outline of village huts. I knew that I was safe, but I still had the problem of locating Mr. Limbani's house.

I emerged from the bush and asked the first person I encountered for directions to Edward's house. The man knew Mr. Limbani and his family and was kind enough to walk me to my destination. Mr. Limbani's house was the only modern one in the village. I could see that the roof was metal, and the house was fairly large compared to the traditional houses in the village. Mr. Limbani came out upon hearing the call "Odi." I was never happier to see someone as I was to see Mr. Limbani and his family. His wife told me to come in and get some food. I related in great detail my exhausting and frustrating travel experience. I told Mr. Limbani how disappointed I was in the priest who refused to help me in any way. Mr. Limbani expressed his surprise since he was raised in the Roman Catholic Church and attended the school run by the church. It was late. As soon as I finished eating, everyone was ready for bed.

The next morning when I got up, Mrs. Limbani had already fixed tea and made butter sandwiches. Canned margarine was a staple in rural areas because it can be kept without refrigeration. We took our breakfast on the porch as people started to walk over to the house to see this village celebrity—me. As was the custom in a village, everyone came over to greet me. Mr. Limbani and I sat on the porch as visitors stopped by to see this Peace Corps volunteer who was *not* White. Generally, when people found out that I was educated in and was from America, I was considered European. In this case, they wondered who this brown-skinned man was who came to visit their village.

During the day, an old man, who obviously had been drinking, came by to greet me. He had a small ketchup bottle filled with an almost-clear liquid. He wanted to share his homemade gin with me. I could not imagine drinking gin or anything else at that time of day. I made up the excuse that I could not drink straight gin, that I needed orange juice to mix with the gin. I knew there was no chance that he had any orange juice, and therefore I would not have to drink the gin. Well, to my amazement, he reached into his pocket and pulled out a little pill that turned out to be an orange

Neighbors visiting the Limbani home.

fizzy. He dropped the fizzy in the bottle, and once it stopped effervescing and turned the gin orange, he gave it to me to drink. What could I do? He had made an orange blossom. So I took a drink.

By afternoon, many villagers had gathered and began passing around a calabash full of freshly made mowa, or African beer, an elder woman had brought over to share. The large calabash was passed from one person to another. The beer was made from ground corn that had fermented until it turned into a mild form of alcohol. When the calabash reached me, I glanced quickly into the gourd, and it looked as if someone had regurgitated oatmeal. I closed my eyes and drank from the bowl and passed it on to the person sitting next to me. I was very relieved that I overcame my reservation of drinking this strange substance from a communal bowl because this simple ritual endeared me to this village community.

Mr. Limbani was anxious to show me his village area and to give me some respite from being the local celebrity. He suggested a tour of the surrounding areas. His village was at the foothills of the Nkoma Mountains. It was beautiful in the daylight and not frightening at all. Mr. Limbani spoke highly of the Catholic mission and how it had provided him with his basic education. Even though I said that I could understand his admiration for the priests and teachers at the school, I could not forget how I was treated the night before when I asked for their help.

Time passed swiftly. I stayed another night with my newfound

Children in Mr. Limbani's village.

Mr. Limbani and British volunteers at the local Catholic mission.

African family before departing on Sunday. I said goodbye and thanked everyone for their hospitality. Mr. Limbani walked me to the mission, where I returned the loan of the torch and thanked the British volunteers. We waited beside the main highway, M1, for the bus. Mr. Limbani saw that I was safely on the bus. I thanked him and his family for their hospitality and said I looked forward to their return to Mpemba.

After traveling by bus for four hours with stops on the way, I finally arrived back in Blantyre. I walked to the extension aids office and exchanged greetings with the watchman. I retrieved my bike, and I was very pleased to get back to my little house on the hill.

Termination Conference

The Peace Corps office provided what they called a termination conference to debrief volunteers on their experience in the country. The 400-mile trip and conference took a total of six days: two days to get there, two days for the conference and two days to return. It was my first visit to the northern region. When I first arrived in Malawi, my Peace Corps group's plane landed in Blantyre in the southern region. We subsequently had about a week of training in Lilongwe in the central region, but most of us never ventured farther north. We often saw volunteers from the north in and around Blantyre. The two Peace Corps extension aid officers stationed in the north came to Blantyre a number of times during our tour. The volunteers in our group all traveled together in two Peace Corps Land Rovers and spent the night in Lilongwe. Even though it was only about 424 miles to Mzuzu via Lilongwe, the roads allowed only moderate speeds even in the dry season. The roads outside of the urban areas were often sandy and treacherous, so it was prudent to take it slow. We were not in a hurry.

We first stopped in Zomba to pick up John. His sister Liz left for the States the previous week; John said how much he was going to miss her. As we drove to Lilongwe, we talked about the good times we had during her extended visit. We got to Lilongwe in our Land Rovers and met up with the agricultural workers from the central region. The next day, we had a caravan that headed north.

Even though the journey to the northern region was long and difficult, I was glad to get the opportunity to see this part of the country that I had not seen before. Mzuzu was the capital of the northern region and the third largest city in the country. Even so, it was not densely populated and was easy to get around in. The north was pretty mountainous with Mzuzu lying in a depression between two hills. The Chikangawa Forest was located in the Viphya plateau mountain range. The forest was the largest man-made forest in Malawi with beautiful pine trees and native evergreen trees. The idea for the forest was President Banda's who wanted to start a pulp industry in the country.

The volunteers who were assigned to the north had to learn the Chitumbuka language which was spoken by most of the inhabitants of the north. There were some Tonga people who lived in the area, but most were found along the lakeshore. I didn't know too much about the Nyasa Tonga other than they had once been ruled by the Ngoni until they rebelled and established settlements along the lake. Whereas the staple food in the south was corn, many people in the north preferred cassava, which they ground into a flour that was used to make a nsima-like porridge. Although many people liked this starch, I found that it was too gooey for me. Mzuzu also had a large East Indian population. Like in most Malawi towns, the Indians were shopkeepers and generally monopolized the commercial businesses. The town itself was quaint.

It was good to hook up with our extension aids team as well as other members such as Doug MacDonald, Carl Scott, John Hunter and Bob Thomas who worked in the south. Missing from our little group was Dick Caldwell who had been expelled earlier in the year. We were glad to see Roy Adams and others from the central region. Outside of our little group of visual aids workers, we did not know the other agricultural volunteers very well.

Despite the dusty, sandy roads, we made good time traveling to Mzuzu. I was pleasantly surprised at how beautiful the area was. We were already in the dry season, but the area was still lush. The grass was light brown against vast strips of controlled-burn areas that left long swaths of a darker sienna brown landscape. We were first introduced to controlled burning when we arrived in the country in the fall of 1967. You could see smoke from controlled burning for miles and miles as farmers prepared their gardens for planting and the coming rains.

The Peace Corps had rented a lodge for our retreat that accommodated all of our numbers two to a room. The lodge was located on the outskirts of Mzuzu where it was possible to see animals roaming around at twilight. The lodge had three meeting rooms plus a dining hall. We had the whole lodge, so food was prepared according to Peace Corps instructions. We were generally pleased to get some real hamburgers and pizzas for a change.

We were divided into two groups that met all day with breaks in the mornings and afternoons and lunch at midday. We reviewed the training that we had in Tuskegee. We all thought it was good overall, especially with bringing in Malawians to teach us the language but most important, to teach us about the culture. Having Malawians at camp was the best part of training and the most useful. Getting to know the culture firsthand made our in-country adjustments that much easier. I did not expect that one trainer, David Chiwanga, would end up as one of our colleagues in the southern regional office.

Rolling hills in the northern region.

Chapter Three. Second Year in Malawi 183

The White volunteers had a lot to say about their experiences being White in a Black country. Some accepted being categorized European, but not all liked being called "bwana" or "azungu" (foreigner or White); most wanted to be accepted as just another human being here to serve where they could. The problem was that they were White and they could not erase that. When Malawians met White Peace Corps volunteers for the first time, they assumed that the volunteers were expatriates and treated them accordingly. This often quickly changed for those who spoke Chichewa fluently, lived modestly in a village area and made a special effort to fit in to the extent that they could. I thought that Dick was a good model for a volunteer until he was kicked out of the country by the Peace Corps. I thought that people like Tom and Doug did a good job but sometimes found it awkward fitting in. Volunteers who were paired together found that they generally associated with each other more than they should have. Some found that their familiarity made life easier and more comfortable. Bob Brown, who was a veterinarian, was more highly qualified than anyone else. He provided a real service in teaching others and in solving problems related to animal husbandry. John Hunter, working in the national extension aids office in Zomba, probably had one of the best experiences. Not that he spoke the language that well, but he was committed to his job and even more committed to fitting into his community. John lived in an urban community in an African township. He was what some might describe as "going African," meaning that he tried to blend in and really become part of the community. John worked with a lot of expatriates and could have easily become one of them, joining the Zomba Club like Bill Wyatt did.

Most volunteers had a positive assessment of the Peace Corps staff and the support that they provided during our tour of duty. From what I observed over the last two years, many liked the idea of coming into Blantyre, spending time around the Peace Corps office and going out to Todd Mayes's house for his weekly Saturday pancake breakfast. Although I never went because I lived in Blantyre and did not want to become too entwined with other members of the Peace Corps, I thought the pancake breakfast function was a good one and was appreciated by all. Todd Mayes and Howard Carter both received very positive feedback for their work and commitment. Ed Marsh, as a director, did not fare so well. Whereas most thought he was pompous and epitomized the gung-ho cowboy image, I had the most negative impression of Ed as a director. I still felt that he was wrong in sending the volunteers home.

The Peace Corps held these termination conferences as part of its overall assessment of the programs and utilized the results to improve the programs for incoming groups. Howard asked me to give an overview of my experiences as a Black volunteer, which I had earlier provided him in writing. I acknowledged that my major problem was with the expatriates and the way they treated the Africans and the deference that they continued to demand or at least expect from Malawians. I said that living in Blantyre had kept me from learning the language as well as some who lived in the rural communities where English was seldom spoken. The locals wanted to improve their language skills, so they mostly talked to me in English. My good Malawi friends wanted me to make more of an effort to speak Chichewa and seemed disappointed that I did not speak the language fluently. Because I had made a special effort to be considered a brother, or "achimwene," since I was Black, not being fluent in the language was a major flaw in my cross-cultural experience, but it did not keep me from being accepted by my friends and colleagues.

While I talked about my reaction to expatriates, I also confessed that I had been greatly influenced by my own experience as a civil rights activist in the 1960s and even more by the Black Power movement, which emerged from the Civil Rights movement. I admitted that I carried some resentment toward Whites when I entered the Peace Corps. I also said how I really resented the Peace Corps assessment that I might not have been fit to represent the United States as a Black man in Black Africa. If I had been de-selected, it might have radicalized me even more. I finally said that I had moderated my views toward Whites. Of course, getting to know some of the volunteers helped, but also developing friendships with people like Anne and Dick Oliver turned out to be very positive for me in moderating my views of Whites. I think that I gave a fairly good assessment of my experience.

We talked for two days about everything from our initial training in Alabama to in-country training (some of us talked about the great experience we had training in London), adjustment to the new culture, our individual jobs, vacations and finally travel to the end-of-duty conference. I was about the only one who did not experience culture shock initially. It actually took me a year before I really went into culture shock. I had difficulty accepting "African time" because I took my job so seriously and set some goals that I was determined to achieve. It was only after I had accepted the culture, like other volunteers, and did not try to change it that my experience once again became positive and I was much happier. Overall, we all gave top rating to our personal experiences as volunteers and felt that we had made a contribution to the people. Above all else, we felt like we had gained more than we had given. We all acknowledged that we had changed and for the better. We believed that the Peace Corps experience would always be part of who we were and would shape our lives forever.

When the Peace Corps termination conference ended, some of us traveled to Nkhata Bay on Lake Malawi to catch the *Ilala* boat south. I had

Chapter Three. Second Year in Malawi

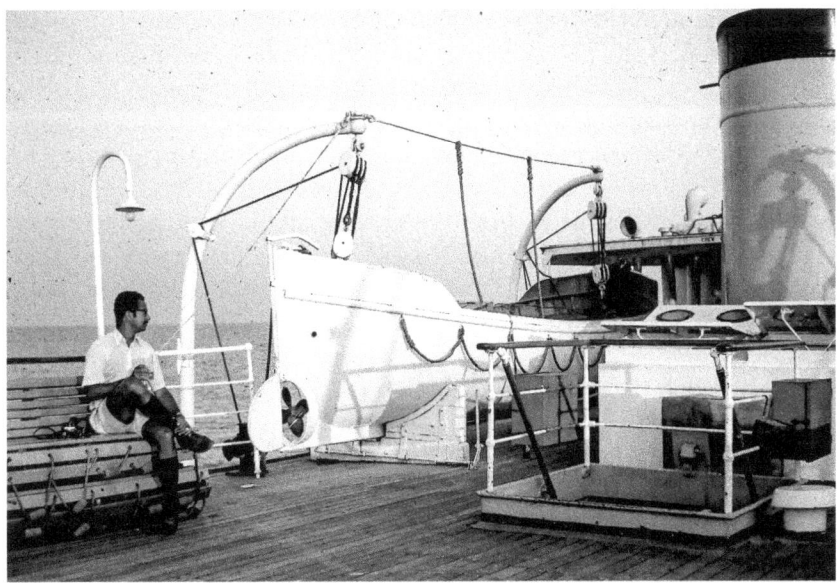

Here I'm on the deck of the *Ilala*.

been fascinated by the *Ilala* since arriving in Malawi. I thought it might have been an old German ship left over from colonial days, but it turned out to have been commissioned by the Nyasaland Railroad in 1949. The *Ilala* had been in continuous use ever since. The ship had four decks and held more than 400 people. We reserved standard cabins on an upper deck equipped with sinks, but we had no toilet and shower. Only the captain's cabin had its own shower. I was not sure how most Malawians were accommodated since there were only 20 cabins. When the ship was being loaded, I noticed that most people carried on their own sleeping mats since the other decks did not have separate individual sleeping quarters. People brought on board lots of baggage and a variety of animals from chickens to goats. A number of people loaded their bicycles to be used for transport once they disembarked the ship. I assumed that the large quantities of vegetables and fruits were being taken to a local market. I understood that only three ports on the lake were deep enough to allow mooring of the ship. In areas that could not accommodate the large ship, people and goods were transported to the *Ilala* by smaller boats.

It took nearly a day and a half to sail to Monkey Bay, where we departed for Blantyre by Land Rover provided by the ministry. Our trip on the *Ilala* was comfortable but by no means luxurious. There was a dining room and bar to serve mainly second- and first-class passengers. Most Malawians traveling in economy class could not afford the price of a beer, much less food in the restaurant. During the two days we were on board, we had peri peri chicken and then oxtail. I had oxtail once before, and in both instances, this dish was superb. I asked the waiter what was being served to the passengers below deck, and he said generally they got rice and beans or rice and vegetables. We made a couple of stops including on one of the larger islands in the lake. Lake Malawi is the second largest lake in Africa and one of the deepest. We were told that a major storm on the lake could sink a seafaring ship. I appreciated the time spent on board, which provided time for me to relax and unwind.

Thoughts on Work and Other Subjects

I began to wonder if the price of success was unhappiness. When I started work nearly two years ago, I found my job not only very satisfying but also very rewarding as I accomplished one goal after another. I wanted to work with Malawians and to train them to do the jobs I had been doing. I had a staff of five people and would be getting another one to take over the office as extension aids officer. Yes! I will be replaced by a Malawian, which was one of my primary goals in setting up the office nearly two years ago. I was no longer doing the more creative work of editing the newsletter, making posters and puppets, designing puppet theaters, designing brochures, etc. All the things that required some creativity I had passed on to the staff, so I was stuck doing administrative work. I really enjoyed working with my hands. I especially liked my field work, traveling to district offices and our rural training centers and interacting with our field staff, many of whom I now called my friends. Traveling around villages and seeing new areas of the country made my job interesting and stimulating.

As I thought about my role as an administrator or "boss," I had tried to be an egalitarian supervisor. As a Peace Corps volunteer, I had made special effort not to identify with the expatriates. I wanted to be friends with my employees, to be one of the guys. Eating lunch together did much to make my office feel like we were all equal. This was especially true since we sat around the conference table eating with our hands out of a central dish with our ndiwo and nsima. Since I was not an authority figure, people began to feel like they could have as much say as I did about running the office. I had learned that egalitarianism came with a price, though. Some of my employees perceived me as being a lenient supervisor, some viewed my leniency as weakness, and maybe they were right. But I had learned that it was not easy to switch roles from becoming one of the fellows to the boss. I finally was forced to deal harshly with only one employee. I did what I had to do in meting out the appropriate punishment for insubordination.

Chapter Three. Second Year in Malawi 187

I considered this a lesson well worth learning. I don't think I would make that mistake again.

What I had really liked doing was working in the darkroom, which became more like a hobby than work. I had developed hundreds of pictures. The problem was that I was developing pictures before I even knew how. When we were in Tuskegee working with the AV supervisor at the Tuskegee Veterans Administration, we were being trained on how to take and develop photographs. Seven of us were crowded into this little darkroom trying to learn the intricacies of developing pictures. I don't think that any of us learned very much. By the time I got to Malawi and got a darkroom set up, I had forgotten what little bit I had learned. It was kind of funny how some of the pictures turned out. I did not have so much of a problem developing the negatives, but I did have problems burning the images onto the photographic paper and then knowing how long to leave the paper in the developer and then the stop bath. Initially, I was more concerned about just getting decent pictures rather than developing art images. I wish that I had spent more time in taking quality pictures and developing quality images. In spite of always being rushed to get the job done, I really liked being in the darkroom. Maybe it was the sense of being alone that I liked. In the end, I had to train a staff person to do the darkroom work. So even there, I had to give up a very pleasant aspect of my job in the interest of Africanizing the office. I had no regrets; I just missed the actual work.

Barbara told me in her last letter that she was getting tired of working for IBM in New York. She said that her office was a cold environment in which to work and that people were not that friendly. She said that most of her colleagues were more interested in getting ahead than in developing friendships. Under these circumstances, it would be easier for her to leave and move to D.C. We thought that I should try to get a job in New York and move in with her in her Harlem apartment. Because I would not get back to the States until the end of the year, I didn't plan to start Howard University until the fall of 1970. By working in New York, I could save some money to get settled in D.C. My only concern was living in the largest city in the country. I was not sure how I would make the transition from rural Malawi to the metropolitan area of New York. I liked the idea of living in Harlem, which was an all–Black community. It would lessen the impact of moving back to a majority White country. I also liked the idea of going to a majority Black university in a majority Black town. Howard had some outstanding professors including Rayford Logan, Chancellor Williams, and Sterling Brown. It had a strong history department with lots of courses in African American and African history.

I had some regrets about leaving my house, the construction of which was a labor of love working on designing and overseeing the construction. I had tried to fix it up as time went by, but I never managed to paint the exterior. My dog, Thako, was a good companion. He followed me around everywhere I went. Everson and I raised him from a little pup. I would hate to leave Thako. I had already told Everson that he could have the dog when I left.

Over the last two years, I had developed into a pretty good cook. I did not know what I would have done without Fannie Farmer, whose cookbook was provided by the Peace Corps office. When I was living in my apartment in Lexington, Kentucky, I really could not cook and rarely tried. I found it was easier to make sandwiches. I would have the oddest combination of things for dinner: pickles, olives, cottage cheese, sardines, cold cuts—anything that did not require cooking. I learned to visit neighbors and friends around dinnertime and would sit and wait to get invited to dinner. I started that practice when I was a student at Berea. Joe and Beth Mouledous were my best "adult" friends. I served as Beth's research assistant my last year in college. They had three children. The youngest child once asked me at their dinner table why I was always there when dinner was being served. I was embarrassed but replied that it was good planning on my part. It was habit that I continued in Malawi. And who would not want to be at Joe and Beth's house during dinner? Joe was a fantastic cook and loved cooking. He had been a cook in the navy, and he had learned his creole cooking when he was growing up in New Orleans. He made the best spaghetti and was famous for his gumbo.

My attitude toward White people had changed a lot over time. Now that I reflect on my experiences over the last few years, I realized that my dislike for White people was never based on their whiteness but rather on their character. Even during my so-called Black Power days in Kentucky, I had good White friends. I do not know what I would have

Me taking pictures for the *Southern Advisor*.

done if it had not been for my friends Bonnie and Archie Allen and the many meals that I shared at their home in Frankfort. Our southern roots provided a bond that allowed us to talk about anything. It was good to have unconditional friendships. Archie was my colleague at the Kentucky Human Rights Commission. He was a little older and had a little more experience than I did. He came out of the Civil Rights movement in the Deep South and was a friend of John Lewis's. I think Archie told me that he and John were classmates at the American Baptist Theological Seminary in Nashville. Bonnie was just a lovely person, very genuine. I was surprised to learn that she had gone to Fisk University as the only White student on campus during the years of the mass sit-ins and protest demonstrations in Nashville. I never thought about it until now, but it seemed as if all of my really good friends were southerners. Both Bonnie and Archie talked with a southern accent. Even in Malawi I ended up with an Alabama boy as a good friend. So in retrospect, it was not the fact that I could not get along with expatriates whether from South Africa or Great Britain; it was the fact that they felt superior and acted on their feelings of superiority. It was this that I could not accept, especially as it impacted not so much me but my Malawi colleagues and friends.

The Four-Color Newsletter

We have had our offset press for some time now. Although we were doing various jobs for other departments, our focus was to produce audio-visual educational materials for the Ministry of Agriculture. One of my first tasks was the development of a newsletter I named the *Southern Advisor*, published every month since I had been in Malawi. It started off as a modest operation, but it had now matured into a sophisticated newsletter.

Ever since we got the press, my ambition was to produce a color image for the cover of the newsletter. Our most ambitious project to date was the creation of a two-color cover, black and yellow or black and blue. Now I wanted to move the newsletter to the next level and create a cover in four colors. I finally got enough money and permission to purchase two reams of coated semi-gloss paper to produce the *Southern Advisor* cover in four colors. I had been talking with Alton Brown, the South African sales representative who sold the press to the department. He had taught me how to run the press to create a color image. I selected the image of smallholder tea producers with Mount Mulanje in the background. It was a beautiful image and would make a wonderful color cover for the newsletter. It would also emphasize the number of Malawi tea producers. I took the picture over to Alton's office, where using filters, he separated the colors into cyan, magenta, yellow and black and burned four anodized thin aluminum plates for each color.

He emphasized how important it was to print the colors in proper sequence to get the true four-color image we wanted. He labeled each plate.

When I got back to the office, I told Mr. Ntungama that we would try our hand at producing a color image for the October issue of the newsletter. This would be my final issue before leaving Malawi. Mr. Ntungama had become very efficient at running the offset press, making sure the plates were secure in place and making sure the registration was correct. He cleaned the rollers after each run if we were using more than one color. He always cleaned the rollers after each day's printing and did a good job maintaining the press.

This time was a little different. To achieve a color image, he would have to run the press four times for the four colors of black, red, yellow and blue, cleaning the rollers after each run-through. The real trick was to make sure that the color registration was absolutely aligned, otherwise the final image would be slightly blurred and the color off. Mr. Ntungama ran the plates in the sequence Alton had listed. He used cross marks to make sure at the beginning of each run to properly align each color. We had 1,000 sheets of paper to produce 800 covers needed for the newsletter, so we had to get it right. We did not have a lot of paper to waste. We held our breath following each run. With the second run, we had printed nearly 100 copies before I realized that the registration was off just ever so slightly. The third run also needed the registration adjusted. We were running out of paper. We completed the total job with only a couple of extra sheets to spare. I looked at the final product and realized that Alton had given us the wrong sequence for the color printing, which resulted in more of a greenish tint to the image. Although one could tell that it was a color image, it was by no means of the highest quality I desired. I wondered to myself if Alton Brown, a South African, had deliberately sabotaged our project. Nevertheless, the job was done. We were out of paper, so this would have to do for this issue. I just hoped that the staff would be encouraged to attempt to produce future issues of the newsletter in color. I personally took issues of the newsletter to the regional office and to the office in Zomba to show what this African staff had accomplished, even if we had not achieved perfection the first time.

Extension Aids Office in Zomba

When I took a copy of the newsletter to Zomba, I realized that this would be my last trip to our national headquarters. It never occurred to me how hard it would be to say goodbye to my friends and co-workers. Derrick McKinley had retired and left for Nigeria. He gave his address to John

Hunter and invited us to visit him when and if we traveled through Nigeria. Derrick had spent most of his adult life in Africa and could not see himself back in England. As much as expatriates disliked Nigerians and talked about how arrogant they were, just the opposite of Malawians, I was a little surprised that he would take a job there. I understood that he worked for an agency of the United Nations.

The staff at the headquarters all came out for our goodbye luncheon; at least 50 people were at the event. Some of our Malawi colleagues made speeches about the Peace Corps and what it meant working with us. I thought that we were greatly appreciated because we were so egalitarian, unlike the British. What really got to me were the personal sentiments expressed by my co-workers and friends. I did not realize that so many people were so fond of us Peace Corps volunteers.

The New Director Arrived

Nigel Murphy sent for me to come to the regional office to meet the new extension aids officer, Edmund Nkona. I would have liked to have been involved in the selection process, but I never had a chance to interview or recommend anyone for the job. I understood that the new director was chosen by the Minister of Agriculture in Zomba from new graduates of the polytechnic. He must be among the first graduating class since the polytechnic became part of the University of Malawi in 1967. The university itself was not organized until 1964. Mr. Nkona received his degree in management specializing in environmental management. In his early 20s, Mr. Nkona appeared to be a smart, young man having gone straight from secondary school to the university. After Nigel introduced me to him, we talked for a while before we drove over to Kabula Hill where I introduced him to the staff. I could see right away that he might be too young and inexperienced for the job. Everyone in the office was older except for James Kalenga, the office assistant. Mr. Ntungama was smart enough to know that it would be in his best interest to help acclimate Mr. Nkona to the job. I couldn't say the same for Mr. Chirwa, though. He had always been ornery and no doubt would challenge Mr. Nkona's authority if he thought he could get away with it.

I set Edmund up in my office and gave him my desk and chair. I sat at a smaller desk next to the window. I wanted him to know from the start that he was in charge, and I would do everything that I could in the short time left to make the transition as smooth as possible.

Rather than having our traditional lunch in the office, I invited Mr. Nkona to have lunch with me downtown at my favorite little Mediterranean restaurant. It gave us a chance to get to know each other on a one-on-one basis. I talked briefly about my background and why I came to Malawi as a Peace Corps volunteer. More important, we talked about the history of the office and how I was the only non–White who served as a regional officer. Now he would be the only African with that title. I told him how the office started off as a one-person operation, and now with his presence, there would be six people on staff. I reviewed the positives and negatives of each person and indicated that overall, I thought we had a good staff. I also talked about the expatriates in the regional office and their personalities and how I thought he could best work with each. Mr. Nkona, unlike most Malawians, asked me to call him Edmund. He told me a little about his background and how he happened to be selected for this position. Altogether, Edmund was pretty easygoing and would generally follow the directions of the regional director. He was educated by White teachers both in secondary school and in college, so he was used to working with expatriates. I thought he would get along well with his regional colleagues. I told Edmund that I wished he had come on board sooner so that we could have had more time to work together. As it was, my service as a Peace Corps volunteer would end next month.

Getting Ready to Go Home

The office was running smoothly with Edmund on his third day. After checking in, I decided to take the afternoon off from work to write to Barbara and my family letting them know my travel schedule. I was traveling home with John Hunter. We originally wanted to travel from Malawi through East Africa and up through Sudan, Ethiopia and Egypt and then to Europe. I had mixed emotions about this route since I wanted to see both Ethiopia and West Africa. John's idea was that we would travel down the Nile from Lake Victoria through Sudan. I had the foresight to check a map. When the Nile leaves Uganda, it spreads out into a great marsh called the Sudd. It is nothing more than mass swampland. I told John that I was sure we would die trying to navigate such swampland. We then decided to go home through West Africa. Our itinerary now was to leave Blantyre on October 14 and go to Nairobi, Bujumbura, Kinshasa, Lagos, Accra, Abidjan, Madrid, Paris, London and New York. The travel agent said that we could make as many stops as we liked as long as we did not backtrack on our journey. The Peace Corps paid for a basic airline ticket home, and we had to pay any additional charges. Even with our complex schedule, we had to add only an additional $110 for each ticket. I thought this was great, but it left me with only $500 for six weeks. That worked out to be about $10 a day for all in-country expenses. I knew that I was spreading my funds too thinly, but the way I saw it, this was a chance of a lifetime to see as much of the world as I could, especially African countries. I would not get to New York until November 28. I was not telling my parents exactly when I would arrive in the States because they wanted me to come directly home, but I wanted to spend at least a week in New York with Barbara before heading to North Carolina. I hated leaving Malawi as much as I hated the thought of having to return home and to face racism again, even though being in Blantyre surrounded by Whites from Southern Africa did not allow me to completely escape racism.

The entire Agriculture Department in the southern region gave the agricultural volunteers a going-away party, which was fantastic. The party was held at the Tuchila Training Center where John Scott worked and where we had spent a number of days over the past two years developing AV resources for the center. The regional officers came down in their own cars while other Malawi staff came down in the office's fleet of Land Rovers. People came from all over the region, from Fort Johnston to Nsanje and from Dedza to Mulanje. Many of the people we had worked with over the past two years came to bid us farewell. It was one of the few times that expatriates and Malawians socialized on a somewhat equal basis. Of course, all of the agriculture volunteers in the southern region were there. It was a very festive occasion with lots of food. The center's cooks had prepared roasted chickens and goats, rice and lots of vegetables and fruits. There was also a lot of beer available.

My entire staff was there. For the first time it hit me that by next month, I would be leaving Malawi and probably never see most, if not all, of my friends and colleagues again. I felt very sad because I had gotten to know them so well. A very important part of my life was coming to a close. Before my thoughts lingered too long on my departure, someone handed me a beer and encouraged me to join in with the African traditional dancers who were providing entertainment for the group. It took only three beers before I was out there with everyone else. It reminded me of our first Christmas in Malawi when our African colleagues took us to a neighboring village around 10 at night and woke up most people in the village. Our colleagues suggested that the villagers build a fire and show us some of their traditional dances. With little or no encouragement, they were dancing in a counterclockwise circle and we all joined in. These activities were some of the most enjoyable that I had experienced during my time in Malawi. So we were closing out our experience in Malawi the same way we began that Christmas in 1968, with traditional dances.

After we all had our fill of food and drink, the formal part of the program began. I always marveled at how seriously Malawians take ceremonial occasions, with speaker after speaker making formal remarks. Nigel Murphy opened the program and spoke of our service to the ministry and to the country. Despite our differences, I felt that Nigel was sincere in expressing his gratitude for our service. Next came Troy David, Nigel's second in command and Mr. Bower, the head of the cotton project. Mr. Chiphwanya spoke next and was very elegant in his expression of gratitude not only for our service but also for the friendships that he had established with many of us. David Chiwanga spoke next. Our group had become very fond of David. He taught us Chichewa at Tuskegee, but more important, he taught us about the culture and the people. He spoke elegantly about his involvement with the Peace Corps office and with his friends, the volunteers. Edmund Nkona spoke next but did not talk long because he had just begun work in the office. It was Mr. Ntungwama who really spoke on behalf of the staff. He talked about the "John" that they had all come to love and respect. He recounted the many office meals we shared. Needless to say, I was moved to tears by his comments regarding my leadership of the office. Mr. Ntungama mentioned how well the office staff were treated and how they were given the opportunity to learn new skills. He said I was more like their friend—no, more like a brother—than their boss. Several of the area supervisors spoke about their friendships with the other volunteers. Obviously, we had all made an impression on the people with whom we had worked and lived over the two years. When the official program was over, we returned to merrymaking and drinking beer. It was a good night, and I was pleased to know how well my staff and colleagues thought of me and the other Peace Corps volunteers with respect to the service we provided for the country we had come to love and call home.

 The weather had changed into the hot and dry season. There was so much to be done before leaving. I wanted to be sure that the office was in good shape. I felt good about the training of the staff and their ability to carry on without me. I was sorry that Mr. Nkona had not arrived until a month before I was scheduled to leave even though I was promised an assistant long before then. I had devoted much of my time to orienting Edmund to his new duties and transferring my files and other information he would need to run the office. Now I wanted to make sure that they had enough supplies to get them through the rest of the year. It was not easy to get supplies when you needed them, so it was best to order in advance and have them on hand. Like so many items, we got a lot of our office supplies from South Africa. But what could I do? The supplies were much cheaper even though it supported the racist regime there.

 Since I would be carrying only one suitcase with me as I traveled home, I decided to sell most of my clothes. Some things like the African shirts I had made, I would forward home in my trunk along with gifts for the family. I would keep a few shirts for travel, but I hoped to buy a few items along the way, especially as I traveled through West Africa. I had not gained weight, so Malawians could fit my clothes. They liked jeans and khaki pants, dress shirts, towels and the like. I sold my loafers to my messenger and bought some suede Bata shoes. Mr. Kapanela took my worn shoes to the market and came back with what looked like brand-new loafers all polished and shiny. It almost made me wish that I had kept them. After selling everything I owned that I did not need for traveling home, I made a total of $30. Well, every little bit helped toward my expenses. Daddy loaned me $200 to be repaid from the resettlement allowance. I got a total of $1,200, which was more money than I have ever had at one time.

Everyone I knew wanted to take me out in the evenings before I left. I had not been home all week except to go to bed. Beer drinking was a habit in Malawi, so that was how we celebrated by going to bars, dancing and maybe getting something to eat along the way.

Of course, there were things that I had to do for the Peace Corps to officially end my tour of duty. I had already had my physical. The doctor determined that I had an inflamed liver that he wanted checked out by a specialist when I got home. He said that I had had so many attacks of malaria that there may be some slight liver damage. The doctor did not seem overly concerned, so I was not either. I decided that I would have my dental work done at home at Peace Corps expense. The last thing that I would have to take care of once I got home was to see a skin specialist. It looked like I had developed a tropical fungus and not been able to get rid of it. Overall, I felt pretty good and was pleased with my service over these last two years. I thought that my physical health was good, but I had taken out travel insurance, which covered any health issues I might have on the way home.

A Near-Fatal Accident

Some Malawi friends invited me out to celebrate my departure. I normally would not accept so many invitations, except that I would not see these people again for years, if ever. I was so sad to leave my friends. We decided to go to a local club in Limbe. We all had a good time. Four beers was about my maximum over a couple of hours if I was to drive home safely. Well, this night, I drove back into Blantyre from Limbe and was driving along the Chileka Road toward home. It must have been after midnight as there were few cars on the road. I was traveling about 35 miles per hour when a car pulled to a stop on the side of the road next to the Catholic church. I knew that the driver saw me coming because I saw him stop at the stop sign. Then he let his car slowly move across the road directly in my path. As soon as I saw that the car was moving, I slammed on my brakes as hard as I could but to no avail. Rather than hit the car head on, I slid off the road into a gully. I sat there in the gully unable to speak or move when tears began streaming down my face. I could not stop crying. I realized that if I had been going a little faster, I would have hit the car head-on and probably gotten killed. As I sat there, I thought of the poor Malawian who was driving his motorcycle on the airport road when a car pulled right in front of him. He hit the side of the car head-on and was immediately killed. That was what I thought about as I sat in the gully. I continued to cry for several more minutes and then got up and went over to the driver and asked why the hell did he pull out right in front of me. I knew that he had seen me because he initially had stopped. He was an old expatriate, and I soon realized that he was totally drunk. He tried to talk but just mumbled some words. I knew that he had taken his foot off the brake that allowed his car to roll across the road. I felt like cussing him out, but I knew he was too drunk to understand anything I said. I pulled my bike out of the gully and drove off as the wind dried my tearstained face. This was the closest I had come to death. I had been in Malawi for two years and was nearly killed during my last few weeks in the country.

Thoughts on Leaving Malawi

Two years ago, we arrived in Malawi for the first time. It was hard to believe that two years had passed. One of the most difficult things that I had to do was say goodbye to all my friends. I had been saying my goodbyes for well over two weeks. I think it was easier leaving home than leaving Malawi, maybe because I was going on an adventure to Europe and then Africa for two years.

I had many mixed emotions about leaving and about my experience. I wrote down my thoughts in a journal as I had time. I came to have great respect for all people and learned to treat all people the same, no matter their status in life. Most people in Malawi had very little, yet were willing to share what they had. I found Malawians to be very friendly but can sometimes be cruel when taking justice into their own hands, like when I hit a pig with the Mini Moke and killed it. I was certainly willing to pay for it but was told to just leave because I would be stoned—a form of immediate justice for such transgression. I was not sure that this would have happened to me, but I left anyway.

I never liked having a houseboy, but my living conditions required that I had some help just dealing with the chores of everyday life. Our first houseman did not work out, so a neighbor suggested that I hire Everson, a young man from his village who had to drop out of school for lack of school fees. The five or six pounds we paid him plus room and board was more than he could possibly make in his home village. I gave Everson my dog Thako, but I don't think that he would get fed in his village as well as I had fed him. Tom and I withheld two pounds a month from Everson's salary. We gave him the 20 pounds we had saved for him. I gave Everson my home address and told him that if he stayed in touch, I would pay his school fees until he graduated or could not go any further in school.

I will miss the office staff. I think we worked well together as a team. I wished I had more patience with the staff, but it seemed the choice I had was that I could be patient and allow the work schedule to slip or have less patience and maintain my work schedule. I saw more Africanization taking place in the southern region toward the end of my tour. Edmund Nkona was finally selected as my Malawian replacement. I think that eventually all the expatriates would leave the country. I know that many did not want to go back to the United Kingdom where their standard of living would drop appreciably. They got hardship pay (as if working in Malawi was a hardship), a very nice modern ranch-style home, private (White) schools for their children and allowance for overseas education for their older children, paid leave in Europe, etc., etc. What more could they have asked for? They would be lucky to get half that when they returned to Great Britain. I heard that some were trying to secure jobs in other African countries.

Now that I was leaving, I have time to assess my work over the last two years. I had often been unable to see the forest for the trees. I felt good about my work with my staff and my ability to leave them with skills that would serve them well for the rest of their lives. Much of what I was able to accomplish, I had to teach myself first. I learned how to develop film and print images, knowledge that I then used to teach one of my staff members. I improved on the making of puppets by creating a puppet head that allowed movement of the mouth. Such a simple thing actually had a lot of impact, as area extension agents used the puppets to teach improved agricultural methods. I taught the staff how to make farm relief models, posters, display boards and displays for agricultural shows; design, lay out, and edit the monthly newsletter; develop publications, textbooks, leaflets and booklets for the extension staff; use audio-visual aids equipment; and introduced them to general administration and evaluation. By the time I left, I had my replacement on board, a college graduate. The other staff consisted of a printer, photographer, artist, general office assistant, a carpenter and a messenger. I supervised the construction of my house, which I have now left to my Malawi friend Mr. Katembe and his family. Together

Tom and I raised a couple of sheep and some chickens and planted a vegetable garden. In the evenings, we taught basic English to local children in the village. I was leaving dozens of friends who would always remain in my memory and heart.

My health was good. I had gained some weight. I weighed 160 pounds—too much nsima. I was concerned about getting malaria again. The Peace Corps doctor gave me some chloroquine tablets to start taking when I got to Europe and out of the tropics. I did not think that I would ever forget the brush with death when the car pulled out in front of me. If I had not witnessed a similar accident earlier in the year, I don't think I would have been as visibly shaken by the incident.

I would love to return to Africa one day, but I was convinced that I could never return as a missionary. I saw so many negative aspects of missionaries' behavior, especially how they treated Malawians, the very people they came to serve. I believe that missionaries paved the way for colonization and that other volunteers and I experienced the last vestiges of colonialism as Malawi faced its future as an independent African country. I had given a lot of thought to becoming a teacher. I liked the idea of teaching at one of the African universities, especially in East Africa. I had a lot to think about as I faced the future.

Chapter Four

Departure Home

I could not believe that my tour of duty in Malawi had ended and that I was on East African Airways heading for Dar es Salaam. Four of us left from Blantyre airport together. I would travel to East and West Africa with John Hunter while the other volunteers would head north into Ethiopia and Egypt. We had a choice, but we could not travel to northern and western Africa unless we were willing to pay extra for our ticket home. I was barely able to pay the extra $110 for our current itinerary. Howard Carter was kind enough to drive us to the airport. Many of my friends from the regional agricultural office came to bid us farewell. My good friend Mark Chiphwanya as well as Mr. Limbani and Mr. Katembe all came to see us off. These were my closest friends. It was very sad to say goodbye to all of them as well as my office staff. As we flew over Blantyre and the surrounding countryside, it seemed like yesterday that we were landing for an adventure of a lifetime.

I had not heard a word from Salome. I wrote to tell her that I would be back in Nairobi on my way home, but I did not receive a reply. I was concerned. It was unlike Salome to not respond.

East and Central Africa

Our first stop on our trip home was in Dar es Salaam to get some more Mkonde art and anything else affordable that I could find. We then flew on to Nairobi where Harry Mbui met us at the airport and transported us into Nairobi. I met Salome's brother who was kind enough to entertain us but only said that Salome was out of town. I then had dinner my last night with the English couple I had met on my last visit. They were very friendly and hospitable but strangely silent regarding Salome. They indicated that she was back home in Kisumu and had taken ill. They said that she would be there for a while recuperating from whatever was ailing her. I assumed that I would not be seeing her on this trip before heading to Bujumbura.

We flew from Nairobi to Bujumbura, Burundi. I did not know much about this central African country other than what I saw in the movie *The African Queen*. Burundi is located on the northeast shores of Lake Tanganyika. The major groups of people are the Hutu, the Tutsi and the Twa. Unfortunately for us, there was an attempted military coup and the country was in lockdown. We failed to secure a visa to enter the country before leaving Malawi. I was surprised at how rigid African countries were in requiring entry visas while European countries were much more relaxed about visa policies. Upon entering the airport, we were told by the military that we could not remain in the country. We were immediately ordered to reboard East African Airways, which was now headed to Kinshasa in the Congo. It was very disappointing and a long flight over the Congo Basin. You could see nothing but dense vegetation for hundreds of miles.

We landed in Kinshasa again without a visa and were told that we could not enter the country. I could not believe that we were going to be denied entry into another country. I asked myself if this was the way we were to be treated as we travel throughout Africa. Negotiating with the security staff at the airport was not easy. We assured them that we were there for only a short visit and would be heading to Lagos in three days. After a long discussion, we were given temporary papers to enter the city but were allowed to stay only overnight before we had to leave for Lagos. We were thankful that we were not forced to return to Nairobi as the security officer had first suggested to us. I could not help but notice that *Air Force One* was parked to the side of the airport, which I thought was odd. I had not heard that the president was going to be in the Congo.

Once we arrived in the city, we learned that the American *Apollo 11* astronauts were visiting the capital. Neil Armstrong, Michael Collins and Buzz Aldrin had arrived in the Congo the day before we got to Kinshasa. People from all over the country had come into the city to welcome the astronauts. We managed to get a glimpse of them in a passing motorcade. Because of their visit, every hotel in town was booked. We were at a loss for what to do for accommodations for the night. I suppose we should have planned better, but after all, we were Peace Corps volunteers and very resourceful. We sat on a bench in a well-manicured tropical park in the middle of town thinking that as a last resort, we would spend the night on a park bench. Again, fortunate for us, a Belgian lady, walking her dog, stopped to talk to the two guys with two suitcases sitting on the park bench. We explained our plight. She told us of a family that rented rooms and gave us directions to the house. We immediately headed out each carrying our one suitcase. The Belgian family welcomed us and provided accommodations for a modest fee. We were lucky in spite of our previous misfortunes.

Kinshasa was a beautiful city. One could still see the impact of Belgian architecture surrounded by exquisite parks. We spent the remainder of our day touring the city snapping many photographs. I was truly impressed with the mighty Congo River that was much wider and longer than the Shire River in Malawi, stretched for a mile before reaching the other side where Brazzaville, capital of the Republic of the Congo, was located. While we were taking pictures of the massive expanse of the river, a Congolese soldier wanted to know what we were doing and even threatened to arrest us as we tried to explain. In English, mixed with broken French, we attempted to explain that we were tourists just taking pictures of the river. We did not realize that there was a railway in the background and of course the city of Brazzaville. I guess we were suspicious characters in an environment where hostilities existed between the two countries dating back to when the French and Belgians were colonial rivals. When the soldier demanded that we give him our cameras, John got angry and refused to give up his camera that had the film we used to take pictures in East Africa. He kept shouting, "We are tourists! WE ARE TOURISTS!" Trying to remember some of my high school French, I said, " Bonjour, excusez-moi. Je ne parle pas français, mais nous sommes touristes." I opened my camera, took out my film and gave it to the soldier. John reluctantly did the same. We were allowed to keep our cameras but told to move along. "Passez rapidement!" We quickly left. In no way did I want to end up arrested and in a Congolese prison.

During my two years in Malawi, I never had an encounter with the police or military. I wondered what else could happen to us in this beautiful city of Kinshasa. We walked over to the market where I purchased some very pretty ivory carved figures. We then walked back to our boarding house, rested a bit before heading out to a nightclub. The club was crowded. There was a live band that played African highlife music. I was surprised at how much American country and western music was being played. I was told that the most revered musician was Jimmy Dean. People just loved his music. People in East Africa also were very fond of country music. I could not believe that I had to travel to the heart of Africa to be entertained by an African band playing American country and western music.

Nigeria

The next day, we left for Nigeria where we found ourselves in Lagos under similar circumstances. This time, we had visas but no plans for once we arrived. The trip from the airport by taxi cost us $8.40, which was nearly a day's living allowance. As was typical for us, we had not made accommodation arrangements for any of our stops in Africa and Europe. We were living on blind faith that we would find a hotel that we could afford. Well, we did not find one in Lagos, but we remembered that Derrick McKinley had told us about a very nice "Y" in the suburbs of Lagos. When we arrived at the YMCA, the manager, an Englishman, told us that the Y was booked. When he saw that we were at a loss for a place to stay, he offered us the possibility of sharing accommodations in the houseboy quarters in the back of the Y. Sight unseen, we agreed. The quarters housed an Igbo, Yoruba and a Hausa, representing the three main ethnic groups in Nigeria. The quarters were dormitory-style accommodations with six bunk beds in one large room with an adjoining bathroom. The men were responsible for cleaning the rooms in the Y and generally maintaining the place. The manager introduced us to Ehene, Aheo and Danjuma, and we in turn introduced ourselves and said that we had been Peace Corps volunteers in Malawi.

We arrived in Nigeria at the height of the civil war between the breakaway state of Biafra and the rest of the country. Although there were men in military uniforms, there was no other evidence that a civil war was taking place, at least in the Lagos area. I was sure it was a different story in the east where the fighting was taking place. I had always heard that the Igbo were the most industrious of the three main ethnic groups. With the discovery of oil and the flow of money into the country, the Igbo declared themselves independent of Nigeria. There was very little talk of war, except for our conversations in the servant quarters. I thought of the insurgency that occurred in Malawi before we arrived. It was nothing like the war now going on in the newly declared independent country of Biafra.

Of the three men, Ehene, the Igbo, was the friendliest, even offering to wash and iron our clothes as a way of making additional money. After being there for a day, we found him to be very nice. He even offered to share his dinner with us. Being on a budget, we agreed. He boiled some rice over a hot plate that he kept under his bed and brought out a pot of grease, colored red from pepper, with a big piece of fat meat in the middle of the pot, which provided additional seasoning for the grease. Dinner consisted of a piece of the fat pork for each of us and a couple of spoonfuls of seasoned grease over our rice. It was either quite good or I was very hungry.

Other meals were taken at the local gas station near the Y. We were surprised to find a small restaurant that served simple Nigerian food. We found that we could eat jollof rice with plantains very cheaply. If we wanted to add chicken or beef, we would have to pay a little more. I found Nigerian food similar to what we ate in Malawi except a little spicier. During our stay, we ate a lot of fufu with various Nigerian stews. Fufu is generally made from cassava as well as yams and plantains, all of which are pounded into flour and boiled. Fufu is very starchy and not as good as nsima or ngaiwa in Malawi. I suppose it was just what I was used to eating. Sometimes for convenience, we would just stop in a grocery store and purchase a bottle of wine, bread and some cheese for a cheap dinner. One good thing about traveling on a Peace Corps salary was that you get to sample a variety of the local food.

Locating My African Ancestor

I found that Nigerians were very friendly and were not as aggressive as many of the Europeans in Malawi led me to believe. The rainy season in Nigeria was just about as bad as the rain in Malawi. The exception was that it was not as humid in Blantyre as it was in Lagos. As I sat there listening to the rain fall on our metal roof, my mind wandered back to my youth when my grandfather told me about our African ancestors. I began to think that maybe I would be able to identify the area from where he came by asking about the name Tomishan, which was the name my grandfather told us about and the name I found written in our family Bible. I suspected that it was Americanized, but that was all I had to go on. Tomishan was one of the very few enslaved Africans allowed to return to Africa. He was enslaved in the late eighteenth century and taken to my hometown of Morganton by William Walton, a local merchant and slave trader between Morganton and Charleston. Tomishan lived on Waighstill Avery's plantation, where he was very unhappy with his lot in life. He said that he was of noble birth and could read and write Arabic and speak seven languages. Avery would have him read from the Koran as a form of amusement for his fellow slaveholders. Yet he agreed to allow Tomishan to return to Africa out of fear that Tomishan would cause a slave uprising. So when Tomishan asked to return to Africa in exchange for four Africans, Avery agreed. He instructed Walton to take him to Charleston and tell the captain of the vessel not to allow him to go ashore alone. During the trip, Tomishan impressed the ship captain with his knowledge. When the ship reached the West African coast, the captain allowed Tomishan to go ashore alone. After four days, Tomishan returned with $400 in gold dust to send to Avery in exchange for his freedom. He said that he could not enslave his fellow Africans for his own freedom. I had heard this story many times and vowed to search for my African roots if I ever got to Africa. I asked a number of people in Lagos if they recognized the name or its derivation. Several said yes, but I had also learned that Africans will often tell you what you want to hear rather than disappoint you. I did not gather any hard evidence during my research for my ancestor. However, my one of my Nigerian roommates, Aheo, told me that the name sounded like it might be Yoruba. This was a project of discovery that I would undertake seriously one day.

John and I walked just about everywhere we went, covering five to 10 miles a day. We traveled to the market and generally walked around the city of Lagos. I was surprised at how dirty the city was, especially around the market. People just discarded their waste on the streets and sidewalks. There were open water drains that men often used to relieve themselves right there in public.

Traveling to Ibadan

When Derrick McKinley retired as head of the extension aids office in Zomba, he got a job with the United Nations and was stationed in Ibadan, which is the capital of the Oyo State. We promised that we would visit him when and if we got to Nigeria. We traveled the 80 miles from Lagos to Ibadan by bus. I was surprised to see how thick the jungle was along the way, almost impenetrable. There were lots of abandoned automobiles that were now being consumed by the jungle. With several stops, we made it to Ibadan in less than three hours. Once we got into the city, we had no trouble locating Derrick's house. I fully understood why expatriates did not want to leave Africa. They got these palatial houses manned by numerous servants. They lived in tropical splendor. Derrick invited us to stay for dinner and then drove us to a hotel. Derrick knew that we were traveling on a limited budget, so he said that he had selected a modest but clean hotel located in the central part of town. Once settled, we explored one of the largest cities in Africa. I was truly impressed with the dress of both men and women. They all donned beautiful African robes, many with very sophisticated embroidery. I priced one outfit, which was more than I made as a Peace Corps volunteer in a month.

We stayed at a local hotel that catered to the Nigerian market. I generally liked to stay in hotels that cater to the European market, but those were more expensive. Our hotel was a modest hotel, priced right but the rooms could have been cleaner. As long as there were no bedbugs around, I was fine. The bathrooms left a lot to be desired. I did not think that I have had a warm shower since arriving in Nigeria. I couldn't say that the water was cold. Nothing was ever cold in this hot and humid climate. I found that I had to change clothes to stay dry. That meant I was washing out my clothes, usually in a sink or bucket, and hanging them up to dry in the room.

African market in Ibadan, Nigeria.

The African markets in Ibadan were filled with vendors, mainly women. The market seemed to stretch for miles, but I was told that there were three markets that run together. I think that you could purchase just about anything in the world in these markets from fruits and vegetables to kitchen utensils to clothes to furniture. I was surprised at how many billboards there were advertising skin lightening creams. I never thought I would see this in Africa. I just assumed that all Africans were proud of their blackness. Nigerians loved to barter. I really did not like the idea of haggling over something that I wanted, but after being in Malawi for two years, I think I became good at it. I purchased some beautiful fabric for Barbara and a few other items. John and I enjoyed walking in the market and around this all-African town. We spent several days in Ibadan before heading back to Lagos.

Ever mindful of our budget, we decided to take an "African mammy wagon" back to Lagos. Most mammy wagons were trucks or small buses outfitted with wooden benches. The drivers charged such low rates that they packed them to capacity to make up for the low fares. We decided to take a station wagon that accommodated 11 people packed into three rows of seats, our luggage and a crate of chickens tied to the top. We had no idea how reckless these mammy wagon drivers were. We left Ibadan going 90 miles an hour it seemed. The driver passed everything on the road. John shouted at the driver to slow down but to no avail. Finally, the driver came up behind a lorry. We were temporarily relieved because we were convinced that this would slow the driver down. To our astonishment, he chose to pass the truck going full speed around a 90-degree curve. An 18-wheel petrol truck was fast approaching us. I knew then that we would all die in a split second. The driver instantly swerved to avoid a head-on collision with the gas tanker by pulling in front of and side-swiping the lorry. I had never been so frightened in all my life. The driver stopped to inspect the damage. We all got out to see what nearly caused our death. We could have been in one of the many vehicles that wrecked on the road between Ibadan and Lagos that were now rusting away in the jungle next to the highway. People were cursing in English and raising their voices in Yoruba. All nine people, women and men, had to have their say before everyone was satisfied. Even we were expected to chime in. I decided not to say anything because it would have just prolonged the conversation and delayed us even more getting back to Lagos. When everyone was satisfied that they had sufficient input into the conversation, we all crawled back into the mammy wagon with the driver assuming his self-appointed role of race car driver. It was too much. By the time we reached the outskirts of Lagos, John screamed, demanding the driver, "Stop this goddamn car!" Not knowing how we would get back to town, we got out of the wagon, unloaded our bags and waited to see if a bus would arrive soon. Over the course of two years in Malawi, I had a number of serious accidents on my motorcycle but nothing compared to the accident we almost had traveling back to Lagos. If we had hit the truck head-on, we all would have been killed. I thought about how fortunate we all were.

We arrived back at the Y later that evening. All we wanted was to shower and go out for a beer. We turned in early in preparation for our departure to Ghana.

Ghana

We spent more time in Nigeria than we originally planned. Since we were literally expelled from Burundi and Congo, we had extra days to explore West Africa. Lagos was a good home base because of the cheap living conditions. But it was time we proceeded on our journey. We arrived in Accra, Ghana, where we made a change in our itinerary. We learned that it was too expensive for us to travel in the Ivory Coast, a francophone country, so we stayed a little longer in Ghana before heading to Madrid. When we arrived in Ghana, we gathered our bags and took a bus into the city. We traveled on a very impressive four-lane highway into the city but later learned that the highway did not go beyond the airport. On the other end, the highway took us into the city, where we found a small hotel. For the first few days, we walked throughout the city and then spent an afternoon at the ocean at a place called Labadi Beach. There was a restaurant and bar and a lovely beach with no one on it. I thought that Africans must not enjoy the beach and probably did not like to swim in the ocean. Of all the things that we did not bring on the trip were our swimming trunks. In fact, I did not own any swimming trunks. If we had been on Lake Malawi at our retreat, we would have gone swimming in the nude, but we thought better of it on a public beach near Accra. We stripped down to our underwear and went wading in the ocean. It was awfully strange that not a single person was on the beach. I just thought it was due to it being a cloudy day. I really didn't swim in the ocean but did a little wading. I could not help but think about the millions of Africans who had been captured and sold into slavery. It was a sobering moment for me.

We soon dressed and went up to the bar to enjoy a Ghanaian beer. Although I liked the Nigerian beer, I found that I liked the Ghanaian beer called Club better. It had been brewed in Ghana for a while and seemed to be stronger than anything we had had in Lagos. For our meal, we had fufu and grilled tilapia. I asked the waiter why there were no people on the beach and he said that there was a strong undertow and swimming was not allowed that day. Well, that sure was a surprise. If we had gone swimming in the ocean, we could have drowned.

My plan was to spend time in Ghana with my Berea classmates Rodney and Cynthia Hamilton. They were older than me and graduated ahead of my class at Berea. I think Cynthia was a home economics major while Rodney was an agriculture major. When they graduated from Berea, they went on to get advanced degrees from Cornell before heading back to Ghana to accept appointments at the University of Ghana at Legon. I had written to them to let them know when I would be in Accra and hoped that we could get together. They were gracious to pick us up and took us to their suburban ranch home in Legon. Their neighborhood was beautiful, full of tropical flowers and lush greenery. They had invited us to stay with them and said that they would take us sightseeing. They gave us a tour of the university and the neighborhood where the faculty and staff lived. The university was much larger than the university in Malawi. They took us out to dinner at a very elegant restaurant with tablecloths. I certainly was not used to such fine dining. It was a great evening and the best meal we had had on this trip. It never occurred to me while a student at Berea that I would ever see so many of my classmates in Africa. Both my Kenyan and Ghanaian friends could not have been more hospitable and generous with their time.

Our stay in Ghana was all too short. I really enjoyed being with the Hamiltons. Rodney dropped us off at the airport in Accra. I certainly appreciated the hospitality of Rodney and Cynthia. I was really impressed with the University of Ghana at Legon and would love to return to the country to teach. Of course, I said the same thing about the universities in East Africa.

Travel Home

We left Accra on Saturday morning, November 8, and boarded our plane to Madrid. I had some concerns that we were heading for Europe in the middle of the fall, where the weather was bound to be much cooler than in West Africa. We traveled in Spain, France and England for nearly three weeks before heading for the States.

My plane arrived on time, and Barbara was waiting for me on the other side of the exit from the customs gate. She was absolutely beautiful! She had gotten even prettier from our college days. She was tall and slim, had a beautiful Afro and wore a close-fitting knit pants suit. She was my African queen. I couldn't remember being filled with more emotions than I was at that moment. I rushed up to her and gave her the biggest kiss. She

Here I am in front of the Williams home in Legon, Ghana.

jokingly told me later that I looked like a homeless person and wanted to know where I got the pointed-toe suede shoes. I guess wearing and washing the same clothes for nearly six weeks had taken its toll. As soon as she got the opportunity, she bought me some stylish clothes.

Barbara had a nice one-bedroom apartment on 135th and Lenox Terrace. As we drove to Harlem, I kept thinking about how different it would be living in New York. The taxi dropped us off in front of her 16-story apartment building. We were met at the door by the doorman and went straight up to the 14th floor. Barbara's apartment was toward the end of the hall. Throughout the hallway, you could smell the aroma of chicken frying and greens seasoned with pork cooking. I was home. Barbara had purchased some secondhand furniture, which she had painted black. With her new Afro, her mother said that this must be part of the new Black Power movement. I laughed when she told me.

Lay Lady Lay

I had been in New York for a week when Barbara took a train to Boston where she was the maid of honor in Lou Outlaw and Freida Hopkins' wedding. Freida was Barbara's roommate at Berea. They both wore minidresses and knee-high leather boots with Freida in a mini wedding dress.

Freida walked into the church to Bob Dylan's "Lay Lady Lay." They had to rush through the ceremony because there was a meeting of a church ladies' group that was scheduled for the same afternoon. One of the ladies arrived early, and when she saw the wedding crowd and heard the Dylan song, she said, "What the hell is going on in here?" I had to laugh when Barbara told me this. I was glad when she got back. Even a day away from her seemed like an eternity.

Epilogue

I stayed in New York for two weeks to the chagrin of my dad and mom. Dad even offered to buy me a roundtrip ticket so I could come home for a few days, but it was too soon to leave Barbara. Plus, I still had anxiety about flying. Barbara and I planned to get married as soon as I got a job. We decided that I would look for a job in New York since she already had an apartment in the city. We would then move to D.C., where I would apply for the graduate program at Howard University. Barbara had been working now at IBM for nearly two years and was making a good salary as a computer programmer. I had been to New York several times as a student, so the city was not unfamiliar, but the immensity of her apartment complex and the city itself was almost overwhelming. For the first time I was experiencing reverse culture shock.

I immediately began looking for employment. I literally walked the breadth and length of Manhattan searching for employment. Every day, I looked in the want ads and would follow up on any leads I could find. No offers came.

After two weeks of looking for work and not finding any, I decided to go to D.C. and look for a job there. I stayed with my sister, Patricia, who by this time was separated from her husband and living in a high-rise apartment in Silver Spring. During my stay with her, she complained bitterly about me bringing trash from the trash closet into her apartment. She did not understand that having lived in an undeveloped country where resources of any kind were limited, I could not ignore picking up so many good items that were still useful. When I brought back to her apartment a brand-new telephone book, Patricia asked me why I did that. I said it was new, and in Malawi, people could use it for toilet paper. She kindly informed me that it was last year's phone book, she already had the new edition and she had plenty of toilet paper.

After about a week, my parents insisted that I come home. I took the train to Morganton, and my parents met me at the little train station in town. They were so happy to see me, as were all my other relatives, and I was very happy to see them and to be home again. Barbara later joined me at home for the Christmas holidays, and then we drove to Birmingham to spend New Year's with her mother, Mrs. Rosa Durr, and sisters. Barbara had shown her family my pictures from Malawi. There was one picture of my neighbor's children that she showed her mother. They were children between three and six years old. Barbara's mother asked Barbara if they were my little children. I had to laugh since I had been in Africa for only two years and the youngest child in the picture was three. After the New Year, I headed back to D.C. to look for a job and Barbara went back to New York.

I had been out of the country during a very turbulent time in America. People were now active in the Black Power/Black Arts movement from coast to coast. I still felt guilty about being in Africa when Dr. King was killed. I now wanted to again be involved in the movement. I felt like my service in the Peace Corps provided me with skills to work among my own people—to work among the poor, disadvantaged and disenfranchised.

To friends and family, I expressed my frustration about not being able to find a job in D.C. My good friend and former colleague from the Kentucky Human Rights Commission, Kenneth Cox, now living in Washington, introduced me to Marion Barry, who had been an organizer of the Student Nonviolent Coordinating Committee along with John Lewis and others. Ken knew Marion from Memphis, Tennessee, where they grew up, and from the Civil Rights movement. He set up an interview for me to meet with Marion, who now headed Youth Pride Inc., an organization dedicated to working with the hard-core unemployed and unemployable, especially Black men. Pride Inc. not only worked with young people in the city but also with addicts, ex-addicts and ex-offenders. Having missed much of the Civil Rights movement, I wanted to work for an agency that would make a difference. I could not have selected a more relevant organization to work for. I would make any sacrifice to get a job at Pride.

Youth Pride Inc. was in an old building on 16th and U Street, NW, across from the Women's Congressional Club. I thought, how appropriate. The interview with Marion went well, but he said that I would have to talk with his co-director, Margaret Wells. I went across the hall to her office and told her secretary that I had an appointment to see Miss Wells. She went in to inform her that I was there. She told me to have a seat and that Miss Wells would be with me shortly. Well, "shortly" meant four hours. I sat there until eight o'clock at night waiting for her to come out, while numerous people walked into and out of her office. I wanted this job, and even more, I needed this job if Barbara and I were to be married. Finally, she came out and invited me into her office. Margaret was from a middle-class family in Columbus, Ohio, but she played the role of a tough, authoritarian lady. She inspected me up and down while asking numerous questions about my background. As I answered her questions, she carefully watched the expression on my face. She knew that I had no experience working with inner-city people, but I had worked with poor Africans. Yet, at the end of the interview, she offered me the job as skills development supervisor. I worked at Youth Pride for over a year developing seven levels of skills development. Many people fear ex-addicts and ex-felons, but not once was I concerned about my safety. Even at midnight when Margaret called her employees to go to Youth Pride's service station on 14th Street to protect the station during the riots, I did not hesitate.

Me as a returned Peace Corps volunteer in Washington, D.C.

While working at Youth Pride, I stayed with my sister and traveled to New York every weekend to visit Barbara. We decided that she would move to D.C. as soon as I was able to secure an apartment. The end of February, I rented a U-Haul, packed Barbara's belongings, and headed to D.C.

Barbara and I were married on March 7 at People's Congregational Church on Upper 13th Street. Just before leaving for the church, Barbara put a large turkey in the oven and we drove in my small green Toyota across town during a near-total solar eclipse.

For several years, I maintained contact with my friends and colleagues in Malawi. I constantly wrote to my old employees at the extension aids office. I would shop at thrift stores to purchase clothes that I would ship to my former office for the staff to share. I would list on the duty forms that the clothes did not have a value so that the staff would not have to pay any duty.

I kept in close contact with Mark Chiphwanya and his wife, Beatrice. Mark informed me that they had had another boy and assured me that it would be his last. He was still waiting on a promotion that depended on an expatriate retiring. Nigel Murphy retired as head of the regional office and went back to the United Kingdom. Mr. Nanthambwe, a regional officer

My wife, Barbara Fleming.

from Lilongwe, was his replacement, the first African to head the southern regional office. Mr. Katembe, my friend and neighbor, wrote to say how much everyone missed me and was thoughtful enough to say that they think a lot about the contribution I had made during my tour of duty. This meant the world to me. He said that he added four more rooms to the house that we had built together and had whitewashed the house, which I had left unpainted. He was promoted to head the credit branch of the Chikwawa Cotton Development Project as senior credit officer. He and his wife welcomed their fifth child since my departure.

I promised Everson Kachale, our houseboy, that I would pay his school fees as long as he remained in school and that he was to keep me informed of his progress. Everson was able to finish form eight but did not pass his exams to move on to secondary school. He asked if he could take form eight over. I agreed and sent him his school fees for the year. Although he passed his exams the second time, it was not at a high enough level to allow him to move on. He repeated his grade again and passed but failed again to secure a spot in a secondary school. Of the 46 boys in his class who passed that year, only 3 were selected for secondary school.

I gave our dog to Everson when I left Malawi. He was glad to get him because he had become attached to Thako. In one of Everson's letters, he said that Thako had been hit by a car, which broke his leg. He carried the dog to the vet's in Blantyre, where his leg was set for six pounds. He paid half and I sent him money to cover the remainder. I also sent clothes and books to Everson and his family. He asked me for a heavy coat because the winter was approaching, which I gladly sent, having experienced Malawi winters firsthand. After several years, I lost touch with Everson.

Dick and Anne Oliver eventually went back to California. We remained good friends and continued to write and stay in contact over the years. They were among the finest people I met in Malawi or anywhere else, for that matter. Howard Carter and his wife moved to Philadelphia. Some years later, he sent me my assessment of living among expatriates. He was impressed with my thoughts and kept the document in his files. I was pleased. I was very saddened to learn that Edmund Nkona, my long-sought-after replacement, was killed in 1973 in a motorcycle accident.

I had not kept up with many Peace Corps volunteers. I lost contact with Tom Barker. John Hunter went on to graduate school and received his doctorate in agriculture. He eventually went back to Africa to work and live. Doug MacDonald got married, had a daughter and finished law school. Bob Brown became a veterinarian, which did not surprise me.

Our daughters, Tuliza (left) and Diara, at our D.C. home.

My last physical connection to Malawi came the summer following our marriage: I came down with a terrible case of malaria. I woke up with a fever of 104 degrees with chills. Barbara did not know what was happening. I remembered that I had lost my chloroquine tablets that I was to take once I left the tropics. I told Barbara that I needed to go to the hospital. She drove me to George Washington University Hospital because of it being a teaching hospital. Unable to find the exact location of the hospital, I told Barbara to stop in the middle of K Street and blow her horn to get the attention of a policeman, who then had us follow him to the hospital.

I was immediately admitted. I soon recovered, but for nearly a week, I was prodded and poked by medical students who had never seen a case of malaria. People came in to see me at all hours of the day and night checking my vitals and drawing blood. On the sixth day, I had had enough. I checked myself out of the hospital and had Barbara pick me up. I was weak for a few days but recovered and never had another bout of malaria.

I started graduate school at Howard University on a Ford Foundation Fellowship, completing my studies and dissertation under my professor and friend Rayford Logan. Our first daughter, Tuliza, was born while I was a graduate student. Four years later, our second daughter, Diara, was born. We gave them both African names. Barbara later enrolled at Howard and completed her doctorate in psychology. We moved to Columbus, Ohio, where I began a 40-year career developing and directing museums. It's been a half century since leaving the Peace Corps, an experience that shaped and continues to shape my life.

Index

Abrams, Michael 23–24
Adams, Michael 100
Adams, Roy 16, 181
The African Queen 200
Aheo 202
Aldrin, Buzz 200
Allen, Archie 189
Allen, Bonnie 189
Allison, Jack 7, 95, 98–99, 175
Anderson, Susan 124
Anderson, Tom 124
Armstrong, Neil 200
Ashcroft, David 92
The Autobiography of Malcolm X 59
Avery, Waighstill 203

Banda, Agnes 145
Banda, David 30–32
Banda, Pres. Hastings 13, 29, 52, 59, 69–71, 103, 134, 147, 152, 162, 171–172, 176
Barker, Tom 26, 27, 29, 32–36, 37, 47–48, 52–53, 55, 61, 65–67, 71, 75–76, 78, 79, 82–84, 94, 143–144, 151, 156, 160–161, 165–167, 183, 197–198, 215
Barry, Marion 212
Batjargal 140
Berea College 6, 9–12, 18, 22, 25, 28, 30, 43, 51, 58–60, 92–94, 102, 104, 109, 121–123, 125–128, 130, 157–158, 162, 164, 169, 188, 208–209
Black Power movement 6, 23, 58, 157, 184, 188, 209, 212
Bonomi, Mr. 81–82
Bower, JW 82, 194
Branson, Jim 13
British Overseas Visual Aids (OVA) 15
Bronson 88–89
Brown, Alton 189, 190
Brown, Bob 37, 43, 183, 215
Brown, H. Rap 56
Brown, James 103

Brown, Sterling 187
Brown v. Board of Education 33
Caldwell, Bob 181
Caldwell, Dick 26, 27, 29, 32–34, 45–46, 69, 71, 78, 79, 82, 94–95, 116, 153–155, 181, 183
Carmichael, Stokely 6, 23, 56
Carson, Hester 130
Carter, Howard 18–21, 27–28, 54, 104, 149, 162, 183, 199, 215
Chipenbere, Henry M. 70
Chiphwanya, Beatrice 61, 143, 145–148, 171, 213
Chiphwanya, Mark 61–62, 143, 145–148, 171, 194, 199, 213
Chirwa, Henry 76, 80, 98, 173, 191
Chiwanga, David 182, 194
Chomba, Stone 35–36
Clark, Mike 157
Cleaver, Eldridge 158
Collins, Michael 200
Congress of Racial Equality (CORE) 6, 23–24
Cornell University 145
Corydon, Sir Robert 132
The Cotton Manual, a Field Work Guide to Modern Cotton Growing for Agriculture Extension Workers in the Southern Region 174
Cox, Kenneth 166, 212
Cox, Ronald 170

Danjuma 202
Dare, R.J. 173–174
Darwin, Charles 109
David, Salome Nolega 10, 92–93, 120–135, 199
David, Troy 28, 46–47, 54, 73–74, 82, 104, 173, 194
Dean, Jimmy 201
Durr, Barbara 22, 27–28, 44, 51, 60–61,

63–64, 67, 92, 103, 142, 144, 151–152, 157–161, 164–166, 168–169, 171–172, 187, 192–193, 206, 208–216
Durr, Rosa 63, 212
Dylan, Bob 210

Ehene 202

Farmer, Fannie 188
Fellowship of Reconciliation 125
"Feteleza Achulukitsa Zokolola" 95, 98
Fleming, Barbara 7
Fleming, Diara 215–216
Fleming, Tuliza 215–216
Flowers, Dr. Raymond 21
Franklin, John Hope 150

Hamer, Fannie Lou 60
Hare, the Rev. Delmar 9–10
Henderson, Margaret 15
Holloway, James 169
Hopkin, Freida 209
Hunter, John 16, 25, 27, 48–49, 82, 101, 102, 105, 106, 110–113, 115, 117, 120, 134–137, 139, 161, 168–169, 181, 183, 190–192, 199, 201, 204, 206, 215
Hunter, Liz 168–169

Ilala 184–185
"I'm Black and I'm Proud" 103

Johnson, Larry 13
Johnson, Lyndon B. 56, 157
Johnson, Marie 13
Johnson, Robert 13, 21, 149
Johnson, Robert, Jr. 13
Johnson, the Rev. William 84
Jones, Franklin 13

Kachale, Everson 55–56, 61, 143, 151, 188, 197, 214–215
Kadzamira, Cecilia 172
Kalenga, James 191
Kapanela, Joseph 50–51, 74, 77, 81, 195
Katembe, James 53–54, 60, 67, 72, 91, 197, 199, 214
Kaunda, Kenneth 6
Kennedy, John F. 157
Kennedy, Sen. Robert 62–63, 146
Kenya African National Union Party 123, 134
Kenyatta, Jomo 123, 126, 133–134
King, Martin Luther, Jr. 56–59, 62–63, 67–68, 126, 146, 212
Kundecha, A.S. 174

Leakey, Louis 109, 132–133
Leakey, Mary 109, 132–133
Lewis, John 189, 212
Limbani, Edward 29–30, 35, 83, 171, 175–180, 199
Livingstone, David 11, 13, 112
Lodge, Tom 6
Logan, Rayford 187, 216
Luangwa Game Reserve 81–83, 85, 87, 102

MacDonald Doug 26, 27, 29, 32–34, 44, 46, 69, 71, 75, 79, 82–83, 116, 152, 156, 167, 174, 181, 183, 215
Makerere University 122, 139
Malcolm X 6, 58–59
Mama Tisa 127, 130–131
March on Frankfort 6
Marsh, Ed 152–155, 183
Mayes, Todd 43, 143, 152, 183
Mbui, Harry 133, 199
McIntosh, Mr. 157
McKinley, Derrick 25, 27, 49–50, 72, 75, 76, 190–191, 202, 204
Mkandawire, Simplex 174
Mouledous, Beth 188
Mouledous, Joe 188
Mount Mulanje 36–43, 80, 101, 147, 189
Mozambique Liberation Front (FRELIMO) 6
Mphiri, Sandy 54, 74, 98–99
Muhammad, Elijah 59
Murphy, Nigel 28–29, 32–33, 35, 38, 44, 46, 65, 72–73, 82, 98–99, 104, 167, 191, 194, 213
Mutesa, Sir Edward Frederick 140
Mutoka, Brenda 128
Mutoka, Rodney 128

Nairobi Game Reserve 134–135
The Naked Jungle 48
Nanthambwe, Mr. 213
Ndonga, Frank 86
Ndungi, Harriet 120–121, 123–124
Ndungi, Michael 10, 92, 120–121, 123–124, 133–134
Nixon, Richard 157
Nkona, Edmund 191–192, 194, 197, 215
Nkrumah, Kwame 102
North by Northwest 167
Noss, George 162
Ntungama, J.B. 75, 156, 173, 190, 191, 194
Nyerere, Julius 6, 102–103, 109

Obote, Pres. Milton 140
Olive Hill High School 157
Oliver, Anne 67, 94–95, 184, 215

Oliver, Dick 67, 94–95, 184, 215
Outlaw, Lou 209

Patel, Mujeeb 19–20
Pentecostal Methodist Christian Church 83–84

Rather, Matt 21
Rustin, Bayard 126–127

St. Stephen's Episcopal Church 9–10
Scott, Carl 33, 37–43, 45, 71–72, 79, 82, 89, 181
Scott, John 193
Serengeti National Park 121
Sharpeville: An Apartheid Massacre and Its Consequences 6
Slades Chapel African Methodist Episcopal Zion Church 9
Society of Friends (Quakers) 125–126
The Southern Advisor 73, 167, 173, 188–189
Speke, John 137
Spelmon, Diara 7

Tembo, Mr. 80
Tomishan 203
Trans-Zambezia Railway 119

Tsavo National Park 120
Tsiranana, Philibert 162
Tuchila Training Center 193

"Ufa Wa Mtedza" 175
Uganda Technical College 140
Unilateral Declaration of Independence 6
University College 140
University College London 140
University of Chicago 150
University of East Africa 122, 126
University of Malawi 145
University of Nairobi 126

Wade, Richard 150
Walton, William 203
Wand, Patricia A. 1–3, 7, 93–94, 211
Ward, Charles 58–59
Wells, Margaret 212–213
Williams, Chancellor 187
Woodson, C. Vann 150
Wyatt, Bill 50, 183

Young Pioneers 71
Young Turks 70
Youth Pride Inc. 212

www.ingramcontent.com/pod-product-compliance
Ingram Content Group UK Ltd.
Pitfield, Milton Keynes, MK11 3LW, UK
UKHW041710160525
458631UK00013B/105